GREAT WALKS OF THE WORLD

GREAT WALKS
of the
WORLD

From Your Armchair or from the Trail,
a History and How-To for Some
of the World's Best Hikes and Walks

D. LARRAINE ANDREWS

RMB

Rocky Mountain Books
www.rmbooks.com

Library and Archives Canada Cataloguing in Publication

Andrews, D. Larraine, 1953-, author
      Great walks of the world / D. Larraine Andrews.

Includes bibliographical references and index.
Issued in print and electronic formats.
ISBN 978-1-77160-000-2 (pbk.).—ISBN 978-1-77160-001-9 (html).—
ISBN 978-1-77160-002-6 (pdf)

    1. Hiking—Guidebooks. 2. Trails—Guidebooks. I. Title.

GV199.5.A63 2014   796.51   C2013-908257-3
                                              C2013-908258-1

Front cover photo: Jinshanling: "Great Wall with Sunrise," 2012-09-25 © Zhudifeng.
Page 2 photo: Scarlet blooms of the claret cup cactus perch on the edge of Big Bend's South Rim © Richard Reynolds/ Texas DOT.
Page 6 photo: Glaciar Grey as seen from Lago Grey © Robert A. Mitchell Jr.
Page 10 photo: Carthew Lakes at the summit of the Carthew-Alderson Trail © D. Larraine Andrews.

Printed in Canada

Rocky Mountain Books acknowledges the financial support for its publishing program from the Government of Canada through the Canada Book Fund (CBF) and the Canada Council for the Arts, and from the province of British Columbia through the British Columbia Arts Council and the Book Publishing Tax Credit.

This book was produced using FSC®-certified, acid-free paper, processed chlorine free and printed with vegetable-based inks.

Disclaimer
The actions described in this book may be considered inherently dangerous activities. Individuals undertake these activities at their own risk. The information put forth in this guide has been collected from a variety of sources and is not guaranteed to be completely accurate or reliable since changes inevitably occur as trails get modified or operators and facilities come under new management. Many conditions and some information may change owing to weather and numerous other factors beyond the control of the authors and publishers. Individual climbers and/or hikers must determine the risks, use their own judgment, and take full responsibility for their actions. Do not depend on any information found in this book for your own personal safety. Your safety depends on your own good judgment based on your skills, education and experience.

    It is up to the users of this guidebook to acquire the necessary skills for safe experiences and to exercise caution in potentially hazardous areas. The authors and publishers of this guide accept no responsibility for your actions or the results that occur from another's actions, choices or judgments. If you have any doubt as to your safety or your ability to attempt anything described in this guidebook, do not attempt it.

To my parents, Joan and Budd Andrews.
You are with me every step of the way.

Solvitur ambulando.
It is solved by walking.

—SAINT AUGUSTINE

I am not sure I ever completely solved anything by walking. I have, however, learned one simple truth – as long as I keep moving forward, I will eventually arrive at my destination. Whether I will have arrived at a solution is another matter ...

—LAINE HENRY

Why do you walk? ... Can't you ride a horse?
People round here hate walkers.
They think they're madmen.

—BRUCE CHATWIN, *In Patagonia*

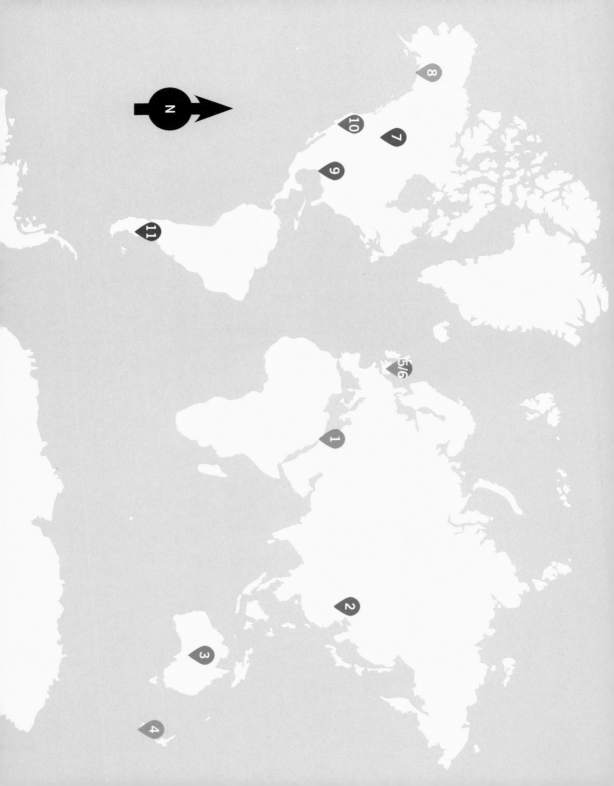

CONTENTS

ACKNOWLEDGEMENTS

Several people have been instrumental in seeing me through what turned into a long and difficult journey to the end of this project. My mother, Joan, and my sister, Arlene, gave me unflagging support and encouragement that kept me going on even the bleakest days. Arlene read the manuscript from the perspective of a non-hiker, while Megan Ballard read each chapter with the critical eye of a hiker who has walked many of the trails described. Their suggestions were invaluable and always insightful. But I take full responsibility for any deficiencies in the final product where I failed to heed their advice.

Walter and Marjorie Danylak propped up my sagging confidence, while Walter displayed the patience of Job when it came to my many phone calls and emails about photo resolution and the mysteries of the camera. To these good friends I say many, many thanks.

I would also like to thank the following people, whose contributions of time and photographs were essential to the completion of this project. Many were hiking buddies on the trails described in this book. My sincere apologies if I have missed anyone along the way.

Chapter 1, Mount Sinai: Sally Ma, Wendy Fung, Kent Klatchuk and Marjorie Danylak.

Chapter 2, Great Wall of China: Tristan Cossey, Sally Ma, the Hong Kong Tourism Board and Jackie Peers of Walk Hong Kong.

Chapter 3, Larapinta Trail: Colin Mann, Chris Buykx of World Expeditions, Shelagh O'Brien of Glen Helen Resort, Monika Tonkin, Carly Saunders and Lucy Stark of Tourism NT and Amy Warren of Uluṟu-Kata Tjuṯa National Park.

Chapter 4, Milford Track: Peta Bamber of Ultimate Hikes and Lindsey Shields and Clare Manners of the New Zealand Department of Conservation.

Chapter 5, Cotswold Way National Trail: Audra McSherry of Bath Tourism and James Blockley, National Trail Officer of the Cotswold Way.

Chapter 6, Offa's Dyke Path National Trail: Rob Dingle, National Trail Officer of Offa's Dyke Path.

Chapter 7, Waterton Lakes National Park: Nathan Andrews, Pat Hughes, Walter Danylak, Colleen F. Bains, Bernie McMahon, Carey Tetzlaff of Waterton Outdoor Adventures, Adria Lund at the Glenbow Archives and Jennifer Burnell at Parks Canada.

Chapter 8, Chilkoot Trail: Bobbie-Lynne Brock, Sylvia Fowler, Mark Waldbillig of Sea to Sky Expeditions, Leighann Chalykoff of the MacBride Museum of Yukon History and Adria Lund at the Glenbow Archives.

Chapter 9, Big Bend National Park: Megan Ballard, Bernie McMahon, Betsy Devlin, Johan Maertens, Samuel Feldman, Anne Cook of the Texas Department of Transportation and Claudia Arnberger of the United States National Park Service.

Chapter 10, Yosemite National Park: Lisa P. Freeman, Paul Lycett, Sandy Brennan, Gwenyth Barrow of the Yosemite National Park Archives and Linda Eade of the Yosemite Research Library.

Chapter 11, Patagonia: Robert A. Mitchell Jr. and Debra Garside. Check out Debra's outstanding collection of professional photographs at **www.truenorthfineimages.com**.

INTRODUCTION

Walk, amble, hike, foot it, hoof it, meander, perambulate, ramble, saunter, slog, stroll, tramp, trek, trudge, wander, yomp

Few ... know how to take a walk. The qualifications ... are endurance, plain clothes, old shoes, an eye for nature, good humor, vast curiosity, good speech, good silence, and nothing too much.

—RALPH WALDO EMERSON, 1858

Emerson's list of qualifications is simple, really, but it's one that many of us often overlook, even now, over 150 years after he first recorded it. Keep that list in mind and it will serve you well along many trails – walking or otherwise.

There is endless discussion about why people walk or hike or trek. Whatever you decide to call it, and whether you are doing it to contemplate life, solve a problem, get fit, enjoy nature or simply get from one place to another, the fact is, people walk.

So while this book is aimed at the walkers of the world, it is also aimed at anyone interested in learning the story behind some of the world's great hikes from the comfort of their armchair. An eclectic collection of 12 walks and treks, it includes destinations from every continent except Antarctica – everything from one-day adventures to two-week odysseys. For ease of reference, the sections are arranged alphabetically by continent and then alphabetically by hike within each continent/region.

The book is filled with historical information and factoids along with a superb collection of images, both contemporary and archival. Each chapter begins with a visual reply to the question "What will I see?" featuring a stunning photograph from the trail or area that you will see if you decide to make the journey. Photographic contributors come from around the world; many were walking companions I met along the way.

You will also find maps illustrating where in the world you will find the trail, as well as a hike profile and a detailed trail map. The profile is a visual representation of the elevation gain or loss you can expect to encounter. Some chapters don't have a profile, due to the nature or length of the trek.

Each chapter then proceeds to answer, in some detail, many of the questions a prospective walker, or an interested armchair traveller, would have about the hike.

Expect to find a section on "Claim to fame": many of these walks are located in or near designated World Heritage Sites or, in Great Britain, Areas of Outstanding Natural Beauty. This is followed by a written summary of the "Hike profile" and a discussion of "Hazards" specific to the destination. A separate box on "The Essentials" helps you plan for how to get there, the currency used and any special gear you might need to consider. (Specific information on passport/visa requirements, vaccinations and travel insurance is not included. It is your responsibility to ensure you meet all the rules before you set out. Check out **www.travel.gc.ca** for current Canadian travel information and be sure to consult a travel health professional prior to departure. Good summary material on this topic can also be found at **www.mdtravelhealth.com**. Before you leave, always get travel insurance that will cover evacuation costs!)

The "Hike overview" provides a concise description of what to expect on the trail, while the "Why would I want to?" section explains some of the reasons you might want to consider putting this walk on your list. Advice on "When to go" is included to help you pick the best time to tackle the trek.

"What's the story?" is packed with fascinating historical information and facts specific to the trail. Each walk has its own particular story to tell and this section tells it with a combination of words and photographs. Many of the chapters, such as chapter 8 on the Chilkoot Trail and chapter 7 on Waterton Lakes National Park, include archival photos. They help to visually describe the history unique to the area where you are hiking.

Once you know some of the background, it's on to a detailed description of "The hike." Some of the walks described are one-day saunters, some are loop trails, and some are one-way traverses. Some take a week, some take two weeks or more. The routes range in length from as short as 14 km (8.7 mi.) to close to 322 km (200 mi.). (Note that appropriate mileage conversions are supplied throughout the text for the convenience of US readers.) The narratives are not intended to replace the detail you would find in a guidebook specific to the walk. Packed with interesting facts and information, they provide a visual and written feast to keep you entertained and informed along the way.

"The hike" section is followed by the practical details of "How to do the hike." Information for solo and group hikers is provided, along with links to trusted outfitters/tour operators. Each chapter offers a selection of operators based on my own personal experience. A section titled "How do you say that?" will help you navigate some of the unique language you will encounter in the area you are visiting.

"Consider this: Before or after the hike" provides suggestions on what to do in addition to the walk. Many of these treks will involve significant travel commitments, so you will want to get the most you can out of your visit. The section is not intended as a detailed guide. Depending on the destination, it provides ideas for additional hikes or historical/cultural sites not to be missed while you are so close. For example, chapter 1 on Mount Sinai in Egypt includes a "Consider this" section on the ancient city of Petra in nearby Jordan, while chapter 4 on the Milford Track in New Zealand provides suggestions on Queenstown, the jumping-off point for the Track.

In many of the chapters, this section provides additional historical information and photographs to give you some context for your visit.

"Are you ready to eat?" supplies information on what you can expect when it comes to hygiene standards, tipping and services for vegetarians. Again, there is no intention to provide a detailed guide on where to eat. Along with the practical matters, you will find stories about food specialties and rituals unique to the area. For example, the ritual of drinking yerba mate tea in Patagonia is described in sensuous detail in chapter 11, with an excerpt from Bruce Chatwin's classic book *In Patagonia*; while chapter 3, on the Larapinta Trail in Australia, offers a bewildering array of slang terms for Aussie edibles.

Each chapter concludes with sections on "Internet resources" and "Recommended reading." Internet links are provided to help you begin your search for information. The reading section is based on my research, during which I read almost all of the books listed for each chapter. The reading list is not intended to be a detailed bibliography, merely a summary of books I used and liked, with my personal comments and opinions included throughout the list. Many are standard classics relating to the hike or the region, plus a few gems I found along the way. You will also notice that when I have a choice between guidebooks for the area, I have recommended the *Lonely Planet* version. This reflects my own particular bias – there are many great guidebooks out there to choose from.

I haven't provided a list of books on walking in general. There is a plethora of these and I leave you to your own devices to find your favourites. I will, however, recommend one of my all-time favourites: *Wanderlust: A History of Walking*, by Rebecca Solnit, is an inspiring read on something we all have in common – a love of walking and an abiding curiosity about the world around us, whether we view it from the trail or from a comfortable armchair.

Finally, near the end of each chapter, you will find a section called "Fauna facts." This describes, both visually and in text, an animal you may encounter along the specific trail.

That is a basic summary of what this book is. But there are several things the book is not.

It is not a gear guide, nor does it tell you what to do if you've "gone for a ball of chalk" – a brilliant British slang term that essentially means you are lost. This book doesn't tell you how to read a map or a global positioning system receiver, or what to do if you have blisters or a sprained ankle. It doesn't tell you how to get fit, how to take a poop in the woods, purify your water or build an emergency shelter. There are plenty of excellent guidebooks that already do all that in meticulous detail.

Finally, this book makes no attempt to rate the walks described in the following chapters.

What I can say is that I have walked every kilometre described, with three exceptions when I was briefly forced off the trail. One such episode was on the Larapinta Trail in Australia, because of injury. The other two were on the Offa's Dyke Path National Trail in Great Britain and the W Circuit in Parque Nacional Torres del Paine in Patagonia, both because of bad weather. But these missing miles are clearly noted in the text.

What I cannot say is which walk is the best or the second best or the twelfth best. Every walk presents its own particular challenges and appeal. Some, like the Chilkoot Trail in chapter 8, have great historical significance and are very challenging. Others, like the Cotswold Way National Trail in chapter 5, while steeped in history, follow delightful paths through paddocks full of sheep, picture-perfect villages and ancient beech woodlands filled with bluebells and a symphony of birdsong, just for the sheer joy of it. Whether you decide to put boots to the trail and go see for yourself or read about it from the comfort of your living room, the choice is entirely yours.

CHAPTER 1 – EGYPT – MOUNT SINAI

{ Mount Sinai – *Jebel Musa, The God-Trodden Mountain,*
Mount Moses, Mount Horeb, the Holy Peak }

I can't believe Moses made this walk in sandals.

—BRUCE FEILER, *Walking the Bible: A Journey by Land*
through the Five Books of Moses (2001)

✳ HIKING RULE 1: Moses may have made it in sandals, but he had divine assistance. Since you probably can't rely on that type of backing, always invest in sturdy, waterproof boots with good ankle support, and never start a long hike with a new pair. Although modern lightweight boots tend not to require the break-in period that older, heavier versions did, you should still make sure you have used them on a few shorter walks to identify any potential rub spots or problems. Blisters and sore feet can quickly turn a glorious day of walking into nothing more than a painful endurance test.

WHERE IN THE WORLD?

SINAI PENINSULA

JORDAN

SAUDI ARABIA

Monastery of St. Catherine

EGYPT

GULF OF SUEZ

CLAIM TO FAME

The Jewish, Islamic and Christian traditions hold Mount Sinai to be the biblical mountain where Moses received the Tablets of the Law in the form of the Ten Commandments. The giving of this Covenant to the Chosen People is said to mark the true beginning of the Jewish nation.

Saint Catherine's Monastery and the surrounding area is a UNESCO World Heritage Site. Saint Catherine's is the oldest remote monastic community to have survived intact. It has been used for its original function without interruption since the sixth century. UNESCO describes it as an outstanding example of human genius that "demonstrates an intimate relationship between natural grandeur and spiritual commitment."

WHAT WILL I SEE?

The view from the summit of Mount Sinai.

HIKE PROFILE

This is a day hike with an altitude change of approximately 672 m, or 2,206 ft. The hike starts from just outside the monastery at 1600 m (5,249 ft.) and climbs to the top of Mount Sinai, which is 2272 m (7,454 ft.).

Hazards

None, other than the usual risk of injury from turning an ankle or falling on the uneven steps and rocky path.

The essentials

The mountain and the nearby Saint Catherine's Monastery are located near the southern tip of the Sinai Peninsula, which is part of Egypt.

Getting there: Cairo is the main access point. It is serviced by many major airlines or their partners, including, among others, Air France, British Airways, Emirates Airlines, KLM, Lufthansa, Royal Jordanian and Singapore Airlines. Egypt Air provides direct flights from Cairo to Sharm el-Sheikh. Bus service to the village of al-Milgaa (also known as Katriin), located about 3.5 km (2 mi.) from the monastery, (which is at the foot of the mountain), is available from Dahab, Nuweiba, Sharm el-Sheikh and Cairo. Many hotels in Dahab, Sharm el-Sheikh and Nuweiba can organize trips to the monastery and Mount Sinai. It is also possible to hire a taxi for the drive from nearby towns as well as from Cairo.

Currency: Egyptian pound, or E£. E£1 = 100 piastres, or pt. For current exchange rates, check out **www.oanda.com**.

Special Gear: if you are planning on climbing the Stairs of Repentance you will need good sturdy walking boots and plenty of water. Consider walking poles, since the stairs are rough and uneven. A headlamp or flashlight is essential, because you will probably be doing one way of the walk in the dark. Depending on the time of day, water, snacks and rented blankets to ward off the cold are available from small kiosks operated along the camel trail by the local Jabaliya people.

HIKE OVERVIEW

There are several alternatives for completing the hike up Mount Sinai, depending on the time of day you undertake the trek and whether you decide to watch the sun rise or set from the summit. Two well-defined routes exist: the camel trail and the Stairs of Repentance. Both trails meet just below the summit at Elijah's Basin. From there, all hikers must climb the remaining 750 steps to the top.

As suggested by the name, it is possible to hire a camel to ascend the camel route to the basin, but the trail itself follows a relatively gentle slope and can be easily navigated by anyone capable of walking up a hill for about two hours. Most pilgrims and walkers take this path up before dawn in order to see the sun rise over the magnificent panorama of mountain peaks that can be seen from the top. Be sure to take a flashlight with you to navigate the trail in the darkness.

The Stairs of Repentance are rough and uneven and should only be tackled in the daylight. Many walkers will ascend the camel trail in the predawn darkness and descend via the steps after sunrise. There are approximately 3,000 steps to the basin, where the two trails converge, plus another 750 to the summit, so you need poles and strong knees to navigate this trail. Our group ascended the steps in the late afternoon, watched the sun set over the mountains and then descended in the darkness down the easy slopes of the camel trail. A flashlight or headlamp is essential when coming down. Of course, it is possible to do both trails in the daylight. This alternative allows you to see the impressive scenery both ways, but misses the climax view of the sun rising or setting while at the top.

Why would I want to?

Mount Sinai has been the site of Christian pilgrimage for centuries, a place where the devout still come to do physical penance as they toil up the Holy Mountain to be closer to God. But the God-Trodden Mountain has also been a magnet for tourists, naturalists and scholars for hundreds of years. They were, and continue to be, drawn by the prospect of a wild and desolate land of red granite and stunning topography that has changed little in thousands of years.

English naturalist Edward Hull, writing in the late 1800s, exclaimed, "Nothing can exceed the savage grandeur of the view from the summit of Mount Sinai," while French diplomat, artist and historian Léon de Laborde, obviously awe-struck by the great and terrible wilderness spread out before him, declared, "If I had to represent the end of the world, I would model it from Mount Sinai."

Hyperbole aside, no other place combines a trek to the top of one of the most sacred spots of three great religions with the chance to stay in and explore the oldest Christian monastery in continuous existence in the world.

When to go

Remember that Mount Sinai is located in the southern part of the Sinai Peninsula, which is essentially desert, so even in the summer it can be cold in the evenings. The Bible refers to the Sinai as "this terrible and waste-howling wilderness, a land of fiery snakes, scorpions, thirst" where the sun dominates the landscape.

The monastery is located at 1600 m (5,249 ft.). In July and August the mean maximum temperature at this elevation is 30°C (86°F) but can easily exceed this. Snow is not uncommon at higher altitudes by November. The best compromise if you are visiting other parts of Egypt, where the weather could be quite different than in the southern Sinai, is probably to stick with spring (March to May) or fall (September to October). I visited in January, and although there was no snow at the top, it was very cold, even during the day.

What's the story?

Mount Sinai is sacred to the world's three great monotheistic religions: Judaism, Christianity and Islam. But while Jews and Muslims have no established custom of pilgrimage to the site, Christians have long felt the need to physically identify the actual Holy Peak that is so central to the biblical story of Moses.

As early as the third century, Christian ascetics identified this specific mountain

THE STORY OF MOSES

Whether or not you believe in the "truth" of the story of Moses as told in the Old Testament book of Exodus, there is little doubt it has had a profound impact on three of the world's great religions. The story begins as the Egyptian pharaoh, fearing the prolific increase of the Israelites in his country, orders every newborn boy thrown into the river. One small babe, who is placed in a papyrus basket and hidden in the reeds, is discovered by the pharaoh's daughter, who hires the child's mother as a nursemaid. The boy is named Moses because he was "drawn from the water."

When Moses kills an Egyptian for striking an Israelite, he flees into the desert, where he marries Zipporah, the daughter of Jethro. While tending Jethro's sheep, Moses wanders to Mount Horeb, the Mountain of God. Here Yahweh (God) calls to him from a blazing bush which is not consumed by the fire. He tells Moses that the place is holy ground. Yahweh orders Moses to return to Egypt and lead the Israelites out of their slavery, back to the sacred mountain where they are commanded to worship God.

The pharaoh rejects Moses's plea to release his people. Finally a series of ten plagues, concluding with the deaths of all Egyptian first-born and the Passover of Hebrew children, convinces the pharaoh to agree. Moses then leads his people back to Mount Horeb. They escape the pursuing Egyptian army when God parts the Red Sea to allow the chosen ones to pass while the army is drowned.

Yahweh tells Moses that he will descend on Mount Sinai and warns the people not to touch the mountain or they will be put to death. The entire mountain is wrapped in smoke and shakes violently as God comes in the form of fire.

Moses climbs the mountain to receive the stone tablets with the inscription of the law and the commandments. There he spends forty days and nights, but when he descends he finds his people have become corrupted and he throws down the tablets, shattering them at the base of the mountain. He pleads with God to spare them for their sins and Yahweh agrees to cut two new tablets which Moses brings to his people, passing on the words of the Book of the Covenant. The Israelites eventually leave Mount Sinai in their quest for the Promised Land.

as the "real" one, and began using it as a place to pray and come closer to God. In his book entitled *Mount Sinai,* Joseph Hobbs notes that Daniel Silver surmised the mountain's identity was "probably based on little more than the vision of a desert monk … who had a revelation that this was the famous Mount Sinai where Moses had spoken with God."

It is a statement the monks of Saint Catherine's would no doubt strongly dispute. They believe with certainty that this is the true sacred mountain, based on the oral traditions of the local Bedouin and the existence, right from the beginning, of the

"AND THE BUSH WAS NOT CONSUMED"

And the angel of the Lord appeared unto him in a flame of fire
out of the midst of a bush: and he looked, and, behold, the
bush burned with fire, and the bush was not consumed.

— Exodus 3:2 [KJV]

When writer Joseph Hobbs visited the monastery, the monks of Saint Catherine's explained to him that "this bush is what the whole thing is all about. This is what attracted the monastics to come to the area in the very beginning. It is unique. No other plant like this is alive anywhere in the Sinai." In his book *Mount Sinai*, Hobbs says he couldn't bring himself to tell the monks that he had seen other specimens of the plant known as *Rubus sanctus* during his treks in the Sinai mountains. But he admits that botanical experts at the University of Cairo confirm the plant is an extremely rare endemic species with a range limited to the immediate vicinity of Jebel Musa, or Mount Sinai.

As far back as the fourth century, two hundred years before the establishment of the monastery, the Spanish nun Etheria recounts that "having made the whole descent of the mount of God we arrived at the bush ... out of which the Lord spake in the fire to Moses, and the same is situated at that spot at the head of the valley where there are many cells and a church. There is a very pleasant garden in front of the church, containing excellent and abundant water, and the bush is in this garden." According to Hobbs, experts agree it is quite plausible the plant that continues to thrive at the monastery is the same plant Etheria saw on her pilgrimage over 1,700 years ago. They believe it is not out of the question for plants of this species to live for "thousands of years."

The bush, which never bears fruit, is tended by the monks, who water it from the nearby Well of Moses, where Moses met his wife Zipporah. They claim the well never goes dry. In fact the bush thrives to the point where it must be regularly pruned. The extra foliage is either distributed to pilgrims as a memento of their visit or burned. Bruce Feiler, in his book *Walking the Bible*, says one of the monks who watched a burning admitted to him, "Yes, well, it did burn." Feiler notes with some amusement the presence of a fire extinguisher "perched at the base of the bush ... At first I thought it was an eyesore, but then I realized the unintended humor. Was this in case the burning bush caught on fire?"

SALLY MA

The Burning Bush located within the walls of Saint Catherine's Monastery.

Bible's "burning bush." In fact, the site that would eventually be occupied by the monastery at the foot of Mount Sinai was often called "the Bush."

Scholars have pondered and debated the issue of the sacred mountain's location for centuries, often undertaking arduous desert journeys to "prove" they found the Bible's Mount Horeb and many of the other holy places associated with Moses's journey.

One intriguing argument for the southern route to Mount Sinai focuses on three factors critical to survival in such a harsh environment. These include the availability of adequate water and pastures for the people and the herds, as well as the "bread from heaven" that God rained down each day to feed them as described in the book of Exodus. It is depicted as a "fine and flaky substance, as fine as the frost on the ground." The Israelites called the bread "manna" and there is ample evidence of its existence along the route.

In the end, despite the identification of competing locations in the northern and central parts of the peninsula by many experts, this spot remains the favourite.

Whether you come as a pilgrim or an interested visitor, you have the opportunity to actually stay at the guesthouse located adjacent to the monastery. The food is plain but filling and the rooms are comfortable, with plenty of extra blankets and electric heaters to ward off the evening chill.

Remember you are in the desert, so expect it to be cold at night. In *Walking the Bible* Bruce Feiler recalls the warnings he had from former visitors to be prepared for the "coldest night of my life." As a result he came armed with "enough equipment for Everest." In the end he didn't need it. Take it from someone who is always cold, I was also quite comfortable there, once we figured out the heater! There is also the option of staying at the nearby village of al-Milgaa (also called Katriin), which offers ample alternatives for all budget levels.

BREAD FROM HEAVEN

Research shows that manna is the product of two insect species that infest tamarisk trees growing in the mountainous southern part of the peninsula. These insects suck the sap from the trees and deposit any surplus on the branches. The small globules crystallize and fall to the ground, where they must be harvested each day before the ants find them or they dry up.

During a visit in 1844, Constantin von Tischendorf reported eating the "excrescences hanging like glittering pearls" from the tamarisks at the monastery, describing the taste as greatly resembling honey. Early rabbis claimed manna had unusual properties: no one ever tired of eating it, because it adapted to each individual who consumed it. And best of all there was no need for bowel movements, since it "was entirely dissolved into their bodies."

Mount Sinai looms behind Saint Catherine's Monastery.

Pressure from an ever increasing number of pilgrims and tourists has forced the monastery to restrict access in order to allow the monks to observe their own daily ritual of work and prayer. As a result it is open to the public from 9:00 a.m. to noon on most weekdays and Saturday, except religious holidays. Expect large crowds gathered at the gate and a press of people within the walls.

The Monastery of Saint Catherine on the God-Trodden Mount Sinai, as it stands today, is the oldest Christian monastery in continuous existence in the world. The walled monastery was not built until the sixth century, but we know a church and tower existed here in the fourth century based on the account of the Spanish nun Etheria (also called Egeria). During her pilgrimage to the holy sites in the area, she described "many cells of holy men there, and a church in the place where the bush is, which same bush is still alive today and throws out shoots."

Tradition holds that the tower and church were built under the auspices of Saint Helena, after her son, the Roman Emperor Constantine the Great, made Christianity a legal religion in 313 CE. Consecrated as the Monastery of St. Mary, it was built as a refuge for the many monastics who were coming to pray at the site of the Burning Bush. The name recognized that, like the famous bush that was not consumed by the fire, Mary was a virgin who contained God and was not destroyed.

In the sixth century, the Roman emperor Justinian built the fortress that still exists today. Although he is said to have constructed the fortified monastery to protect the monks from warring nomads, he probably viewed the structure primarily as a defensive outpost. Once established at the site of the Burning Bush, it seems likely the rugged Mount Sinai that rises up behind it earned its permanent status as the biblical Mount Horeb almost by default.

The monastery was well known as a place of pilgrimage but did not begin to thrive until after 1000 CE when it became linked to the venerated Catherine of Alexandria.

The Romans built granite walls 18 m (60 ft.) high and 2.7 m (9 ft.) thick, as well as a basilica, the Church of the Transfiguration. The church doors are the oldest functioning ones in the world according to the monks.

The fact that the monastery has survived for over 1,500 years is a miracle in itself. Sheer isolation probably explains part of it, but a series of protectors over the years also helped ensure its continued existence. Arab, Crusader, Ottoman, French, British, Egyptian and Israeli armies have all left their mark on the peninsula but the monastery has survived, even thrived.

Legend maintains that the prophet Mohammed actually visited the monastery on one of his merchant trips. And in response to a request from a delegation of monks who visited Medina in 625 CE he granted the Covenant of the Prophet, ensuring protection of the Christian monks who had treated him so well during

THE BRIDE OF CHRIST

Catherine was a high-ranking woman of exceptional intelligence born in Alexandria in the third century. She spurned all her potential suitors as unacceptable. Catherine converted to Christianity and claimed through prayer and vision to have met and married Christ. She tried to convert the Emperor Maximinus, but when she refused to renounce her mystical marriage, he ordered her execution.

It was a rather gruesome affair. Catherine was attached to four wooden wheels studded with steel blades and spikes designed to tear her to pieces. But an angel miraculously released her uninjured. (She is regarded as the patron saint of clockmakers and others who work with wheels.) The emperor was eventually successful in having her beheaded, at which time her body was transported by holy angels to the summit of Mount Catherine (Jebel Katarina), the highest peak on the peninsula, located close to Mount Sinai, or Jebel Musa.

When monks climbed the mountain in the ninth century, they found Catherine's uncorrupted body. It released a holy oil, which they collected in small bottles. One of the monks accidentally broke off three of her fingers. The relics became associated with various healing miracles as he carried them throughout Europe. Pilgrims began flocking to the area to view her remains, prompting the monks to place them in a silver casket in the basilica and rename the monastery in her honour.

his stay. During Napoleon's conquest in the late 1700s, protection was provided under a written proclamation that remains preserved at the monastery.

Still, the monks were not immune from attack. In fact for several hundred years and even into the twentieth century, visitors and monks alike gained access to the interior via a basket suspended on a thick rope from a pulley on the north wall. According to Feiler, the monks refer to it as the "first passenger elevator in the world."

The monastery houses many treasures and should not be missed unless you are unfortunate enough to be there on a day when it is closed. About the size of a city block, it encompasses an incongruous collection of buildings, built at different times and connected by a maze of corridors and narrow passageways. Chapels, towers and monks' cells are jumbled together with the Burning Bush, Moses's Well, a library and a mosque. Much of the monastery is closed to the public but it is still possible to visit the Chapel of the Transfiguration and the Chapel of the Burning Bush as well as to view the actual bush and the well.

A recently restored museum, called the Sacred Sacristy, contains some of the monastery's many treasures including examples of some of its world-famous Byzantine-era icons. The collection is recognized as one of the oldest and richest in the world, mainly because of a good piece of luck: its geographical isolation helped it escape the iconoclasm. (During the Byzantine iconoclasm, which began in 726 CE, Christian art depicting religious figures in icons was considered heretical and was largely destroyed.)

Over the centuries, the monastery has been a magnet for scholars coming to study its magnificent collection of religious manuscripts. With over 3,000 documents, the library is said to be second in importance only to the Vatican. Unfortunately, history has not been kind to the monks when it comes to the integrity of some of the researchers.

The most notorious example is that of Constantin von Tischendorf, who journeyed to the monastery in 1844 to study the *Codex Sinaiticus*. Dated from the fourth century, the codex is considered the oldest and most complete edition of the Bible, According to Janet Soskice in her book *The Sisters of Sinai: How Two Lady Adventurers Discovered the Hidden Gospels*, it predates most other known copies by close to 600 years. Written in Greek, it was a "magisterial Bible" too heavy to be carried by one man. Over the course of several visits, von Tischendorf managed to convince the monks to let him "borrow" the entire text.

Von Tischendorf promptly presented the codex as a gift to the Russian Tsar Alexander II and it was eventually sold by a cash-strapped Stalin to the United Kingdom in 1933 for £100,000. It now resides in the British Museum. Of course, the monks maintain the manuscript was only a loan and belongs back in their monastery.

One amazing story with a happy ending concerns the discovery of the *Codex*

THE TWIN SISTERS OF SINAI

This is the improbable story of how identical twin sisters, who grew up in mid-nineteenth-century Scotland, found and deciphered one of the earliest known copies of the Christian Gospels. The text was written in ancient Syriac, a dialect of Aramaic, the native language of Jesus, and was one of the most significant scriptural discoveries in history.

In her eponymous book about the famous sisters, Janet Soskice transforms what could easily have been a dry, scholarly treatise about an obscure manuscript into a thrilling narrative of discovery, intrigue and drama, full of suspicion, academic snobbery and perhaps some "Greater Providence."

Agnes and Margaret Smith were well-educated and wealthy and had lost both their parents early in life. Even though they were girls, their father had insisted on a rigorous education. Not only were they fluent in French, Spanish, Italian and German, they also mastered Arabic and Greek. And when called upon to help translate the Syriac texts they found, Agnes learned that language as well.

The two sisters refused to be restricted by the Victorian times in which they lived. Their wild eccentricities were unheard of for unmarried women of their age. Not only had they "astonished their neighbours by taking exercise on parallel bars in their back garden – in their bloomers," they also owned one of the first cars in Cambridge and dared to travel unescorted to Europe and the Middle East.

In 1892, through a series of unlikely events, Agnes and Margaret tackled a dangerous nine-day camping trip across the Sinai by camel to Saint Catherine's Monastery. Fuelled by a strong interest in old biblical texts, they were in search of a hidden treasure thought to be kept in a mysterious "dark closet." The scholar J. Rendel Harris had told them of finding chests of Syriac manuscripts in the cupboard off a "dark chamber beneath the archbishop's rooms." He had found the trove on a previous visit but had run out of time to investigate.

Despite the negative legacy left by von Tischendorf, the sisters were welcomed by the monks, partly because they spoke fluent Greek. It was Agnes who discovered the manuscript. She recalled, "It had a forbidding look, for it was very dirty, and its leaves were very nearly all stuck together through their having remained unturned since the last Syrian monk had died, centuries ago, in the Convent."

She had found a palimpsest. When vellum was scarce, the monks often scraped off the original writing and wrote something new on top – an ancient and effective approach to recycling. The original text lay hidden beneath, eventually restored through the use of a chemical reagent. Over several years and a number of camel trips by the sisters back to the monastery, the texts were restored, translated and released to the world. The precious manuscript is kept at the monastery in a specially built box presented by the twins.

Sinaiticus Syriacus, one of the earliest known manuscripts in the world that preserves the text of the four gospels in Old Syriac. This codex resides in the monastery in a special box presented to the monks by the famous Sisters of Sinai. Their tale of scholarly sleuthing certainly proves the old adage that truth is often stranger than fiction.

Just outside the walls lie the monastery gardens. An oasis in a sea of barren rock and desolation, the gardens are fed by wells and a series of tanks that trap rain and snowmelt from the mountain. During her fourth-century visit, the nun Etheria talks of "a little plot of ground where the holy monks diligently plant little trees and orchards," and even now peaches, almonds and olives thrive among the towering cypress trees.

In the midst of the garden is the ossuary, a stark reminder to all the monks of their ultimate fate. Soil is precious in this land of rock. So monks are interred in the small cemetery for a period of time. Their bones are then removed, washed and added to the rather grisly pile stacked in the charnel house. The empty grave awaits its next occupant.

THE HIKE

Whether you believe this is the sacred Mount Sinai of the Bible or not, there is no denying that the rugged desolation of these "wild and tortured" peaks evokes powerful responses. Léon de Laborde, writing in 1836, described a "chaos of rocks," exclaiming, "If I had to represent the end of the world, I would model it from Mount Sinai." Edward Hull, in 1884, saw "the face of Nature under one of her most savage forms," viewing it with "awe and admiration." Suffice it to say that whichever route you decide to take, it will be well worth the effort. You will be rewarded with spectacular views of a "sea of petrified waves" in a jumble of red and purple hues stretching to the horizon.

The hike begins just outside the walls of the monastery. As noted in the "Hike overview" section there are basically two choices for climbing the mountain: the camel path and the Stairs of Repentance. Your choice will depend on the time of day you do the climb, whether you decide to watch the sun rise or set at the summit and the strength of your knees. Stairs, however, cannot be avoided. The two trails meet about 300 m (984 ft.) below the summit at Elijah's Basin. At this point all hikers must climb the remaining 750 steps to the top. Don't forget your flashlight, and take some warm clothes since it is almost guaranteed to be cold at the top.

The Camel Trail

This is the easier but longer route. It begins immediately behind the monastery and follows a relatively gentle slope up the mountain to the basin. Anyone with reasonable

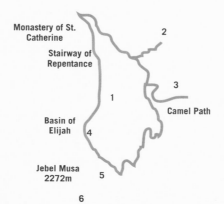

1. Shrive Gate
2. Monastery of St. Galaktion and St. Episteme
3. Chapel of St. Theodore of Tyre and St. Theodore the Recruit
4. Church of Elijah
5. Church of the Holy Trinity
6. Fatimid Mosque

Monastery of St. Catherine
Stairway of Repentance
Camel Path
Basin of Elijah
Jebel Musa 2272m

1
2
3
4
5
6

A "sea of petrified waves" greets hikers nearing the summit of Mount Sinai.

walking ability should be able to navigate this path in two to three hours. It is possible to detour on two different side paths to see the Monastery of St. Galaktion and St. Episteme, where the nun Episteme and her husband (!), the monk Galaktion, came during the Roman persecutions, and the white Chapel of St. Theodore of Tyre. Since most people will do this trail in the predawn darkness, these chapels are generally bypassed unless you descend on the same path in the daylight.

This is the most popular route, so expect to be sharing it with many other climbers on their way to watch the sun rise. Along the way you will pass kiosks selling drinks and renting blankets to help with the cold and often fierce winds at the top. At the start of the trail, it is possible to hire camels which will take you to the basin, but that is technically cheating! From here everyone must navigate the 750 uneven steps to the summit. From the summit you have the choice of descending the same path or taking the Stairs of Repentance.

The Stairs of Repentance

Local Bedouins call it "the Path of Our Lord Moses." It is the shortest, most direct route but definitely not easy. You should only consider doing this in the daylight, as the stairs are rough and uneven and dangerous to navigate in the dark. You will need extra water, since there are no kiosks along here until you reach the basin. Many people will climb the camel path in the darkness to see the sun rise and then descend the stairs. Either way, poles are essential if you value your knees. Our group ascended the stairs in the late afternoon, watched the sun set at the summit and then descended in darkness down the easy slopes of the camel trail.

The rough, uneven steps of the Stairs of Repentance.

WENDY FUNG

The steep path begins southeast of the monastery. Tradition states that the stairs were carved by monks during the sixth century over a period of about fifty years. There are said to be 3,000 of them up to Elijah's Basin (I lost count), but in 1836 de Laborde was sure it was 50,000! The monks hold that climbing the stairs provides the proper ritual preparation required to ascend the Holy Peak.

You will need to take your time going up. Far fewer people tackle this ascent, so you shouldn't have to contend with the crowds that are common on the camel trail. Once our group had spread out and everyone found their own pace, I was struck by the profound, almost spiritual silence of the place, broken only occasionally by the sound of a dislodged rock as the hikers toiled upward. As you climb, look out for the so-called "Rays of God" in the rocks.

RAYS OF GOD

Rocks in the area often display the mark of plants resembling palm fronds. They are said to have been created by the intense heat when God descended on the Holy Peak in the form of fire. Pilgrims called them the "Rays of God" and believed they were not found on any mountain other than Mount Sinai, proving it was the Mountain of God. Modern geologists identify the imprints as manganese deposits that form a pattern called dendritic pyrolusite.

Over halfway up you will pass two stone arches. The lower one is called the Shrive Gate of St. Stephen. According to Hobbs, this is where St. Stephen "took pilgrims' confessions and tested their knowledge of the Bible." Those who passed the test were granted certificates and allowed to continue.

The two trails eventually meet at the Basin of Elijah, a welcome relief for weary stairway climbers. It's a beautiful spot marked by a small chapel called the Church of Elijah and a towering cypress tree thought to be more than 500 years old. The deep green of the cypress provides a striking contrast to the barren landscape surrounding it. At the base of the tree a cistern called the "Well of Our Lord Moses" collects rain and snowmelt for the flocks of the local Bedouin, or Jabaliya, people.

SALLY MA

The Shrive Gate of St. Stephen.

The final ascent to the summit passes market stalls of the local Bedouin.

From this point all hikers must climb the last 750 steps to the summit. They are steep, rocky and uneven, so take your time. If you are doing the hike to watch the sun rise, don't be surprised if you have to pick your way around people who have spent the night huddled in sleeping bags to catch the first rays of the sun.

The actual summit area is quite small. Here the Christian Church of the Holy Trinity and a mosque cling to the rocks overlooking a stunning 360-degree panorama of barren, jagged peaks stretching to the horizon. It is not hard to understand why de Laborde thought it resembled the "end of the world."

The present church building dates to 1934, but a series of chapels are thought to have continuously occupied this spot since at least the fourth-century pilgrimage of the nun Etheria. After the "infinite toil" of her ascent, she speaks of visiting a church "not great in size," but "great in grace."

Because we did the hike to catch the sunset, and were there in January when it was freezing cold, we were lucky enough to have the entire site to ourselves. But it is not unusual for as many as two to three hundred climbers to be jostling for the best views while they eagerly await the sunrise.

Ironically, the monastery has extended its hospitality to pilgrims and visitors for centuries, but like many spectacular destinations that formerly could be reached

The Church of the Holy Trinity at the summit of Mount Sinai.

only by an arduous journey, modern transportation and accommodation alternatives now make the site accessible for literally thousands. This has created tremendous pressure on the monks and their sacred mountain.

Bruce Feiler, in his book *Walking the Bible*, describes the crowded site at the top as an "ecclesiastical strip mall" filled with people, religious buildings and a Bedouin tent selling supplies. The monks and the local Jabaliya, who have a rich tradition of religious ritual dating back centuries, have been forced to stop the ceremonies that were becoming a "tourist spectacle" at the top of the mountain. The church and the mosque are now kept locked because visitors were sleeping and even defecating in them. It should go without saying that you are in a sacred spot, so please respect that fact.

One other word of caution before you begin the hike. If you are descending the camel trail in the dark as our group did, take note of the door where you need to re-enter the monastery. We wandered around in the inky darkness for some time until we finally stumbled on the entrance. Flashlights were of little use in the pitch black night, and believe me, no one heard our shouts for help through the massive stone walls. We were hoping someone would notice we had not returned for supper, but they were obviously too busy eating!

HOW TO DO THE HIKE

As noted in the section called "The essentials," there are a number of alternatives available to access the site, including bus, taxi, private car or air. Many churches and religious institutions offer trips to Mount Sinai as part of a Holy Land tour. For those looking for a more in-depth experience that combines a visit to the mountain and the monastery with the chance to see more of this fascinating country, consider a small group trip that specializes in the region. This avoids the hassle of trying to organize something on your own. The language (spoken and written) as well as significant cultural differences (especially for women) can often create problems when it comes to negotiating details about service and payment (see the sidebar about baksheesh). It may be well worth it to leave the planning to the experts.

Recommended outfitters

I have travelled with all three of these outfitters in various parts of the world. In my experience they are all reputable and reliable operators. Each company offers different hiking and sightseeing choices. I booked my 17-day Egypt and Jordan adventure with G Adventures and found it good value for money.

- G Adventures (formerly GAP Adventures) **www.gadventures.com**. This is an excellent trip because it combines many of the archeological and historical wonders of ancient Egypt and Jordan with a trip to the monastery, including accommodations at the monastery guesthouse. Unlike many other tours of the area, the trip also travels into Jordan with the chance to hike in the Lost City of Petra (see the "Consider this" section below) and stay in a local Bedouin desert camp.

- Exodus **www.exodus.co.uk**.
- Explore! **www.explore.co.uk**.

HOW DO YOU SAY THAT?

Arabic is the official language of Egypt. Unfortunately for most foreigners the script in which it is written has the appearance of an unreadable, if graceful, sequence of squiggles. Some form of transcription into words using the Roman alphabet would help, but apparently no single standardized system has yet been developed to do this. For those looking for a more complete guide, check out Lonely Planet's *Egyptian Arabic Phrasebook*. Here are a few common phrases to get you started:

- hello – sa·lam'a·lay·kum
- goodbye – ma'·as sa·laa·ma
- thank you – shu·kran
- Do you speak English? – En·ta bi·tit·kal·lim in·glee·zee? (addressed to a man)

- Do you speak English? – En-tee bi-tit-kal-li-mee in-glee-zee? (addressed to a woman)
- Where is...? – Fayn...?
- How much is it? – Bi·kam da?
- I don't understand – A·na mish faa·hem (addressed to a man)
- I don't understand – A-na mish fah-ma (addressed to a woman)

CONSIDER THIS: BEFORE OR AFTER THE HIKE

If you are this close, my unqualified recommendation is to consider a side trip to the rose-red City of Petra in nearby Jordan. You may know it from Steven Spielberg's popular film *Indiana Jones and the Last Crusade*, in which the famous Siq and Treasury had starring roles along with Harrison Ford in his quest for the elusive Holy Grail.

The hidden city of Petra was lost to history for centuries until it was "rediscovered" by the Swiss explorer Johann Ludwig Burckhardt in 1812 during a trip from Damascus to Cairo. (The city had fallen into obscurity after it was shattered by devastating earthquakes.) During his journey, Burckhardt heard rumours of some magnificent ruins located in the mountains of the Wadi Musa, the Valley of Moses. The location was a closely guarded secret, known only to local residents.

Burckhardt convinced his Arab guide to take him to the site by vowing to have a goat slaughtered in honour of Aaron, whose tomb lay at the end of the valley. In his journal he explains that "by this stratagem I thought that I should have the means of seeing the valley on my way to the tomb."

His ploy worked, but the full extent of what he had stumbled across was not appreciated until after his death, when the inevitable flood of archaeologists, travellers and artists began visiting the site. Although excavations have continued since the nineteenth century, it is estimated that as little as 5 per cent has been uncovered.

Petra was probably occupied by the Nabataeans, a nomadic tribe who came from Arabia, around the early third century BCE. The tribe gradually established control over a vast region that eventually extended from the Hejaz of northern Arabia, the Negev and the Sinai to the Hauran of southern Syria.

KENT KLATCHUK

The famous Siq and Treasury of Petra had starring roles in Indiana Jones and the Last Crusade.

Their fabulous wealth came from the taxes they imposed on camel caravans coming from the east and along the Incense Route from southern Arabia. By far the most profitable was the trade in frankincense, myrrh and other spices from Arabia, but the city was also an important link in the Silk Road.

With their expert knowledge of hydraulic engineering the Nabataeans were able to control water resources in the valley, building an elaborate series of dams, cisterns and channels. With secure access to water and the protective barricade of the surrounding mountains, they began building a magnificent city out of the rose-coloured rock (Petra means "rock"). They combined Greek and Roman design with their own unique local style to create an extraordinary place that is pure magic.

Getting there is relatively easy from Mount Sinai. (Note that both the G Adventures and Exodus trips described in the "How to do the hike" section include Petra in their itineraries.) Bus service is available from al-Milgaa to Nuweiba, where excellent fast-ferry service departs for Aqaba in Jordan. From here, minibuses depart regularly for Wadi Musa (the town outside of Petra) with ongoing connections to various destinations in Jordan, including Amman. It is also possible to rent a car or hire a taxi from Aqaba.

Petra covers a huge area. You can spend days hiking around the site and never see it all. Specialized tours are available to help you do this; check out **www.go2petra.com** for information on all things Petra. In my humble opinion, here are a few highlights that should not be missed.

The Siq: You can't really miss it, since you must walk down its length in order to gain access to the ancient city. It may look like it is the product of water erosion, but it was actually formed by tectonic forces that have split the rocks apart. The Siq winds for just over a kilometre past towering walls that sometimes almost meet overhead. The clever Nabataeans harnessed the floods that hit the narrow passage each winter

The multi-hued sandstone of the Siq with the channels of the water control system clearly visible along the side.

KENT KLATCHUK

and devised a water control system to supply the city. As you walk you will see the channels cut into the walls along with carvings hewn from the rock. The Siq seems almost mystical as it winds through the multi-hued sandstone and opens into the fairy-tale land of Petra.

The Treasury of the Pharaoh, or Khazneh el-Far'un is probably the best-known monument in the city. The elaborately carved facade will take your breath away as you leave the twilight of the Siq and catch your first glimpse of it in all its glorious rose-coloured brilliance. There is no consensus on when it was built (probably near the end of the first century BCE), but the abundance of funerary symbols in its design indicate an association with the Nabataean cult of the dead. Wrested from the solid rock walls by men using little more than pickaxes and chisels, the level of craftsmanship is astonishing. Tradition holds that an Egyptian pharaoh hid his treasure in the urn in the middle of the second level. If you look closely you will see the solid-rock urn is pockmarked from bullets aimed at shattering it to reveal the gold inside.

The Monastery, or Al-Deir: One of the largest carved facades in Petra, it resembles the overall design of the Treasury, but dwarfs its famous counterpart in terms of scale. Its colossal size indicates the monument had some special significance. The monastery can only be reached by climbing an ancient stone pathway of more than 800 steps.

The elaborately carved facade of the Treasury of the Pharaoh.

The rugged path leading to the monastery.

The climb up to see the monastery is worth the effort.

The climb is best done in the afternoon, when the stairs are in the shade. The trail starts behind the Nabataean Museum and is well worth the effort it takes to get to the top.

ARE YOU READY TO EAT?

Egyptian food can generally be described as simple, hearty fare. Drawing on the traditions of its Greek, Lebanese, Turkish and Syrian neighbours, it has been adapted to suit Egyptian tastes with a focus on local ingredients.

Aysh, or bread, is the mainstay of the national diet. You will see freshly baked piles of it for sale every morning in markets all over the country. Along with the lowly bean, the two form the basic ingredients for some of the most popular street food in the country. Fuul combines slow-cooked fava beans mixed with garlic, lemon and spices stuffed into a shammy pocket (similar to pita bread). It is sometimes served with an egg for breakfast. Another popular variant called ta'amiyya (or falafel) is made with mashed broad beans mixed with spices, formed into patties and deep fried before they are tucked into a shammy pocket covered with tahini or sesame paste.

Coffee houses are ubiquitous. They are a gathering place for the locals, who come to sip strong tea or Turkish coffee and smoke the traditional shisha, or water pipe. The shisha has a glass tube filled with water, which cools the smoke and creates bubbles – hence the name "hubble bubble." Hot coals plus the occasional puff keep the tobacco going. Smokers can choose from regular tobacco or various mixtures soaked in apple juice or other flavours such as strawberry or cherry, creating a wonderful aroma as the pipe is smoked. Before you indulge, make sure you get a disposable plastic mouthpiece to put over the end of the pipe.

Whatever epicurean adventures you decide to embark on during your stay in Egypt, here are a few words of caution and advice to help you safely on your journey.

Hygiene standards are often questionable or non-existent. If you decide to eat street food, be sure to have your hepatitis A shots up to date before you leave home, and never eat anything that is not thoroughly cooked.

As a rule of thumb, never eat raw fruit or vegetables you have not personally peeled or washed, unless you are eating in a top-class restaurant, and even then it might pay to be wary. Always be sure to check the seal on bottled water. If it is broken, do not take a chance on it.

Tipping is a way of life in Egypt. The practice is often called *baksheesh*, and you will be expected to tip for virtually any service you receive, real or imagined. In hotels and restaurants, a 12 per cent charge will usually be added to the bill, but beware. This doesn't go to the waiter but straight into the restaurant till. You will still be expected to tip the waiter separately.

Vegetarianism – the concept is not well understood. Although it is easy to find vegetable-based dishes, including plenty of hearty bean soups, they will often be made with a meat stock, so it will be necessary to check if this is a concern to you.

Dining customs – as in any culture, there are certain subtle rules you should be aware of. For example, it is considered to be very bad manners to blow your nose in a restaurant or to eat, drink or smoke in public during the holy month of Ramadan. And it is generally advisable to sit next to a person of the same sex at the dinner table unless instructed otherwise.

INTERNET RESOURCES

There is a wealth of Sinai information available on the Internet. Here are a few reliable sites to get you started:

> *BAKSHEESH*: **TIP OR BRIBE?**
>
> The payment of baksheesh will be expected in almost any transaction you will encounter in Egypt. Everything from the simple opening of a door to delivery of your baggage will require a suitable gratuity. Egyptians regard it as a fact of life. Baksheesh has been described as "lavish remuneration and bribes, rudely demanded but ever so graciously accepted by the natives in return for little or no services rendered." Whether you regard it as a tip or a disguised bribe, there will be no way to ignore the hand inevitably extended to receive it.

www.sinaimonastery.com is the official site of Saint Catherine's Monastery.

www.egypt.travel, the official site of the Egyptian Tourism Authority, features news and a comprehensive range of resources and links.

www.sis.gov.eg, the Egyptian State Information Service, provides information on tourism, geography and culture as well as useful links.

www.go2petra.com has history and general information on Petra.

www.nabataea.net provides in-depth information on the Nabataeans.

RECOMMENDED READING

You may have to search more than usual to track down books on Mount Sinai and the monastery. Most of these were located through my local library service:

Lonely Planet Egypt – *I tend* to be partial to the Lonely Planet series. This one is a comprehensive and useful starting point for planning any trip to Egypt.

Lonely Planet Jordan – another comprehensive and useful planning tool for any trip to Jordan.

Mount Sinai – Joseph J. Hobbs – a very readable and comprehensive view of the history, geography and biblical context, plus a great description of the monastery and the actual climb. By far my best resource.

KENT KLATCHUK

Camels rest near the Treasury in Petra.

FAUNA FACTS: ONE HUMP OR TWO?

Say the word camels and the next thing that probably comes to mind is "ships of the desert." Not only are these creatures capable of hauling large loads of goods for long distances, but their rolling gait can sometimes make the rider "seasick." These amazing animals have thrived for centuries in some of the most desolate, arid regions of the world because they are uniquely equipped to survive even the harshest conditions. Camels in the Sinai are Arabian camels, or dromedaries, with one hump. Contrary to popular belief, the hump is not used to store extra water but up to eighty pounds of fat. Camels' eyes are shaded from the sun by a ridge of bone and they actually have an extra eyelid that can be used to brush away blowing sand or closed to protect the eye while still permitting vision. The animal is well known for an ability to eat almost anything at hand, and is not above chomping down on a tent if one presents itself. Probably its most amazing adaptation is its ability to survive long intervals without water. There are several reasons for this. Camels don't sweat like humans, but are able to increase or decrease their body temperature to track the weather, using only the water they need to live. They are capable of losing up to 30 per cent of their body weight in water and can quickly rehydrate with large quantities of water without inducing water intoxication, something that would kill a human that did the same thing. And just in case you ever wondered how desert nomads cook their food, apparently camel fecal pellets are so dry they can be used to start a fire almost as soon as they hit the ground.

Petra – Maria Giulia, Amadasi Guzzo and Eugenia Equini Schneider – another good one for the historical context, with wonderful photos, though somewhat academic.

Petra and the Lost Kingdom of the Nabataeans – Jane Taylor – a comprehensive source on the history of the fabled lost city, complete with lavish photographs. Taylor also has a shorter guide simply entitled *Petra.*

*Saint Catherine's Monastery, Sinai Egypt: A Photographic Essa*y – text by Helen C. Evans with photos by Bruce White – contains stunning photographs combined with good historical information.

The Hidden City of Petra – an A&E DVD that contains an excellent summary of the history and the sites.

The Monastery of Saint Catherine in Sinai: History and Guide – Jill Kamil – a fine overall guide to the monastery, including good maps and a detailed description of the climb.

The Pilgrimage of Etheria – edited by M.L. McClure and C.L. Feltoe – includes a portion of the narrative of Etheria's pilgrimage to the "Mount of God" near the end of the fourth century. See archive.org for a scanned version of McClure and Feltoe.

The Sisters of Sinai: How Two Lady Adventurers Discovered the Hidden Gospels – Janet Soskice – tells the fascinating story of identical twin sisters who found and deciphered one of the earliest known copies of the Gospels at Saint Catherine's Monastery. The tale sounds dry and academic but is really an astonishing story of grand adventure in the 1800s. Highly recommended.

Walking the Bible: A Journey by Land through the Five Books of Moses – Bruce Feiler. The chapters in Book III, "The Great and Terrible Wilderness," offer the story of one man's journey to the "god-trodden mountain of Mount Sinai."

CHAPTER 2 – CHINA –
THE GREAT WALL OF CHINA

The Great Wall of China –
Changcheng – literally The Long Wall

Unequalled throughout all antiquity, it is a miracle, a historical one-off

—SUN YAT-SEN, creating the myth of the Great Wall

✳ HIKING RULE 2: Use rubber tips on your hiking poles. Not only do the standard pointed, metal tips make an annoying click on rocks and paved walkways, they cause irreparable damage to dirt trails by loosening soil and promoting erosion. This is a big concern on any trail, but particularly on many of the ancient, eroded sections of the Great Wall.

WHERE IN THE WORLD?

WHAT WILL I SEE?

T. COSSEY

T. COSSEY

A restored portion of the crenellated towers and wall at Jinshanling.

A crumbling section of the wall at Luowenyou.

CLAIM TO FAME

The Great Wall of China was designated a UNESCO World Heritage Site in 1987, recognizing its historical, strategic and architectural significance as the world's largest military structure. It is considered the national symbol of China.

HIKE PROFILE

These are day hikes. Expect to encounter plenty of undulating terrain and sections that involve navigating uneven rock and rubble. Altitude change, however, is not an issue.

Hazards

None, other than the usual risk of injury from turning an ankle or falling due to uneven surfaces.

The essentials

Getting there: Beijing is the main access point to begin any exploration of the Great Wall. From North America it is serviced by many major airlines or their partners, including, among others, Air Canada, Air China, Cathay Pacific, Continental Airlines and Delta Airlines.

Currency: Renminbi (RMB), or "people's money"; the basic unit is the yuan, or ¥. ¥1 = 10 jiao or 100 fen. For current exchange rates, check out **www.oanda.com.**

Special Gear: Make sure you have good sturdy walking boots. Even if you normally eschew walking poles as being for sissies and old fogies, you should consider taking a pair to navigate the uneven rocks and often exceedingly steep terrain, especially on unrestored portions of the Wall. Of course hat, sunscreen and water bottles are essential. You may encounter enterprising Chinese who will show up with water and snacks for sale in the most unexpected places, but don't count on it.

A note on spelling: Over the years, various systems of transcription have developed to represent the speech sounds of Chinese characters in a written form based on phonetic letters from the Roman alphabet. The result is a confusing collection of spellings and name references. The spellings used here are consistent with those in Thammy Evans's *Great Wall of China* and Julia Lovell's *The Great Wall: China Against the World, 1000 BC–AD 2000*, both of which use the Pinyin system. (See the "How do you say that?" section for a discussion of Pinyin.) Lovell's book was by far the best and most readable single source of information on the Great Wall that I found.

HIKE OVERVIEW

Let's get one thing straight about the Great Wall of China. Despite what you will read in the tourist brochures, there is no one single ancient stone wall that snakes its way across the breadth of China for a precise, measurable distance – and no, you can't see it from space.

Instead there are many lesser walls built by a series of Chinese dynasties from the Qin (starting in 221 BCE) to the Ming (ending in 1644) that meander across China from the desolate western frontier of the Gobi Desert to the border with North Korea. Most of these are in various states of disrepair, at times not much more than a barely perceptible scar on the landscape.

The massive, crenellated brick and stone structure that has become the national symbol of China dates back about 500 years to the Ming Dynasty, and then only parts of it have been restored for the benefit of the tourist hordes flocking by the millions every year to hike along the pristine ramparts and snap the obligatory photos.

Most visitors with a day to spare opt for one of the many excursions offered to Badaling, 70 km (43.5 mi.) northwest of Beijing, where the Wall was meticulously restored and manicured in the latter part of the twentieth century, mainly by Communist labour. But venture beyond the showcase restorations and there is a good chance you will have the Wall to yourself to explore in all its wildness. That is where this chapter leads us.

Why would I want to?

In 1793 Lord George Macartney stopped at the Gubeikou pass, northeast of Beijing. He was travelling to meet the Chinese Emperor Qianlong at his retreat in Jehol (modern day Chengde) with hopes of convincing him of the benefits of free trade and open ports. In this task he failed miserably, but along the way Macartney paused to have a look at the Wall. He was astonished by what he saw, claiming the structure to be "the most stupendous work of human hands."

The British were not known for flights of hyperbole, but they were clearly impressed. And although they were responsible for perpetuating a number of the

myths and misconceptions that continue to plague many descriptions of the Wall, they were also responsible for launching a Western fascination with the history and architecture of the structure that continues to this day.

The myths persist (see the sidebars on myths below) but there is no dispute that the Wall represents a colossal human achievement in terms of scale and scope. If that sounds intriguing, perhaps this adventure is for you.

When to go

September or October usually offer warm, dry, sunny days but can be quite cold at night. Summer months can be very hot and humid, with peak rainfall usually falling in July and August. Most tour operators with extended trips to various parts of the Wall tend to offer them from June to October.

What's the story?

When Lord Macartney stopped to view the Wall at Gubeikou Pass in 1793, he was in vintage Wall country – where walls and towers snake vertiginously along the ridge-tops of mountains and descend to follow steep valleys as far as the eye can see. And although he was clearly blown away by what he saw, he wasn't the first to be awe-struck by the vista before him – the same vista that continues to be promoted in tourist brochures across China and the rest of the world.

As far back as the seventeenth century, the Flemish Jesuit Ferdinand Verbiest had already seen the same sections of the Wall that would be viewed by Macartney

Located about 10 km (6.2 mi.) east of Gubeikou Pass, the walls and towers at Jinshanling snake along the mountain ridgetops.

over 100 years later. He proclaimed, "The seven wonders of the world put together are not comparable to this work."

Martino Martini, a Jesuit cartographer and contemporary of Verbiest, declared it was "longer than the entire length of Asia," claiming it was built by Emperor Xius, 215 years before Christ. Martini claimed, "In the space of five years … it was built so strongly that if anyone was able to slip a nail between the cut stone, the builder of that part would be put to death. The work is magnificent, huge, and admirable, and has lasted right up to the present time without any injury or destruction."

What was originally viewed by the Chinese themselves as the "long wall" was gradually transformed by the Jesuits from a mere "wall" to "a tremendous wall" to "that prodigious wall" until it was finally agreed that nothing short of "Great Wall" would suffice.

Julia Lovell, in her very readable history *The Great Wall: China Against the World, 1000 BC–AD 2000*, believes this Jesuit "cult of the Great Wall" was one of the most obvious ironies of what she sees as a propaganda campaign by them to promote China to the West. Lovell maintains, "Their critical faculties were blunted by the need to defend their investment in China: they were, in effect, worshipping at the shrine of a structure expressly designed to keep people such as themselves out of the country."

THE CENTRE OF THE WORLD

The Chinese called their country Zhongguo, or the "Middle Kingdom" because they believed China was at the centre of the civilized world. They viewed their culture as entirely self-sufficient with no need to engage in trade with anyone outside its borders. In 1792 when Lord Macartney and his entourage of 700 began the long, perilous journey to China on behalf of King George III to establish trade relations with Qing Emperor Qianlong, the mission was doomed from the outset. When the Emperor finally made his formal reply on October 3, 1793, it had actually been written more than six weeks prior to the meeting. The English were informed, "We have never valued ingenious articles, nor do we have the slightest need of your country's manufactures." But despite the failure of his mission, Macartney was well compensated for his efforts, receiving £15,000 for every year he was away from Britain.

NO TO THE KOWTOW

When the British attempted to use diplomatic means to establish trade relations with the Chinese, they were confronted with the Chinese view that all foreigners were barbarians and therefore intrinsically and undeniably inferior. The Chinese firmly believed the barbarians had nothing of value to offer to the Middle Kingdom. They also viewed their Emperor as the ruler of "all under heaven." So, unlike most countries with some form of foreign affairs department established to deal with envoys from other nations, the Qing dynasty had a Tribute Reception Department. There was a complicated set of rules to govern how visitors should present themselves to the Emperor, one of which involved the kowtow. This required three full prostrations, with the head touching the ground each time. Chinese records indicate that Macartney actually complied with the ritual, but the British maintain he never agreed to submit to what they considered an indignity for a person of his status. In the end, it didn't really matter whether Macartney kowtowed or not. Emperor Qianlong rejected the British advances and the mission failed miserably. It was this failure by the Qing dynasty to fully understand the threat posed by the British and their Western counterparts that would have far-reaching and tragic consequences for China.

MYTHS ABOUT THE GREAT WALL

Myth #1: (Note: there are probably more than six myths about the Great Wall. Those presented here are based on Lovell's discussion in her book *The Great Wall*.) There is one Great Wall, an ancient monolithic structure with one coherent past. In fact, it is a series of walls built over thousands of years by different Chinese dynasties and most of these structures are crumbling or no longer exist. The impressive portions of the Wall that have been restored for the benefit of tourists date back to the Ming dynasty and are no more than 500 years old. And even most of this Wall is now totally derelict, while portions have actually been destroyed to make way for roads or dismantled to use as building materials.

Myth #2: The Wall marks a boundary between the Chinese civilization and the barbarians of the northern steppes. This view completely overlooks the fact that for large parts of its history, China was ruled by these very barbarians. The Wall did little to stop the advances of the Mongols under Genghis Khan and the Manchus of the Qing dynasty. As Genghis Khan is often quoted, "The strength of walls depends on the courage of those who guard them." When the Mongols encountered walls they simply dodged around them or bribed officials who were often languishing in appalling conditions and lacking even the most basic supplies for survival.

Myth #3: The Wall has always been viewed as "Great." For most of its history, the Chinese term for the Wall, Changcheng (which translates literally as "Long Wall"), was not even used by them. Jesuits and Victorian travellers from the West may have been enamoured of the impressive Ming walls they saw northeast of

T. COSSEY

A crumbing portion of the Wall near Jiaoshan Pass overlooks modern greenhouses.

Beijing, but for the Chinese the Wall often represented a symbol of humiliation and military weakness, a desperate defensive strategy for dealing with the barbarians when all else had failed. Not only was it built at huge human cost, sacrificing the lives of hundreds of thousands of forced labourers, but it bankrupted once strong dynasties in the process.

Myth #4: The Wall was built as a defensive barrier to keep out the barbarians, promoting the Chinese view of themselves as non-imperialist, non-aggressive and peace-loving. But this overlooks the fact that some of the earliest wall building occurred far into the Mongolian steppes, making them much more offensive than defensive in nature. And it certainly ignores the fact that throughout Chinese history, a strong sense of cultural superiority clearly pervades the names attached to their forts: "Fort Where Barbarians Are Killed" and "Overawing the Goat-like Barbarians" clearly smack of a not so subtle view of outsiders and aliens.

Myth #5: The Wall is the only man-made structure visible from the moon. This claim was initially made by a US magazine called *The Century* in 1893 and later promoted by Robert Ripley (of *Believe It or Not* fame) in 1932. It was generally regarded as a statement of fact until the Chinese astronaut Yang Liwei admitted he could not see a single section of the Wall during his 2003 space expedition.

Myth #6: The amount of stone in the Wall was equivalent to "all the dwelling-houses of England and Scotland." This amazing statement was made by John Barrow, who travelled with Macartney on his failed trade mission. Not satisfied with this observation, Barrow went on to claim, "it is more than sufficient to surround the circumference of the earth on two of its great circles, with two walls, each six feet high and two feet thick!"

The myths continued to be perpetuated by intrepid Victorian adventurers such as George Fleming, an army veterinarian who in 1861 was granted permission to travel over the Great Wall and into Manchuria. The Chinese had suffered humiliating military defeats in the Opium Wars of the 1800s. Not only had they been forced to cede Hong Kong to the British, but under the Treaty of Tianjin, the Western barbarians now had free access to trade their opium for Chinese goods and to work and travel in the realm of the Middle Kingdom.

Whatever your views on British culpability when it comes to the introduction of the opium trade to China, the country was seen as little more than an historical curiosity, a crumbling empire full of opium addicts sorely in need of an injection of so-called Western civilization. Fleming's account, published as *Travels on Horseback in Mantchu Tartary*, was scathing in its denunciation of practically everything he encountered on his journey. Not only was Chinese calligraphy "grotesque" but villages were described as "wretched" and the smells as "revoltingly vile."

In short, Fleming had nothing good to say about China until he was stopped dead in his tracks by his first sighting of the Wall near Shanhaiguan, where he abandoned himself to unrestrained admiration for this "petrous girdle ... bounding magnificently up hill and down dale." Even Fleming had to admit he was impressed by "the Herculean efforts of a great nation in bygone ages to preserve itself from invasion and subjection."

As these wildly enthusiastic reports from travel writers began to appear in the West and organized tours became available, Wall viewing soon became, and continues to be, an essential part of any trip by foreign visitors.

The Chinese, on the other hand, had no such obsession with the "Greatness" of the Wall. For them it was a symbol of shame, oppression and military failure. It represented the suffering of millions of the Chinese people under cruel and despotic rulers over thousands of years.

But when the Qing dynasty eventually fell in 1912 and the last emperor, Puyi, was driven from the Forbidden City in Beijing, Sun Yat-sen, the leader of the new Republic of China, began looking for a symbol that could restore national self-respect. He looked north to an obvious candidate.

Like his Western counterparts, Sun did not trouble himself with historical facts, but instead perpetuated the myth of the ancient, unchanging Great Wall heralded by the Jesuits and the Victorians. According to Lovell, he proclaimed it as "unequalled throughout all antiquity, it is a miracle, a historical one-off." In the process he ignored the reality of its history, choosing instead to focus on a symbol that could rally the nation.

In the years of turmoil and civil war that followed, the Wall would gain increasing significance as a rallying point for the Chinese. On the famous 13,000 km (8,000 mi.)

Long March of the Communists, as they fled north from the Nationalists of Chiang Kai-shek, Mao Zedong rallied the troops with his famous cry, "If we fail to reach the Great Wall we are not true men!"

His call to action would eventually morph into the quotation now found on T-shirts at every Great Wall tourist kiosk – "You're not a real man if you've never been to the Great Wall." It is a prospect Mao might have viewed with some dismay – especially considering that the Communists, under his guidance, were responsible for the wholesale destruction of hundreds of miles of the Wall during the Cultural Revolution, when materials were carted away for use in road and reservoir construction.

But despite the efforts of Sun and Mao, it was the Japanese invasions during the 1930s and 1940s that ultimately enshrined the Wall as a byword for the strength and patriotism of the nation. The popular resistance song "Defend Our Great Wall" declared that "the blood-stained Great Wall is glorious!" And the national anthem of Mao's People's Republic of China rallies Chinese patriots to "Arise, ye who refuse to be slaves. Let us build a new Great Wall out of our flesh and blood."

The visit of US president Richard Nixon to China in 1972 was a symbolic turning point. Nixon offered official foreign homage to the strength and resilience of the Chinese people when he declared, "This is a Great Wall and it had to be built by a great people." This was followed in 1984 by Deng Xiaoping's national campaign to "Love China, Restore Our Great Wall," which resulted in the massive restorations we see today at Badaling and other points along the Ming wall north of Beijing.

Thanks to the efforts of Deng, millions of tourists now visit this extraordinary destination every year. Rising serpent-like along the contours of the mountains, the structure is without doubt a spectacular achievement of human skill and ingenuity. But it also remains one of the most intriguing paradoxes of Chinese history that a product of such bloody conflict and human suffering has been so successfully transformed into a symbol of national pride.

FROM THE QIN TO THE MING: BUILDING CHANGCHENG, THE LONG WALL

The Chinese have built walls in some form for centuries, but most historians agree that it was "The Only First – First Sovereign Emperor" of the Qin (pronounced "chin") dynasty, Qin Shihuang, who was responsible for the original Long Wall. Legend maintains he flew to the moon in a dream. When he saw that his land was vulnerable to attack from the demon barbarians to the north, he proclaimed, "I will build a Great Wall!" It was decreed that since demons only travelled in straight lines and were unable to turn corners, the wall must not be straight.

The First Emperor's demon barrier eventually sprawled almost 5000 km

(3,100 mi.), from Lintao in the northwest to the northeastern region of Liaodong. This was serious wall building on a grand scale not seen before. The Emperor enlisted the famous general Meng Tian to oversee the project, which he started about 215 BCE. But the cost in human suffering and lives was immeasurable. Hundreds of thousands of men, including conscripts, prisoners and enemies of the state were forced to work under deplorable conditions. It is estimated that only three survived for every ten who laboured on it. When they died of starvation or exhaustion they were simply tossed into the middle of the wall and buried where they fell, so that it eventually came to be called "the longest cemetery on earth." Popular legends ignored the horror but the sad truth is the Wall was built by the sweat and blood of ordinary people.

The First Emperor didn't stop at wall building. Once he had unified China under one rule he proceeded to lay the foundations of a bureaucratic administration that would help define the nation for centuries to come. Not only did he standardize currency, weights, laws and the Chinese script, but he was responsible for additional grand building projects, including a vast network of roads and canals.

He even press-ganged an estimated 700,000 labourers into the building of his mausoleum, a project that took almost 40 years to complete. Many workers were executed when they completed their service, to protect the secret site of the tomb. So effective was this strategy that the location was erased from historical memory until it was revealed in 1974 near Xi'an by Chinese farmers digging wells. Their chance discovery of bits of terracotta arms and legs eventually led to the astonishing revelation of the world-famous terracotta warriors, guarding the First Emperor into eternity.

The First Emperor's achievements may have been monumental, but his ruthless disregard for life and the cruel tyranny of his rule led to the eventual collapse of the dynasty and to his well-earned reputation as one of China's absolute despots.

Wall building continued for centuries after the fall of the Qin. When the Han finally realized that their "peace and friendship policy" with northern nomads was not working, they quickly began repairing Qin walls. They went on to build an estimated 10,000 km (6,200 mi.) of wall to the Qin's 5000 km (3,100 mi.), extending their reach as far west as Yumenguan (the Jade Gate) running along the route that would eventually become part of the Silk Road.

Little remains of these walls that were generally built far to the north of the restored brick and stone Ming walls we see near Beijing. They were commonly built using the hangtu, or tamped earth, method, where dirt was dumped in a frame of wood or bamboo and packed down in layers until the desired height was reached. Then the frame was moved on to build another section.

But it was the Ming who introduced a whole new level of engineering skill to wall building. Although they used the tamped earth method in many sections, they also built thousands of kilometres of the crenellated brick and stone walls we now associate with the Great Wall showcased north of Beijing.

While the tamped earth approach used locally available material, this new method required specialized groups of masons and stonecutters. It meant they needed access to brick kilns and quarries, and men and animals to transport material.

The task was monumental. Bricks weighing 10 kg (22 lb.) were fired and hauled up the wall to be cemented into place with mortar made from a secret recipe containing sticky, glutinous rice. In steep areas, bricks were tied to the horns of goats that were driven up the mountains, or three or four were tied to the backs of men who hiked up to the bricklayers. That's 40 kg (88 lb.) each trip!

An example of bricks in the Wall at Jinshanling.

By the time they were done, Ming walls extended over 6000 km (3,730 mi.) from Jiayuguan – The Last Pass Under Heaven – in the west – to the walls' eastern terminus at Shanhaiguan – The First Pass Under Heaven. They included thousands of towers and forts, often joined with the now famous masonry corridors up to 14 m (46 ft.) high in spots and 6 m (20 ft.) wide at the top.

T. COSSEY

The watchtower – First Pass Under Heaven at Shanhaiguan.

In the end, it wasn't enough to keep out the Manchu invaders from the north. Bribery and deplorable living conditions for Chinese soldiers stationed along the Wall guaranteed the eventual fall of the Ming dynasty to the Manchurians. When the Manchus established China's final Qing dynasty there was no longer any need for walls. The barbarians were now the rulers. The wall became a physical irrelevance, a symbol of shame and humiliation. The final invasion of the Middle Kingdom would be by the Western barbarians. But they came from the sea and there were no walls there to keep them out.

WHO WAS MENG TIAN?

Meng Tian was a great military general appointed by the First Emperor to oversee the building of his wall. When the First Emperor died during one of his tours of inspection, his mentally unbalanced son Huhai seized the opportunity to rid himself of some of his political opponents who were unaware of the death. He forged a command to Meng to commit suicide, accusing him of slandering the Emperor's rule. Meng complied by taking poison. According to Lovell, he admitted he had offended the rules of feng shui in the building of the Wall: "I built walls and dug moats for more than ten thousand li [a li is about 500 m, or 550 yards]; was it not inevitable that I broke the earth's veins along the way? This, then, is my offence." In an odd cultural twist, Meng is considered a semi-divine patron of writers and brush makers, since he is credited with inventing, or at least improving, the writing brush.

LEGENDS OF THE WALL

There are many legends about the building of the Wall. The First Emperor is said to have ridden a magical horse across China. Every 14 to 16 km (9 to 10 mi.) the horse would stomp his hooves and a watchtower would spring up. Other popular versions say the Emperor created nine suns to light up the sky so men could work day and night and always in dry weather, or that a large dragon grew tired as it flew over that part of China, stopped to rest and miraculously turned into the Long Wall. Ming accounts often revolve around worried overseers, terrified of the punishment awaiting them for failing to finish their section on time. In one story, the supervisor at Zijing (or Purple Bramble Pass) meets an old man who knits the pass out of brambles that conveniently turn to stone.

THE HIKE

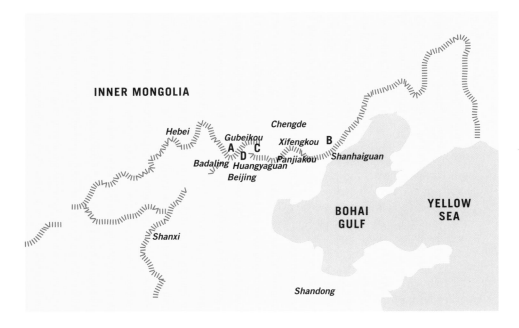

A. JIANKOU

B. JIAOSHAN PASS

C. JINSHANLING/SIMATAI

D. MUTIANYU

The vast majority of options for hiking on the Great Wall are in the area north of Beijing. Most can be done as a day trip or you may choose to spend several days with an organized tour operator in order to get the most out of the time you have available. (See the "How to do the hike" section for more detail on the options available.)

This is prime Ming Wall territory, where you will be able to experience the Wall in all its glory, from extensively restored portions such as those at Badaling and Mutianyu to crumbling, overgrown ruins at places like Panjiakou and Luowenyou. Following are brief descriptions of some of the options available, arranged alphabetically for convenience, and what to expect at each location. I have personally hiked the locations marked with an asterisk. There are many options and they are not all listed here. See the "Internet resources" and "Recommended reading" sections for additional information sources. Note that hiking distances are not provided. In most instances it is entirely up to you to decide how far you choose to walk along various portions of the Wall.

Badaling: not recommended. Located 70 km (43.5 mi.) northwest of Beijing, this is the most heavily promoted and visited section of the restored portion of the Great Wall. Be prepared for a carnival of tourist stalls and pressing crowds every day of the week. This is the part of the Wall where US President Richard Nixon made his groundbreaking speech in 1972 that signalled a significant moment in Sino-American relations and the start of a long, difficult move toward prying open Mao's Bamboo Curtain.

Huangyaguan/Taipingzhai*: highly recommended. This is a quiet section of the Wall located northeast of Beijing. It is possible to hike between Taipingzhai and Huangyaguan Pass or Yellow Cliff Pass (named from the nearby yellowish rocks and hills) in about two hours. This is classic Great Wall country where the Wall and watch towers snake along the mountains in a breathtaking display of architectural triumph. Be prepared for some steep sections that require caution. This part of the Wall is located within easy driving distance of the Eastern Qing Tombs near Zunhua. The tombs are certainly worth a visit if you can fit it in.

HEARTBREAK HILL: LITERALLY BREATHTAKING!

Every May runners from around the world tackle a diagonal stretch of the Huangyaguan Great Wall as part of the Great Wall Marathon. It's called Heartbreak Hill, a tortuous two-mile section rising at a 45-degree angle over 3,600 steps. The marathon is reputed to be one of the most gruelling in the world, taking the best competitors about four hours to complete, compared to the little over two hours required for the Boston and New York marathons.

A steep portion of the Wall at Taipingzhai.

INTO THE VALLEY OF DEATH

The Eastern Qing Tombs near Zunhua are the final resting place of five emperors, 14 empresses and 136 imperial consorts, although the numbers vary depending on what source you check. A highlight is the Ding Dong Ling tomb of Empress Dowager Cixi, who completed its design and building a full three decades before she actually died. Cixi had the audacity to place the symbol of the phoenix (representing the empress) above that of the dragon (the emperor) in the artwork at the entrance to the tomb.

Jiankou: Located just a few kilometres west of Mutianyu and 70 km (43.5 mi.) northeast of Beijing, this section is for serious hikers only. Although it is considered one of the most scenic sections, it has also been called one of the most dangerous and ruined parts of the Wall around Beijing.

Jiaoshan Pass*: recommended. An old section of the Wall, located northeast of Beijing outside Shanhaiguan. This section wanders along barely visible bits of the

T. COSSEY

Wall, with a steep climb up uneven steps to Jiaoshan Pass. Part of the climb requires clambering up a ladder on the outside of a tower (the ladder is actually a "ladder cage" with protective hoops that encircle the climber), but this section can be easily bypassed on a walkway built around the tower. The trail eventually leads to a Daoist temple used for occasional ceremonies. This is a good spot to stop for lunch. On the day we visited, we met the resident caretaker, who lives alone in the temple, protecting it from vandals. On the way down, be sure to opt for the path that circumvents the difficult and uneven climb up, thus avoiding a treacherous descent.

Climbing the Wall to Jiaoshan Pass.

GOOD VS. EVIL AND THE SEARCH FOR ANSWERS

Daoism (or Taoism) includes a confusing array of philosophical texts and legends and thousands of gods and goddesses. It began with the Tao, a text focusing on the unknowable force of the universe "embodying the harmony of opposites: no love without hate, no light without dark, no male without female." Confucianism,based on the tenets of the philosopher Confucius, stressed the need for social harmony and the importance of human goodness. Although Confucianism has exerted a huge influence on the very fabric of Chinese society for two thousand years, it was not always so. In the time of the First Emperor of the Qin dynasty, the Legalists were given full rein to impose absolute control over the people on the basis that humans were intrinsically evil and must be controlled by strict laws.

Jinshanling/Simatai*: highly recommended. This was the highlight of my Great Wall trekking. It is 10 km (6.2 mi.) east of Gubeikou Pass, which was used by the Qing royals on their annual journey to Chengde to escape Beijing's oppressive summer heat. Located 138 km (86 mi.) northeast of Beijing, this unspoiled section of the Wall has few visitors.

The day we visited was a brilliant blue-sky day in October complete with a stunning display of glorious fall foliage covering the surrounding mountains and valleys. We had the entire route almost exclusively to ourselves. Starting at the Simatai end, which involves a long climb up a series of stairs to join the Wall, we walked about 10 km (6.2 mi.) to the Jinshanling side, then along the roadway a short distance to the small tourist complex at the bottom and the rustic Jinshai Hotel.

A large portion of the Simatai section has recently been closed, and guards posted here will ensure you do not go past the official cutoff point. But it is possible to walk parts of the Simatai before backtracking and heading toward Jinshanling. Along the way you will see stunning views across the mountains and a series of towers and elaborate defensive walls. There are also sections in various stages of disrepair that require careful navigation. Be warned: some sections are terrifyingly steep, so it is essential to take your time, preferably with hiking poles to assist on the narrow, uneven descents.

A restored portion of the towers and Wall at Jinshanling.

Luowenyou*: recommended. Located northeast of Beijing, this is a remote and unrestored section of the Wall that requires a guide to locate and traverse. It is quite navigable and does not present the heart-stopping steepness of some areas found along other parts of the Wall. A walk here provides a good example of the crumbling state of disrepair that applies to vast portions of the Wall.

A good example of the crumbling state of disrepair of the Wall at Luowenyou.

Mutianyu: recommended if you are short of time. Located 90 km (56 mi.) northeast of Beijing, this restored section of the Wall is not usually as crowded as Badaling. Mutianyu is known for its Ming dynasty guard towers while its setting in a heavily forested area make it particularly photogenic, especially in the fall.

The Wall plunges into the water at Panjiakou.

Panjiakou/Xifengkou*: recommended. Located northeast of Beijing at the man-made reservoir at Panjiakou, which translates to "Great Wall beneath Water."

A dam on the Luan River has flooded portions of the Wall and surrounding land, forcing local farmers to become fishermen. Hiking here is best organized through a tour operator since it involves several boat trips around floating fish traps

Portions of the Wall at Panjiakou are very steep.

The Wall at Xifengkou is crumbling but easy to navigate.

to various spots on the reservoir with access to crumbling and totally unrestored portions of the Wall. The section at Panjiakou involves very steep, uneven terrain that requires caution to navigate safely, while the portion at Xifengkou (Happy Meeting Mouth) is much easier. There is also a set of extremely steep stairs to the boats that almost did me in.

Shanhaiguan/Laolongtou*: recommended. Located on the coast east of Beijing, Shanhaiguan is the site of the "First Pass Under Heaven," or East Gate. Laolongtou, or Old Dragon's Head, is the spot where the Wall plunges into the Bohai Sea, 4 km (2.5 mi.) from Shanhaiguan, and the easternmost terminus of the Wall. The sections of the Great Wall found here have been restored, including several watchtowers. The

LAUGHING CAN BE HAZARDOUS FOR YOUR HEALTH!

A well-known legend of Qin times tells the story of how Xifengkou, or Happy Meeting Mouth, was named. A father went searching for his son after he was taken away to work on the Great Wall. They ran into each other at Songting Hill, where they were so happy they laughed themselves to death. The pass where they were buried was named Xifengkou Pass to honour them.

The Old Dragon's Head, where the Wall plunges into the Bohai Sea.

Great Wall Museum, located just a few minutes south of the First Pass Under Heaven, is definitely worth a visit.

HOW TO DO THE HIKE

If your time is limited and you have only a few days to devote to trekking the Wall, avoid the madness of the crowds at Badaling (there is no day that is not busy), and consider some of the other spectacular options easily accessible from Beijing.

There are many tour operators offering guided day trips, while those of you seeking more adventure might want to consider hiring a taxi for the day and heading out on your own. Of course, you give up the background commentary supplied by many operators, but since this often gets lost in translation anyway, you may not be missing anything you wouldn't get from a little pre-reading.

There is always the option of navigating the public bus system. Many guidebooks make this alternative sound relatively easy, but keep in mind that the driver almost certainly will not speak English and the time you lose in finding your way is time you could have used walking on the Wall. It all depends on your adventure tolerance and how much time you have.

Two excellent sources of information on planning the logistics of such a visit can be found in the latest edition of Lonely Planet's *China* or Frommer's *Beijing*. Bradt also publishes *Great Wall of China: Beijing and Northern China*, by Thammy Evans, but the latest edition (2006) is already slightly outdated.

For those looking for a more in-depth experience that involves travelling between different sections of the Wall over several days or a week, this alternative is probably not a do-it-yourself project unless you speak at least rudimentary Mandarin and have a basic understanding of Chinese characters. Once you leave Beijing and venture into the countryside on local buses or trains or with a rental car, your chances of finding anyone with even basic English are negligible. So spare yourself the frustration and consider booking one of the excellent small-group guided trips that specialize in hiking the Wall.

Recommended outfitters

I have travelled with all of the following outfitters in various parts of the world. In my experience they are all reputable and reliable. Each company offers slightly different hiking options and additional sightseeing in the area north of Beijing. I booked the ten-day trip with Explore! to hike the Great Wall, which provided excellent value for money.

• Explore! **www.explore.co.uk**
• Exodus **www.exodus.co.uk**
• World Expeditions **www.worldexpeditions.ca**

HOW DO YOU SAY THAT?

There are many dialects and subdialects spoken throughout the country, but the official national language is Mandarin or Putonghua ("common speech"). Here are a few essential phrases to help you navigate:

• hello – ni hao
• goodbye – zaijian
• thank you – xiexie ni
• Do you speak English? – Ni hui shuo yingyu ma?
• Where is ...? – ... zai nar?
• How much is ...? – ... duoshao qian?
• I (don't) understand – Wo (bu) ming bai

CONVERTING CHINESE TO ENGLISH

Pinyin is the system adopted by the Chinese government in 1958 for writing their language using the Roman alphabet. It is also used to spell Chinese names in English. Although the original plan was to eventually replace the traditional Chinese characters with romanized lettering, this plan has essentially been abandoned. Pinyin was developed by Zhou Youguang, who returned to China from New York after the Communists established the People's Republic of China in 1949, believing he was going to help build a democracy. Zhou is sometimes called "the father of Pinyin," but he called himself "the son of Pinyin," since he based the system on the long tradition of use in the Qing dynasty. Pinyin replaced other transcription systems such as the widely used Wade-Giles, developed by Thomas Wade in the mid-1800s and codified in Herbert Giles's Chinese/English dictionary of 1892. The common use of other systems often results in confusing variations in the English spelling of names. For example, under Pinyin, the Wade-Giles conversion "Mao Tse-tung" is "Mao Zedong," while "Peking" becomes "Beijing." You will find a surprising amount of Pinyin on signs in and around Beijing, but don't expect most Chinese people to understand it, nor will you find it in the countryside and smaller towns.

WILL THE REAL EMPEROR PLEASE STAND UP?

Chinese emperors often had at least three names throughout their lives and sometimes more. They normally had a birth name, a reign title and a posthumous temple name as well as additional honorary titles. For example, Emperor Wu (the "martial" emperor) of the Han dynasty had a family name of Liu, a given name of Che, an honorary or courtesy name of Tong (used by more educated Chinese as an alternative to his given name), a reign name of Han Wu Di and a temple name of Wudi. Needless to say, this bewildering array of monikers can lead to considerable confusion, depending on the naming conventions used in the source you are reading. It is always useful to remember that Chinese names give the surname first, followed by the first name. So in the case of Liu Che, Liu is the surname and Che is the given name.

CONSIDER THIS – BEFORE AND AFTER THE HIKE

Beijing

Beijing is normally the beginning and ending point for any trip to the Great Wall. Inaugurated on February 2, 1421, the city was built by the Ming emperor Yongle on the site of the former Mongol city of Dadu, or "Great Capital." The

The Temple of Heaven.

name translates to "The North Is Pacified," although the city would eventually fall to the final barbarian invasion of the Manchurians who formed the last Qing dynasty in 1644.

The Mongols established the city on a north–south grid. Many of the key ceremonial halls built by the Ming follow this axis aligned with the Pole Star. In a headlong rush to destroy symbols of traditional Chinese culture, the Communists demolished and rebuilt much of the original Ming city, following the establishment of the People's Republic of China in 1949 and during the Cultural Revolution from 1966 to Mao's death in 1976. A few iconic structures did survive the wholesale destruction.

There are any number of excellent guidebooks providing in-depth information about everything you would ever want to know about the city and what it has to offer, so it is not the intention of this brief section to even attempt to duplicate such information. But any visit to Beijing should include a visit to at least a few of the remaining historical icons that help define the city and the country. In my humble opinion, here are few that should not be missed.

The Temple of Heaven, or **Tian Tan Gongyuan**, is set in a 267 hectare park. It was originally used by Ming and Qing emperors during the winter solstice to perform various rites and to pray for good harvests and the general health of the empire. The stunning Hall of Prayer for Good Harvests is a circular wooden hall measuring 38 m (125 ft.) high and 30 m (98 ft.) in diameter. The entire structure was built without using a single nail.

The entrance to the Forbidden City.

Tiananmen Square, or **Tian'an Men Guangchang**, is the largest public square in the world. On a typical smoggy day in the city don't expect to be able to see all the way across it. The Square became well known in the West in June 1989 following the violent suppression of student protesters. It is flanked by the Forbidden City to the north, the Great Hall of the People to the west, two museums to the east and Chairman Mao's mausoleum to the south. Every day but Monday, thousands line up to see the mummified remains of the former leader, hustled through by impatient guards wearing white gloves. The story persists that when Mao died in 1976, and the decision was made to preserve the body, his inexperienced doctors pumped him so full of formaldehyde that he swelled to unrecognizable proportions. Apparently they managed to drain the corpse and restore his face to an acceptable shape.

Forbidden City, or **Gu Gong** is home to the emperors of the Ming and Qing, and it is well worth braving the crowds just to experience the sheer, overpowering enormity of the place. It is easy to spend an entire day, perhaps more if you have the time and the stamina. The entrance Gate of Heavenly Peace is famous for the portrait of Mao that continues to hang there and the fact that the Great Helmsman declared the founding of the People's Republic of China from the top of the Gate on October 1, 1949.

The Summer Palace, or Yi He Yuan, was the summer playground of the Qing dynasty where royalty retired to avoid the oppressive heat in the Forbidden City. A favourite residence of the Empress Dowager Cixi, the park is dominated by Kunming Lake, the Hall of Benevolence and Longevity, the Long Corridor and a number of Buddhist temples. A wonderful spot to spend some time on a sunny afternoon.

A marble bridge with seventeen arches connects South Lake Island to the east shore of Kunming Lake.

Hong Kong

If you have the time and can organize a stopover in Hong Kong, don't miss the opportunity. Connections with Beijing are usually easily arranged at minimal extra cost. It may seem like an odd choice. Queen Victoria would probably have agreed. She is said to have remarked, "Albert is so amused at my having got the island of Hong Kong." It was 1841 and a British naval party had landed on the northwest shore of the island, raising the Union Jack on behalf of the British Empire. It was named Hong Kong, the English interpretation of the Cantonese name "heung-gawng" or fragrant harbour. The name is said to refer to the scent of sandalwood incense factories located on the western edge of the island.

The powers that be were not impressed. The Foreign Secretary, Lord Palmerston, fumed that "[it] will never be a mart for trade ...," calling it "a barren island with hardly a house upon it!" The man responsible, Captain Charles Elliot, saw the potential of the island's superb deepwater port, but others, it seems, did not. Jan Morris, in her fascinating account of the island's history *Hong Kong: Epilogue to an Empire*, notes that Elliot was eventually reassigned "in ignominy" to the new Republic of Texas, followed by postings in Bermuda, Trinidad and St. Helena. He is generally snubbed in historical annals, despite being one of the key architects of the cession of Hong Kong to Britain.

To say that Palmerston got it wrong is a bit of an understatement! Over the course of its tumultuous history, the "barren island" became one of the foremost manufacturing, financial and trading centres of the Empire, surviving and thriving despite a series of catastrophic events that would have shattered a less resilient and determined population. Dire predictions of its demise following the 1997 handover to the Chinese have clearly failed to materialize. Now a Special Administrative Region of

*Hong Kong Harbour from Victoria Peak. Increasing
development means smog is a frequent problem here.*

the People's Republic of China, this intensely entrepreneurial trading city is probably
busier than it ever was. With its flashing neon lights, streets filled with frenetic shop-
pers and jumble of skyscrapers lining the famous harbour, Hong Kong announces
loud and clear that making money remains the name of the game.

Given that reality, ask most potential visitors why they would consider a stop in
this tiny territory and the response would probably include the words shopping and
eating. Few would think of hiking. The fact is, about 75 per cent of Hong Kong's land
base is countryside, with an astonishing variety of scenic landscapes, from mountains to sandy beaches to woodlands. Within half an hour you can leave the teeming
streets behind to hike in the quiet solitude of one of the more than 20 country parks.
And the city's outstanding public transport system makes any foray into the countryside an easy excursion to plan.

The Hong Kong Tourism Board publishes a full colour booklet available for
free at any of their visitor information centres, complete with hike descriptions,

Tai Long Wan, or Big Wave Bay.

Shek O Village as seen from the Dragon's Back trail.

detailed information on how to do the hike and excellent maps. Or you may want to consider leaving it to the experts at Walk Hong Kong, **www.walkhongkong.com**. The company has been in business since 2003, offering a broad range of city and country park hikes throughout the region, including transport and a knowledgeable guide. I have used their services a number of times and would highly recommend them. There are many hikes to choose from in Hong Kong. Here are some of my favourites.

Tai Long Wan, or Big Wave Bay: varies from 6 km (3.7 mi.) to 11 km (6.8 mi.) depending on starting point; rated moderate to strenuous. Located in the Sai Kung Country Park, this stunning hike follows part of the long-distance MacLehose Trail and includes white sandy beaches, blue waters and pounding surf. The path winds through old Hakka clan villages and climbs to spectacular mountain and coastal views.

Dragon's Back: 5 km (3.1 mi.), rated moderate. Located in Shek O Country Park, this is one of the most popular hikes in Hong Kong. Voted Asia's best urban hike in 2004 by *Time* magazine, the trail passes through bamboo thickets to follow the undulating spine (resembling a dragon's back) of a wooded ridgeline. On a clear day the ascent is rewarded with fabulous views of Big Wave Bay, Tai Tam Harbour and the tiny fishing village of Shek O with its fine seafood restaurants. Commented *Time*: "The glory of it all is that you're so close to the city but could hardly feel farther away."

Jardine's Lookout: 8.5 km (5.3 mi.); rated moderate. Located in Tai Tam Country Park, this hike involves a few steep climbs to two outstanding viewpoints: Jardine's Lookout and Mount Butler. You will be rewarded not only with fine coastal vistas, but stunning views of Kowloon and the glistening skyscrapers of Causeway Bay and Central. The Lookout was named after William Jardine, co-founder of the famous British trading house Jardine Matheson & Co. Staff used the spot to watch for their trading ships passing through the harbour entrance below.

Lamma Island: length varies depending on which of several routes are taken; rated moderate. Offers a wonderful opportunity to hop on an inter-island ferry and climb to some wonderful views over the South China Sea. The road-free island offers a welcome escape from the traffic madness of Hong Kong, with the chance to explore temples and peaceful, nearly abandoned villages along the way. Be sure to stop for a seafood lunch before catching the ferry back.

The view from the trail on Lamma Island.

Victoria Peak: right in the heart of Hong Kong, but not to be missed. Most people will take the famous Peak Tram to the top and then walk the Peak Circle Walk, an easy distance of 3.5 km (2.2 mi.) with spectacular views of Victoria Harbour and Kowloon at your feet. Consider walking up Old Peak Road from Central, doing the Circle Walk and taking the tram back down. The climb is gradual and well marked. Soon the noise of the city below drifts away and you are surrounded by lush greenery with lots of benches strategically placed for a pause on the way up. You will probably have the whole track to yourself, since most people take the tram both ways.

ARE YOU READY TO EAT?

The Chinese have a saying that "food is heaven for the people," and it is no mere quip. Food is such an intrinsic part of the culture and texture of the nation that it sparks debate at a level commonly reserved for politics or religion in other places. Cooking styles can vary dramatically depending on the region you visit, and since they are heavily influenced by the availability of fresh, local ingredients and spices, you will find a bewildering array of choices that change with the seasons.

As with hikes, there are any number of guidebooks that will help you navigate the culinary delights of the country. (For an interesting account of one person's food odyssey across the country, check out Jen Lin-Liu's *Serve the People: A Stir-Fried Journey through China*.)

Here are just a few words of caution and advice to help you safely on your journey.

Hygiene standards: Since these are often questionable or non-existent, be extremely careful if you decide to eat street food. First be sure to have your hepatitis A shots up-to-date before you leave home. Then, if you do decide to try something, never eat anything that is not thoroughly cooked and hot off the wok. (In general, standards in Hong Kong are high and there should be no worries about restaurants here.)

BEIJING SPECIALTY

The quintessential specialty most often associated with Beijing is peking duck, which has been cooked since imperial times. It was mentioned in a manual prepared by an inspector of the imperial kitchen in 1330 and is considered one of China's national foods. Specially bred ducks are force-fed to a weight of 5 to 7 kg (11 to 15 lb.). Once the duck is slaughtered, air is pumped under the skin to separate it from the fat. The duck is soaked in boiling water, then hung to dry before being roasted to a shiny brown. The dish is traditionally sliced and served in front of the diners with steamed pancakes, scallions and hoisin, or sweet bean sauce. The thin, crispy skin is considered a particularly prized part of the meal.

As a rule of thumb, never eat raw fruit or vegetables that you have not personally peeled or washed unless you are eating in a top-class restaurant, and even then it might pay to be wary. And as a word of caution, always check the seal on bottled water. If it is broken, do not take a chance.

Tipping is not done and is not expected, although you may encounter a service charge at some high-end restaurants.

Vegetarians may have a difficult time finding food that does not contain some type of meat. With the rise of living standards in China, the ability to afford meat is a status symbol. (It is not uncommon to see Chinese people order far more than they can eat for a meal and then leave a staggering amount on the table, as a sign they can afford such flagrant waste of food.) Even if there is no meat in the dish, vegetables will often be fried in animal-based oils, and soups will usually be made with a beef or chicken stock.

Eating customs: Of course the chopstick reigns supreme and it is generally accepted that you will use your chopsticks to take food from a communal dish. (Food is usually ordered for the group and people help themselves.) Just remember not to root around in the dish; take only what you want without touching anything else. It is considered very rude to wave or point your chopsticks and bad luck to drop them. Sticking chopsticks vertically in a dish of rice is considered an omen of death, since they resemble incense sticks in a bowl of ashes. Rice is considered the "staff of life" and the unifier of the table. Chinese people usually eat rice at the end of the meal, so if you prefer to eat it with the other dishes, you will have to order it that way.

INTERNET RESOURCES

Search "Great Wall of China" and you will have millions of hits at your disposal. Many sources provide information of questionable validity and usefulness but here are a few reliable websites to get you started:

www.travelchinaguide.com is a comprehensive and dependable source for all things China.

www.tourismchina.org is the official site of the China National Tourist Office for Canada.

www.cnto.org is the official site of the China National Tourist Office for the US.

www.chinatoday.com has everything you ever wanted to know about China.

www.wildwall.com offers tours organized by British Great Wall researcher and conservationist William Lindesay. (See also reference to his book below.) Lindesay has walked extensive portions of the Ming Wall himself. He is the founder of International Friends of the Great Wall, **www.friendsofgreatwall.org**.

FAUNA FACTS: PANDAMONIUM

© FOTOSEARCH.COM

The Chinese call them "Big Bear Cats" because their eyes have vertical pupils similar to cats. For some reason pandas seem to create a peculiar amount of "pandamonium" as people flock to zoo exhibits to catch a glimpse of the giant white and black bears. Perhaps it is their wide-eyed, cuddly appearance that draws visitors, because they don't really do much except eat bamboo. Since bamboo is hard to digest and low in nutritional content, the bears need to eat as much as 20 kg (44 lb.) every day, which can take as long as 16 hours! They generally feed in an upright position, leaving their forelegs free to manipulate the stalks. Pandas have an extra digit on their paws called the "panda's thumb" that is really an enlarged wrist bone. It provides added dexterity when handling bamboo stalks. The bears, which were considered rare even in ancient China, are declining in the wild as their habitat continues to be drastically reduced. However, they are notoriously hard to breed in captivity. In a clever move to capitalize on their popularity with the public and boost breeding programs around the world, China regularly sends the bears abroad to signal good diplomatic relationships. But the privilege of hosting the bears comes with a few costly strings attached. All the expenses – including exhibit upgrades, an annual "rent" payable to China (plus an extra charge if a cub is born), and food costs that can top $200,000 a year – are paid by the donee.

A panda feeds on bamboo.

www.ebeijing.gov.cn is the official site of the City of Beijing and is packed with information.

www.great-wall-marathon.com is for the runners out there.

www.eatingchina.com features everything you ever wanted to know about Chinese food.

www.discoverhongkong.com is the official site of the Hong Kong Tourism Board, and the best place to start planning any trip to Hong Kong.

www.walkhongkong.com offers a broad selection of well-organized guided walks with a very reputable operator.

A NEW WALL GROWS

Every year from March to June, sometimes called the "Fifth Season," the Yellow Dragon, or Feng Chenbao, can sweep into Beijing from the Gobi Desert, reducing visibility to a few hundred feet. The raging sandstorms carry a toxic combination of sand and heavy metal particulates picked up from the industrial regions of China. The wind is nothing new – it was often viewed as a harbinger of "chaos under heaven" in the Middle Kingdom, bringing with it the prospect of "famine, pestilence and anarchy." China's modern response has been the creation of the Great Green Wall. Begun in 1978, the wall of trees will eventually extend for a distance of 4500 km (2,800 mi.) in the northwest of China along the Gobi Desert. The barrier is designed to hold back the expansion of the Gobi by planting a wide swath of hundreds of millions of trees that are said to constitute the biggest artificial forest in the world. The project is not without controversy. Critics say the monoculture plantations are vulnerable to disease, do not promote the diversity found in natural forests and are responsible for using large amounts of groundwater in an arid region already prone to severe drought. Many experts believe a better solution to the problem would be a non-invasive fencing technique enclosing degraded areas for two-year periods, allowing the land to restore itself.

RECOMMENDED READING

The list of books written about the Great Wall and Chinese history could keep you going for the remainder of your reading life. Here are a few I would recommend for starters:

Beijing Time – Michael Dutton, Hsiu-ju Stacy Lo and Dong Dong Wu – an inside look at a city trying to reinvent itself.

Desperate Siege: The Battle of Hong Kong – Ted Ferguson – an in-depth look at the Canadian experience in Second World War Hong Kong.

Hong Kong: Epilogue to an Empire – Jan Morris – a superb account of the strange history of one of the world's most fascinating destinations by one of the finest travel writers of the twentieth century.

Lonely Planet China – a comprehensive and useful starting point for planning any trip to China.

Lonely Planet Hong Kong & Macau City Guide – a comprehensive and useful starting point for planning any trip to Hong Kong.

The Great Wall: China Against the World 1000 BC–AD 2000 – Julia Lovell – a very readable in-depth history of the Wall with good maps. My best overall source of historical information.

The Great Wall From Beginning to End – Michael Yamashita and William Lindesay – an outstanding pictorial and brief written history of the Wall across China. Yamashita is a *National Geographic* photographer.

The Great Wall of China – History Channel DVD – excellent summary of the history and some of the myths surrounding the Wall.

The Search for Modern China – Jonathan D. Spence – definitive history of China from the Ming Dynasty to modern times.

CHAPTER 3 – AUSTRALIA – WEST MACDONNELL NATIONAL PARK – LARAPINTA TRAIL

{ Larapinta – from the Aboriginal name for the Finke River, Lherepirnte, meaning "salty river" or, alternatively, "permanent water" }

No matter how much I read about the Dreaming, the confidence that I understand it never quite takes root in my mind. To me it is on a par with, say, quantum mechanics, or string theory – ideas you think you grasp until you have to explain them. Each time I attempt it, I have to feel my way into it again, and I am never sure of my ground.

—ROBYN DAVIDSON, "No Fixed Address: Nomads and the Fate of the Planet" (2006)

✳ HIKING RULE 3: If you see smoke along the trail, take it seriously. It may be part of a controlled burn set by park staff, but it could also be a bushfire. Wildfires can sweep through with frightening speed in dry conditions and can be extremely dangerous for walkers. If you are threatened by fire, head for an open, bare area. Try to find a rocky outcrop that offers protection from radiant heat. If you are wearing synthetic clothes, replace them with wool or cotton if possible.

WHERE IN THE WORLD?

ALICE SPRINGS

CLAIM TO FAME

Located in the desert country of Australia's Red Centre, the Larapinta Trail extends for 232 km (144 mi.) along the spine of the West MacDonnell Ranges from Alice Springs to the summit of Mount Sonder. The landscape is rugged, almost primordial, with vast, sweeping views from the ridgetops broken by a series of deep gorges shaped by ancient rivers. The trail is contained almost entirely within the West MacDonnell National Park, where it follows some of the important Dreaming tracks of the local Arrente people and passes several of their sacred sites. Although not well known outside Australia, the track is considered one of the country's classic long-distance walks, often occupying a prominent position on the "bucket list" of many serious Aussie hikers.

WHAT WILL I SEE?

COLIN MANN

Mount Sonder is the prize at the end of the Larapinta Trail.

HIKE PROFILE

The trail begins at a base altitude of 600 m (1,968 ft.) near the Overland Telegraph Station north of Alice Springs and heads west, following the rugged ridges and gorges of the West MacDonnell Ranges. (The MacDonnell Ranges is the name given to the ridges and mountain chains of the Chewings, Heavitree and Pacoota Ranges.) Over the course of the trek, the track rises above 1000 m (3,281 ft.) a number of times before culminating in the ascent of Mount Sonder. At 1380 m (4,528 ft.) it is the fourth highest peak in the Northern Territory. Although the elevation gains and losses may sound moderate, don't underestimate the Larapinta. It is an extremely challenging walk over rugged and remote terrain.

WHITE MAN GOT NO DREAMING

The Dreaming was a term made popular by anthropologist W.E.H. Stanner, who used an expression he got from an Aboriginal, "white man got no dreaming," as a title for one of his books. He actually preferred the term "everywhen." The Dreaming, or Dreamtime, is often described as a creation story passed down through oral tradition. But this simple explanation misses the exceedingly complex and subtle nature of the concept. This is my attempt to capture the essence of it.

In the beginning, ancestral Spirit Beings travelled across the land creating humanity and the social laws and customs to govern them. As they travelled, they sang into existence the natural landmarks that exist today as rivers, mountains, rocks and trees. In the process, they created songlines or Dreaming tracks that criss-cross every part of the country. These songs or "musical maps" are inherited within families, allowing the singer to actually describe the landscape through the rhythm of the song, and to travel great distances by simply knowing the song. They establish a strong and ongoing connection to the spirit world that exists in the past, present and future and that imposes strong social obligations on the owner. When the Creator Beings, or Spirit Beings, were finished, they sank back exhausted into the earth at sacred sites where their creative powers are thought to still be alive. It is believed that damage to such a site disturbs the ancestors and can bring natural disaster or sickness to the community. The Larapinta follows many of the important Dreaming tracks of the local Arrente tribe, passing by several sacred sites along the trail where camping is strictly prohibited. It should go without saying that hikers need to show great respect for these spots, including Fish Hole, Mount Sonder and Inarlanga Pass.

Hazards

This is a strenuous, physically challenging hike that should not be undertaken unless you are a fit and experienced trekker. You must be prepared to deal with steep, rocky, uneven terrain and the potential for walking in cold water up to your waist for much more than just a few metres. Even in winter you should plan for the possibility of daytime temperatures that can promote heat stress or hyperthermia, by ensuring adequate supplies of water and regular rest stops. It is not uncommon for people to die on this trail because they run out of water.

Snake bites are rare since most snakes are nocturnal and will flee any sign of humans. Nevertheless snakes deserve much respect and you should never attempt to handle or threaten one. Bushfires can occur in dry conditions and are capable of covering large distances with alarming speed. Conversely, flash floods can very quickly turn a dry creekbed into a raging torrent. However, once the rain stops, the water will normally recede as quickly as it rose, so waiting it out is often the best choice rather than risk a dangerous crossing.

There are still plenty of feral camels throughout the Red Centre. Although we never saw any along the route, we certainly saw their tracks. When asked about what to do on a trail encounter, the locals tended to laugh off yet another silly tourist question. I haven't seen camels mentioned as trail hazards, but knowing their unpredictable nature, I would give them a wide berth, especially if there were any females with calves.

HUMPING BLUEY

It's yet another of those bits of Aussie jargon that can catch you off-guard. A "bluey" is a swag or bedroll, originally designed to be carried (or humped) by a swagman. They were often shearers travelling between jobs and they used a swag to carry all their possessions. Well-known Australian poet Henry Lawson describes this iconic piece of Aussie gear in "The Romance of the Swag," explaining that it generally included a couple of blue blankets (apparently this colour shows the dirt less), hence the name "bluey." Lawson tells, in exquisite detail, the art of rolling up the swag to hold everything from blueys to books to patches for your pants. Modern day swags are not meant to be carried long distances on foot. It seems we aren't as tough as the bushmen of the past. These days swags are made of waterproof canvas that zip around a foam mattress and easily accommodate a pillow and sleeping bag. There is usually plenty of room to tuck in your pajamas and what Lawson called your "little knick-knacks" before it is rolled up in the morning to carry to the next camp. Then it's just a matter of untying the swag at the end of the day and snuggling into a cozy, ready-made bed each night, either in a tent or under the stars.

The essentials

Getting there: Australia is serviced by a number of major airlines or their partners, including, among others, Air Canada, Air New Zealand, British Airways, Qantas, United and Virgin Atlantic. Qantas is the main carrier to Alice Springs. Depending on your departure point within Australia, travelling by bus may be an alternative. Although the distances can be huge and you can easily spend several days on the road, Australia has an excellent and efficient bus system. Check **www.greyhound.com.au** for detailed information. Anyone interested in a train trip of a lifetime may want to consider The Ghan, which runs from Adelaide to Darwin with a stop in Alice Springs. The train takes its name from the Afghan cameleers who helped forge a permanent trail into the Red Centre over 150 years ago. For many years the tracks ended at The Alice, but in 2004 the final extension to Darwin became operational, making this one of the most famous transcontinental train journeys in the world. Check **www.gsr.com.au** for details.

Currency: Australian dollar, or AUD, or AU$. 1 AUD = 100 cents although the smallest denomination now in circulation is the five-cent coin. For current exchange rates, check out **www.oanda.com**.

Special gear: Make sure you have good, sturdy waterproof hiking boots that are well broken in. They must be able to withstand the rigours of walking on uneven, rocky trails and wading through water well above ankle depth without falling apart. (Unfortunately, it will be too rough underfoot to take your boots off for water crossings.) Hiking poles are highly recommended to maintain balance on the many steep ascents and descents. Sun hats and water bottles aren't optional, but rain gear should also be on your list. Consider gaiters for protection from prickly vegetation such as spinifex, especially if you are hiking in shorts. The trail is usually done in mid-winter when daytime temperatures are moderate for hiking. However, the nights often go below freezing at this time of the year, so warm clothing is essential. When I did the trip in late July, our group awoke to frost-covered tents on several mornings.It is possible to do this trek as a backpacking trip where you take on the responsibility of planning the entire logistics of the expedition. But this is really only an option for backpackers with considerable experience. See the "How to do the hike" section for a discussion of this alternative. Of course, choosing this option means you will need to have all your own cooking gear, tents and other equipment in addition to appropriate first aid supplies. This is harsh, unforgiving territory and you must be prepared to deal with all it can throw at you. The safest and best choice in my opinion is to book through a reputable outfitter. They will supply all your food, water and camping gear in addition to providing highly skilled guides and all the necessary transport. Then all you will need to carry is your daypack, while your personal gear is transferred between camps. If you are lucky, this will include a swag, or Australian bedroll, supplied by the outfitter.

HIKE OVERVIEW

Officially opened in 2002, the Larapinta Trail follows the "backbone" of the ancient MacDonnell Ranges heading west from the Overland Telegraph Station, just north of Alice Springs, to the summit of Mount Sonder. From the Station, the track crosses the railway line that runs from Alice Springs to Darwin and heads up to the crest of Euro Ridge, before passing close to Wallaby Gap and Simpsons Gap with fine views of the Heavitree Range. From here the trail heads onto open plains to skirt the impressive rocks of Arenge Bluff, famous for its sunset colours, and easy walking through mulga woodland to Mulga Camp with its welcome shade. Excellent views of the Chewings Range are a highlight before reaching the campsite at Jay Creek.

Not far along Jay Creek the trail passes Fish Hole, a permanent water hole with particular sacred significance to the local Arrente tribe. Soon hikers have the choice between the Ridge Route and the Lower Route. Spectacular views are the reward for the sharp climb up the Ridge Route to Loretta's Lookout, the highest point on the Chewings Range, followed by a steep descent to Miller's Flat. From the Flat it is hard going over rocky, often steep terrain before emerging onto private Aboriginal land close to Standley Chasm. The Chasm is accessible by vehicle and is a popular stop for tourists who come to see the sheer, vertical red rock walls briefly illuminated by the sun at midday.

From Standley Chasm the trail climbs to Brinkley Bluff, one of the highest points on the Larapinta, then descends steeply on a rough track to Stuart's Pass and easy valley walking to Birthday Waterhole. Expect more hard going through Spencer Gorge and up to wonderful views from Razorback Ridge, before descending to the valley floor at Fringe Lily Creek. The scramble through Hugh Gorge is long and can require wading through cold, waist high water before the trail emerges to the welcome relief of the Alice Valley. The track zigzags to Alice Valley View before descending to Ellery Creek, then continues across a series of low ridges and hills crossing Aboriginal land to Serpentine Gorge. A long climb and hard ridge walking are rewarded with sweeping views of the West MacDonnells from Counts Point finally descending through mulga woodland to Serpentine Chalet Dam.

A tough section follows to spectacular Ormiston Gorge, through the sacred Inarlanga Pass, with good views on the approach to Waterfall Gorge. More climbing to Giles Lookout gives panoramic views to the west before descending to follow the base of the Heavitree Range to Ormiston Gorge, a registered sacred site. From here the trail climbs to more rewarding prospects from Ormiston and Rocky Bar Lookouts. Then it's a relatively easy stage to Redbank Gorge across spinifex-covered plains, with Mount Sonder dominating the landscape. The track ends with the final challenging climb to the summit of this sacred mountain, where sweeping vistas are a fitting reward for all your efforts.

Why would I want to?

Over the course of the hike, the path climbs and descends rugged mountain ridges, winds its way through spectacular rocky gorges and crosses arid, spinifex-covered open plains. Located deep in the heart of the continent, the MacDonnells are some of the oldest mountains in the world. The Larapinta follows them as they march in a succession of red ridges from east to west, traversed by a series of wild, mysterious gorges. The landscape is harsh and demanding, but there is a stark, primal, almost spiritual beauty to this ancient remote land that can only be experienced on foot.

The going is tough, but your efforts will be infinitely rewarded with vast ridge-top views and stunning displays of rich reds, subtle oranges and deep purples magnified to an intense clarity by the clear, desert air. Carved by ancient rivers heading south to the Simpson Desert, the gorges shelter rare ferns and cycad palms as old as 1,000 years within their moist dark shadows. Birds flourish along the trail, with over 150 known species – everything from tall, flightless emus to honeyeaters and tiny finches. And with over 600 superbly adapted plant species, there is an astonishing variety of vegetation, from stately River Red Gums to the brilliant red blooms of Sturt's Desert Pea to the ubiquitous and prickly spinifex grass.

Without a doubt, this is a challenging hike. It is also one of the world's classic long-distance treks through an arid untouched land of unparalleled beauty.

COLIN MANN

The brilliant red blooms of Sturt's desert pea.

When to go

The cooler months from April to September are the best times. Daytime temperatures are generally in the 20 to 25 Celsius range (68 to 77 Fahrenheit) making it ideal for walking. Expect cold nights during winter, often dipping below freezing. Summer months are far too hot and not suitable for such a trek. Although the MacDonnell Ranges are located close to deserts, they are not desert ranges. In fact, they receive fairly significant rainfall throughout the year, with a yearly average of about 275 mm (11 in.). However, it is unpredictable and sporadic, and can fall at any time. So there is a good chance you will encounter rain at some point along the trail.

What's the story?

Central Australia really has two stories. The first is the story of the Aborigines. At least 50,000 years ago, they crossed land bridges from eastern Asia and sailed in small boats to a vast, empty continent. Their migration was made possible by an ice age that lowered sea levels. When the ice eventually melted, they were locked away by the rising waters, isolated from outside human contact for thousands of years.

As they spread out across the land, they became superbly adapted to the harsh environment, living in a symbiotic relationship that allowed them to take what the land could give without damaging it. In the process they developed the world's oldest continuous culture and religion with spiritual roots tied to a creation story called The Dreaming or The Dreamtime.

Although Arrente dreaming stories are strongly connected to the creation of the MacDonnell Ranges and the area around Alice Springs, modern geologists provide a more mundane explanation based on massive earth movements beginning about 350 million years ago. The stratified metamorphic rock was gradually pushed up into a series of parallel steep-sided ridges that were thought to have reached a height of 4570 m (15,000 ft.) before erosive forces over millions of years eventually wore them down to expose the distinctive "sandwich-layered" rock strata we see today. North-south flowing rivers then exploited the softer rock layers forming the spectacular gorges, gaps and chasms that are such a highlight of the Larapinta Trail.

The permanent water holes hidden within many of these gorges meant the region was of particular significance to the nomadic hunter–gatherers who depended on them for survival. And it was the promise of permanent water that eventually began the second chapter of the region's story – bringing the white man and his modern inventions to a stone-age culture that was shattered by the onslaught. The meeting of these two civilizations has been likened to an encounter of inhabitants from different planets.

By the early 1800s, settlers began spilling into the grazing lands west of the Blue Mountains prompting explorers and adventurers to turn their sights on the great white space still left on the map of Australia. It was called "the ghastly blank." It was a tantalizing unknown in the centre of the continent that many speculated held a vast freshwater inland sea and the prospect of fertile land ideal for settlement. The mystery was sparked by the puzzling "problem of the rivers" that flowed inland from the Dividing Range with no apparent coastal outlet. The puzzle prompted a series of epic and often ill-fated journeys in search of the answer.

The debate was partially settled in 1844, when the South Australian government sent Captain Charles Sturt off to find the mystic sea. In addition to 30 bullocks, 200 sheep and provisions for a year, the group was optimistically equipped with a boat. In fact, they faced one of the most brutal summers on record, with temperatures soaring to 69°C (157°F). By the time he stumbled back to Adelaide in 1846, Sturt was convinced that no such sea existed. (He was so emaciated his wife is said to have fainted when she saw him.) The question was resolved once and for all when John McDouall Stuart, (a protégé of Sturt), made the first successful crossing of the continent from south to north in 1862, proving in the process that the "ghastly blank" was in fact a vast, arid and hostile land. There was no inland sea.

Stuart may have returned with bad news about the mystic sea, but he had also accomplished the Herculean task of crossing and mapping the centre and returning to tell the tale. In the process he established a practical route from Adelaide to Darwin, producing meticulous accounts of permanent waterholes and timber access along the way. His route would be followed closely by Charles Todd, the superintendent of telegraphs in South Australia, and his team of builders as they set out to construct the overland telegraph. The route also became a guide for the railway to Alice Springs and the Stuart Highway from Adelaide to Darwin.

"THE SINGING LINE"

The construction of the overland telegraph was a monumental engineering feat completed in less than two years, under the supervision of Charles Todd. The line used 36,000 poles and insulators plus tons of wire, food and medical supplies that had to be transported over vast distances by wagon or camel to the building teams. Spanning a distance of 3178 km (1,975 mi.) the line linked Adelaide and Darwin in August 1872, connecting Australia to the rest of the world through an undersea cable from Indonesia and on to Europe. It made communication within hours possible instead of weeks. Local Aborigines called it the "singing line." They often stole the insulators to use as cutting tools or spearheads.

A TOWN CALLED ALICE

Eleven repeater stations were established, one every 322 km (200 mi.) to relay messages up the overland telegraph line to Darwin. One was located just north of the present-day town of Alice Springs at the site of a permanent waterhole on the Todd River. The Larapinta Trail begins at the station, which is now a restored historical reserve. Both Charles Todd, who oversaw the building of the line, and his wife Alice are well remembered in the area. Originally called Stuart, Alice Springs, or "The Alice," was renamed in 1933, while the Todd Mall, Todd Street, Charles River and Todd River are all named after Charles.

The Arrente name for the area is Mparntwe. They believe that most of the surrounding landforms were created by groups of Caterpillar Ancestors of which they are the direct descendants. Head to the local landmark of Anzac Hill and you will see signs giving the totemic associations of 13 cultural sites plus a 360 degree view of Heavitree Gap and the MacDonnell Ranges stretching from east to west. (The Gap, which also has sacred significance to the Arrente, was widened with explosives when the rail line was put through. Workers at the time recount that the local Aborigines were sent into the bushland so they wouldn't witness the desecration. Of course, by the time they returned, it was too late to do anything about it.) The town has become a major tourist stop, famous for its annual Henley-on-Todd Regatta where racers run barefoot along the usually dry bed of the Todd River with bottomless boats held up around their waists. It must be the only place where a boat race is cancelled if the river has water in it.

TOURISM NT

The Henley-on-Todd Regatta in Alice Springs.

The arrival of pastoralists and gold seekers inevitably led to confrontations with the Aboriginal population over permanent water sources. They were powerless to withstand the push from a white society that forced them to abandon their ancestral lands and to survive in ever more remote locations. The disintegration of a culture built over 50,000 years was the inevitable result. It wasn't until 1967 that a constitutional referendum gave Aborigines full Australian citizenship and voting rights. Land rights have gradually been restored to Aborigines in many parts of the country. In 2009, title for the West MacDonnell National Park was transferred to the traditional Aboriginal owners. It was then leased back to the government under a joint management agreement allowing them significant input into the Park's operation.

THE HIKE

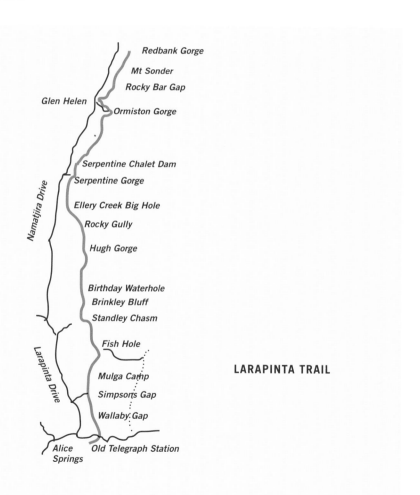

The trail was designed with 12 stages to be completed over an average of 20 days. This is generally based on the assumption that you are backpacking the trail from end to end, which requires organized food drops and assured water access. If you choose to use an outfitter, then you will be fully supported with food, water, transport and camping equipment and will only need to carry a daypack. This allows the trip duration to be shortened, although it involves several long days of hiking. The day-to-day descriptions of the trail that follow are based on the 14-day itinerary I followed with World Expeditions. (See the "How to do the hike" section for more details.)

The trail was planned to be walked from east to west, which is generally more scenic and is the direction in which the cumulative kilometre posts are marked. In places where there is no defined trail, large blue triangular markers are often attached to trees. However, if you are backpacking, walking from east to west can create logistical problems with food drops and access. Although walking from west to east can make planning simpler, some of the climbs are even steeper.

This is a very challenging hike over difficult, uneven terrain, increasing the risk of injury. I will confess up front that unlike every other hike in this book, I did not complete the entire length of the trail, due to an injury from a fall that required a trip to the Alice Springs hospital. Fortunately, because of the nature of a fully supported trip, this did not mean the end of my hike.

Take a close look at the map and you will see the trail is never very far from the main road back to The Alice, although not every stage has vehicle access. Logistically, this allows an outfitter to return to town for fresh supplies almost daily, so I was able to tag along to the hospital and rejoin the group the same day. It's just another reason to use an outfitter. One of the guides said that in the many times he has walked the trail, he has never had an entire group finish the entire route, and that was true for us as well. Of the five guests who started out, only two completed every day of the hike. You can't underestimate the physical and mental resources you will need to draw on in order to deal with all this trek can throw at you, which is considerable. There are no stages rated easy, with the majority graded either hard or very hard. I can safely say it is the toughest long-distance hike I have ever undertaken, but also one of the most rewarding.

Day 1 – Alice Springs Telegraph Station to Simpsons Gap – 23.8 km (14.8 mi.)

The hike begins at the Overland Telegraph Station just north of Alice Springs, following a rough vehicle track that was the original road connecting Alice Springs to Darwin. Parallel to the road are some of the old telegraph poles and wire that linked Australia to the world. The trail passes under the concrete Geoff Moss Bridge and then crosses the railway tracks. With any luck you may catch a glimpse of the famous Ghan on its journey from Adelaide to Darwin. Then it's a steady climb to the crest of

Euro Ridge and fine views of Alice Springs and Mount Gillen, the high point of the Heavitree Range, before descending through mulga woodland to Wallaby Gap.

Desert bloodwoods and tall ironwoods are a highlight before the trail climbs steeply to Rungutjirba Ridge and good views from Hat Hill Saddle. Then it's downhill to Simpsons Gap.

COLIN MANN

EURO DREAMING

A euro is a type of kangaroo, but since they tend to be nocturnal, you aren't likely to see one. Aboriginals believe the highest hills of the ridge are the head and back of a euro ancestor that stopped here. The dreaming story credits the Spirit Being with the creation of the Alice Springs waterhole while digging for water in the Todd River.

Euro Ridge.

Day 2 – Simpsons Gap to Jay Creek – 24.5 km (15.2 mi.)

The trail crosses open, grassy, eroded flats, the legacy of cattle overgrazing from 1872 until farming ceased in the 1970s. The area has been slow to recover, partly due to plenty of introduced buffel grass, an invasive weed that was used as saddle padding by Afghan camel drivers and later planted for cattle feed. The track skirts Arenge Bluff, rising above Rocky Creek to give good views of the bluff before heading to the shady mulga trees at Mulga Camp. (Arenge Bluff is another important Euro Spirit Ancestor for the local Arrente.) The next section marks the last of relatively easy going as you pass through Spring Gap and on to good ridge views of the Chewings Range, then descend through mulga woodland to Jay Creek.

The cool waters of Spring Gap.

Day 3 – Jay Creek to Standley Chasm – 14.1 km (8.8 mi.)

COLIN MANN

Fish Hole.

This is a tough section, especially if you take the Ridge Route. But it is well worth the effort for the spectacular views from Loretta's Lookout. The walk follows the rocky creekbed, with wonderful river views to a waterhole called Fish Hole. The area is a sacred site where a serpent is said to have found a passage through the Chewings Range. Walking is restricted to the creekbed and camping is prohibited at Fish Hole.

The view looking west from Loretta's Lookout.

Above Fish Hole the track follows a historic path constructed for camel trains travelling between Hermannsburg and Hamilton Downs homestead. Then it's on to Tangentyere Junction and a choice between the Ridge Route and the Lower Route.

The Ridge Route involves hard, steep climbing and descending but is highly recommended for the compensating panoramic views at the top. Both trails meet at Miller's Flat, followed by a series of hard, rocky scrambles before the taxing final section around the western side of Standley Chasm. The chasm, which cannot be seen from the trail, is easily accessed by car and is a popular spot for visitors who take the short walk along the rocky floor to see the sheer vertical walls at mid-day when the sun turns them a fiery red. The area is owned by the Aboriginal community of Iwupataka, but its English name honours Ida Standley, who in 1914 became the first school teacher in Stuart or, as it is now called, Alice Springs.

Day 4 – Standley Chasm to Birthday Waterhole Junction – 16.8 km (10.4 mi.)

Another tough section, graded very hard. Along this stage you will see an unexpected variety of plant life, all superbly adapted to their environment – everything from Finke River mallees to hill mulga – clinging to the exposed ridges, to cycads, native figs and corkwoods. The trail follows an old track used for horseback tours, climbing to a small saddle and a short detour to Bridle Path Lookout. From here, ridgeline walking leads to more outstanding views from Reveal Saddle, offering a brief glimpse of Brinkley Bluff, then dips down before the long climb (and several annoying false summits), on to the summit of the bluff with its cairn and logbook. Stunning vistas in all directions are the reward for some hard going.

Ahead is a long, rugged descent to the valley below and Stuart's Pass, named in honour of John McDouall Stuart, who used the pass on three of his attempts to cross the continent. In April 1860, Stuart scaled the bluff, calling it the most difficult hill he had ever climbed.

Now you face the test of descending the bluff into the valley on a very steep and rocky trail that many walkers regard as one of the hardest parts of the trek. Take

Brinkley Bluff in the distance.

TOURISM NT

Birthday Waterhole is worth the short detour off the trail.

your time and exercise caution on the descent. Once you reach the valley, the walking is relatively easy to Birthday Waterhole Junction. It's a short detour off the trail to the waterhole, but it's a lovely spot for camping with a fringe of Red River Gums and lots of bird life.

Day 5 – Birthday Waterhole Junction to Hugh Gorge – 15.1 km (9.4 mi.)

This is another section rated very hard, with your first introduction to some serious gorge walking. The day starts with relatively easy hiking along creekbeds before it enters Spencer Gorge and slow going over boulders and rocks. Subsurface water sources ensure the survival of moisture-loving plant species such as black teatree and native pines. You might even spot the bright red blooms of hill wallflower poison. The scramble up to Windy Saddle can be slow going, followed by another steep climb to Razorback Ridge and the crest of the Chewings Range. The trail heads west along the ridge's rocky spine, with wide views along the range. It narrows in places and caution is required on the loose, slippery rocks on the ridge as well as on the descent to Fringe Lily Creek.

Then it's more climbing up to Rocky Saddle, with its views back to Razorback Ridge, before the descent along Linear Valley to Hugh Gorge, one of the longest and deepest in the area. There is no defined track here, so you need to rockhop and scramble over boulders to find the best route. In several places you must be prepared to wade through cold, waist-deep pools in order to navigate your way through. Our group encountered several such pools along the length of the gorge, making it a

chilling and hard end to a long but rewarding day. You can't take your boots off and carry them because the rocks underfoot are slippery and uneven and the water is very cold. (I always carry spare newspaper with me to stuff into my boots at the end of a wet day. It sops up an amazing amount of moisture by morning. Assuming you don't encounter more water the next day, they will generally finish drying out as you walk.)

COLIN MANN

The view looking west down Razorback Ridge.

Day 6 – Hugh Gorge to Rocky Gully – 15.9 km (9.9 mi.)

This stage is a welcome relief with the going rated medium as you cross the hill country separating the Chewings and Heavitree Ranges. The trail winds through mulga and witchetty bush, rising to Hugh View and good vistas back to Hugh Gorge and the Chewings. From here the trail follows undulating hill country to Ghost Gum Flat and an impressive ghost gum with three large burls on its trunk.

The trail continues over rocky hills and rough, broken terrain, with the Heavitree Range looming in the distance, to a final descent into Rocky Gully. We encountered

The going is easy across the Alice Valley.

rain along this portion of the trail and it was very cold. We were layered up with wool hats and gloves and every bit of clothing we had. It was a good reminder how conditions can change from sunny to freezing cold very quickly, and the need to be prepared.

Day 7 – Rocky Gully to Ellery Creek – 15.3 km (9.5 mi.)

The journey continues across the Alice Valley over rolling hills toward the escarpment of the Heavitree Range, climbing to unrestricted panoramas from Alice Valley View. From here the track continues west, eventually swinging southwest and south toward a high saddle. The trail ascends steeply over loose rock before heading down through rolling valleys and ridges to Ellery Creek. The Aboriginal name for Ellery Creek Big Hole is Udepata, an important gathering point along several Dreaming trails passing through the area.

Day 8 – Ellery Creek to Serpentine Gorge – 13.8 km (8.6 mi.)

This is a relatively short but hard section as the trail follows along the south side of the Heavitree Range over a long series of ridges and hills and many ups and downs. A highlight of this stage is the different rock types of the Bitter Springs Formation that were formed under a shallow sea 800 million years ago, forced up by massive earth movements and then exposed by subsequent erosion. Along the trail you will see white calcrete, dramatic dark outcrops of dolomite, purple mudstone and orange-red ironstone. The track crosses the Roulpmaulpma Aboriginal Land Trust, climbing to good views at Trig Point, eventually descending into mulga woodland before

GHOSTLY ICONS

These graceful eucalypts with their spectral white bark have become iconic symbols of the outback. Made famous by the paintings of Albert Namatjira, the powdery surface of the bark was used by Aboriginals as a pigment for rock paintings or to decorate their bodies for various ceremonies. Namatjira, who was born at the Hermannsburg Lutheran Mission, just west of Alice Springs, became famous for his landscape watercolours and their distinctive blues, purples and oranges. Ghost gums and Mount Sonder figure prominently in his paintings, which depicted important Dreaming sites.

COLIN MANN

Serpentine Gorge.

emerging onto a vehicle track. The side trip up to the fenced lookout provides a spectacular view of the upper portion of the gorge, which is said to be protected by Wedge-Tailed Eagle and Water Serpent Ancestors of the Arrente people.

Day 9 – Serpentine Gorge to Serpentine Chalet Dam – 13.4 km (8.3 mi.)

The trail crosses low hills with wonderful views of Serpentine Gorge before you begin the long, hard climb up to Eagle Landing at the top of the Heavitree Range. (According to the Arrente, the Wedge-Tailed Eagle Ancestor patrolled the area between Serpentine Gorge and the Ochre Pits during the Dreamtime.) Once you make it up, the track follows the almost level ridge, providing vast, sweeping views all the way to the junction with Counts Point. The Point is a not to be missed side trip. The vista looking northwest to Mount Sonder is generally regarded as one of the best on the entire trail.

The trail descends a series of steps into Lomandra Gully (named for the rare iron-grass found here), to the base of the range, swinging west across undulating foothills to Serpentine Chalet Dam. The dam was built in 1960 to service an ill-fated tourist venture, the ruins of which are located south of the trail.

COLIN MANN

The spectacular view west from Counts Point.

Day 10 – Serpentine Chalet Dam to Ormiston Gorge – 28.6 km (17.8 mi.)

This is the longest, most challenging day of the trek and one I did not complete in its entirety, due to severely bruised ribs from an earlier fall on the trail. I walked to Inarlanga Pass, took the 4 km (2.5 mi.) detour to the Ochre Pits, then hopped a ride to Ormiston Gorge for more walking. Because the side trip to the pits is on such a long day, it is almost always bypassed, but provides outstanding views west to Mount Sonder and a chance to explore the pits.

Inarlanga Pass has ritual significance to Aboriginals, but walkers are allowed access. (Inarlanga is the Arrente word for echidna, or spiny anteaters.)

TAKE YOUR MEDICINE

Ochre figured prominently in Aboriginal culture. Not only was it used for body decoration and initiation ceremonies, it was also believed to have medicinal and magical properties. Red ochre mixed with grease and eucalyptus leaves was used as a decongestant, while white ochre was said to cool the sun and calm the wind when it was mixed with water and puffed from the mouth.

COLIN MANN

Inarlanga Pass.

COLIN MANN

Mount Sonder from the top of the Heavitree Range.

As you follow the gorge, expect to see cycads and thickets of spearwood, used by the Arrente to make spear shafts. The gorge opens into a wider valley, eventually heading west over three saddles before descending into the creek junction above Waterfall Gorge.

From here it's a tough climb to a spectacular viewpoint at Giles Lookout overlooking a 160 km (99 mi.) stretch along the West MacDonnells, followed by a trek along the ridgetop with open expansive views along the entire way.

The trail eventually zigzags down to a spot appropriately called Base of the Hill, then turns west through the foothills to Ormiston Gorge.

Day 11 – Ormiston Gorge to Glen Helen Junction – 9.4 km (5.8 mi.)

This is a special day. Not only is it short and relatively easy, but there is the added promise of a well-deserved shower at the end of it – the first one in well over a week. The trail winds through a series of rolling ridges with good views of the mountain ranges, eventually climbing to Ormiston Lookout, sometimes called Hilltop Lookout.

Ormiston Gorge.

EMU DREAMING

Carved by the ancient Finke River (often called the oldest river in the world), the soaring cliffs banded in purple, white and red, the deep waterhole and the superb collection of ghost gums combine to make Ormiston Gorge one of the high-lights of the trek. The multi-coloured crags seem to glow in the sunlight, while the rocks and permanent water make it a haven for plants and wildlife. The waterhole is a registered sacred site and is part of the Aboriginal Emu Dreaming story. You may not be up for adding the 8.4 km (5.2 mi.) Ormiston Pound Walk to your day, but make sure to take the short climb to Ghost Gum Lookout, with its fantastic view over the gorge and the ranges.

Although it's not particularly high, it provides a wide panorama, with the Heavitrees and Ormiston Gorge to the north and Mount Sonder to the west.

From here you gradually descend over undulating ground to the Finke River and the junction to Glen Helen Resort. We made a wild camp along the Finke River. The water attracts a wonderful variety of birds and wildlife making it a special place to relax and enjoy the show.

Mount Sonder.

BARRY SKIPSEY, COURTESY OF GLEN HELEN RESORT

Glen Helen Gorge.

THE BEGINNING OF MAN

The Arrente believe the first human emerged from the large pool at Glen Helen Gorge to gaze upon the world. Closely associated with the Carpet Snake Dreaming, the gorge is a sacred site known as Yapulpa. The permanent water ensures an abundant diversity of birds such as finches and cormorants as well as frogs, lizards and miniature kangaroos. It also brought pastoralists who established a cattle station here in the late 1800s. (The gorge is said to have been named in 1875 by surveyor Richard Warburton after a young woman.) Unreliable rain led to the abandonment of the venture several times. The Glen Helen Resort now operates close to the gorge where you can indulge in a cold beer and a very welcome hot shower. It is possible to walk the 7.0 km (4.3 mi.) from the Glen Helen Junction to the resort, but we drove in style to luxuriate in the beautiful clean showers and take the short stroll to the gorge, where the rugged red cliffs erupt in a fiery display in the glow of the late afternoon sun.

Day 12 – Glen Helen Junction to Rocky Bar Gap – 13.9 km (8.6 mi.)

This is a short, relatively easy section, crossing low, spinifex-covered hills and a plain with mulga trees before tackling a long, steep climb to the summit of Rocky Bar

Lookout (another one sometimes referred to as Hilltop Lookout). Here you get more good views of Mount Sonder, looming ever closer, while a look back east reveals the route already traversed. Then it's another steep descent before reaching Rocky Bar Gap. Our group did this hike in reverse, driving to Rocky Bar Gap, then returning to our wild camp on the Finke River.

Wild camp on the Finke River.

Day 13 – Rocky Bar Gap to Redbank Gorge – 12.0 km (7.4 mi.)

Only one more hard day and today isn't one of them! The trail follows the foothills of Mount Sonder, heading to the final, challenging climb on the last day. The massive mountain dominates this section as you pass through mixed shrubland of mulga and mallee and spinifex-covered plains, finally emerging at the carpark near the entrance to the gorge.

Day 14 – Redbank Gorge to Mount Sonder (and back) – 15.8 km (9.8 mi.)

The mountain – called Rwetypme by the Arrente – has substantial religious signif-icance. Although camping and fires are strictly prohibited, day hikers are allowed access. Many climbers will begin the hike up Mount Sonder in the pre-dawn in order to catch the sunrise at the top. The hike is demanding, (sometimes described as arduous), so be prepared to take your time. The trail winds into the foothills before it begins the longest climb on the entire trail to the highest point on the trail. Once you reach the saddle, the ascent slackens somewhat before the final uphill stretch to the cairn and the lookout. Hope for good weather as a reward for your efforts, because the view out over the West MacDonnells and the surrounding plains is not only the highest but arguably the best on the trail. From here it's downhill all the way as you retrace your steps back to Redbank Gorge and the end of one of Australia's finest treks.

HOW TO DO THE HIKE

Option 1, guided hike: There are two well-known Australian outfitters who specialize in the end-to-end version of the Larapinta Trail: World Expeditions **www.worldexpeditions.com**, and Trek Larapinta, **www.treklarapinta.com.au**.
Both offer fully supported, all-inclusive versions where all you need to carry is your daypack.

I travelled with World Expeditions. They were the first to offer guided and supported Larapinta trekking, beginning with the route's initial construction in 1995. Development progressed to completion in 2002, and World Expeditions has remained the premier operator along the trail. I would have absolutely no hesitation in recommending them. The entire trip was exceptionally well organized, with two extremely knowledgeable and competent guides, good equipment and amazing food throughout. Hikers can also choose from a three- or six-day option if the full 14-day trek seems too much to tackle.

Option 2, self-guided, independent group: In addition to organizing and carrying all your own food and gear, you will need to book the necessary permits, food drops and transportation. You must be a very experienced backpacker to consider undertaking this trek. The Northern Territory Parks and Wildlife Commission provides comprehensive planning information about the trail on their website at **www.parksandwildlife.nt.gov.au/parks/walks/larapinta**.

HOW DO YOU SAY THAT?

You may think you have come to an English-speaking country, but Australian, or "Strine," can be a bewildering language for the uninitiated. It might be worthwhile to pick up one of the books listed below to help with the translation (and I'm not joking, either). Just when you think you understand the basics of the jargon, along comes another tricky bit of lingo to leave you guessing. There are literally hundreds of examples, but here are a few of my favourites:

- arvo – afternoon
- beyond the black stump – the outback, a hypothetical spot somewhere in the centre of Australia; also "the back of beyond" or "the back O'Bourke"
- bonzer – great!
- do your lolly – angry to the point of shouting and raving; also "spit the dummy"
- duck's guts – spot on, right
- fair dinkum – honest or genuine; also "dinki-di" or "ridgie-didge"
- mollydooker – a left-hander, or southpaw
- pom – anyone British; the expression is thought to come from P.O.M.E., for "Prisoner of Mother England"
- reccy – taking a reconnaissance
- sheila – any woman, no matter what her actual name is
- stickybeak – a nosy person
- yakka – hard work

CONSIDER THIS – BEFORE OR AFTER THE HIKE

The hill, as I approached, presented a most peculiar appearance,... When I got clear of the sandhills, and was only two miles distant, and the hill, for the first time, coming fairly into view, what was my astonishment to find it was one immense rock rising from the plain... Seeing a spur less abrupt than the rest of the rock, I left the camels here, and after walking and scrambling two miles barefooted, over sharp rocks, succeeded in reaching the summit, and had a view that repaid me for my trouble ... This rock is certainly the most wonderful natural feature I have seen.

—WILLIAM GOSSE, July 1873

Uluru (formerly Ayers Rock)

Explorer Ernest Giles had seen the wondrous rock in 1872. But it was not until the next year that surveyor and adventurer William Gosse actually scaled it, along with his Afghan camel driver, Kamran, naming it after Henry Ayers, the premier of South Australia.

We now know it as Uluru, the colossal blood-red monolith rising almost ominously from the sandy plains of the Australian desert about 460 km (286 mi.) southwest of Alice Springs.

There is certainly plenty to see and do around Alice Springs before or after you've done the Larapinta, but the relative proximity (in Australian terms) of this astonishing landmark makes it an absolute must-see if you can make it work. It is possible to travel from The Alice on a one-day excursion, but it really deserves more time if you have it.

If you decide to go, there is an extensive list of tour operators offering everything from all-inclusive camping to resort accommodation at the nearby service village of Yulara, or there's always self-drive if you are up for it. You can choose from scenic flights, camel rides or full walking/cultural tours around the base that provide a much more intimate view than you can ever get from the top. The question of climbing the rock always arises, but in my view, that shouldn't even be considered. The sacred site has deep spiritual significance to the local Anangu tribe. Aside from the very real danger of tumbling off the side to an almost certain death, climbing this rock would be akin to trooping into a church and setting up a picnic lunch on the altar. It just shouldn't be done, out of respect for the deeply held beliefs of the rock's custodians.

TOURISM NT

Uluṟu-Kata Tjuṯa National Park, a World Heritage area.

DESERT ICEBERG

We've all seen the pictures. Grooved, pockmarked and monumental, the enormous rock rises from the desert floor in an endless display of shifting colours as the sun moves across the sky. From ominously grey on rainy, cloudy days, to blood-red in the fading rays of the sunset, Uluru is no less astonishing today than it was for William Gosse almost 150 years ago. Nothing can quite prepare you for its sheer, over-whelming size. Geologists describe Uluru as a sandstone monolith that was lifted and buckled above sea level over hundreds of millions of years. Like an iceberg, the majority of its bulk is estimated to lie beneath the sand. The sandstone (called arkose) is eroding in flakes, like human dandruff, or what homeowners will recognize as "spalling," the gradual flaking away of masonry such as sidewalks and founda-tions. Because Uluru's spalling is relatively even, the rock tends to retain its shape even though it is slowly shrinking in size.

Author Ian Moffitt, describing his first sight of the rock in the late 1970s, cap-tured the very essence of the place: "Some people find Ayers Rock beautiful, but at that moment it seemed to me to personify a peculiarly masculine malevolence. I feared the Rock a little then, and I still do; it is dark and brooding, drenched in myth, stained by time and ancient blood."

It should come as no surprise that the rock is a sacred Aboriginal site, sitting at the centre of a number of significant Dreaming tracks no doubt influenced by the permanent waterholes that attract game. The local Anangu believe the landscape was formed by Creation Spirits associated with the mala (rufous hare wallaby), the kuniya (woma python), the liru (brown snake) and the lungkata (blue-tongue lizard). In 1985, ownership of Uluru-Kata Tjuta National Park was transferred to the local Aboriginals, who then leased it back to the government for 99 years, along with the right to certain royalties and significant input into park management.

ARE YOU READY TO EAT?

Australia remains a land where real men don't eat quiche. Meat still reigns supreme here, especially in the outback regions of Central Australia, where steaks will often be served flopping over the edge of the plate, accompanied by a huge plate of chips (French fries) and "dead horse," the inexplicable term for tomato sauce or ketchup. But there is plenty of variety if you want something other than beef, including croc-odile, camel and sweet, tender, purple-red kangaroo fillets. In Alice Springs some restaurants offer an urbanized version of bush tucker, using native Australian ingre-dients like wattle seed and the red berries of the quandong. You might even have a go at witchetty grubs, which have an unsettling resemblance to large maggots.

There seems to be an unending variety of classic Australian slang terms for edibles – words like bum-nuts for eggs, moo juice for milk, rat coffin for a minced meat pie and snags, snorkers or mystery bags for sausages are particularly colourful. Probably no other Australian food elicits such strong reactions as the salty, dark-brown paste called Vegemite. You either love it or you hate it. I tend to be on the love side. Made from brewer's yeast extract, the stuff is a by-product of beer manufacturing and is commonly spread on crackers or toast. Vegemite was invented in 1919 by Cyril Callister when shipments of a similar spread called Marmite that was imported from Britain, were disrupted by the war. Apparently there is no risk that it will fall out of favour – the billionth jar was produced in October 2008.

Hygiene standards on the trail were good and we had no concerns about food preparation. When it comes to eating out in Alice Springs and other Australian towns and cities, standards are generally high.

Tipping is not expected, but is considered a matter of choice.

Vegetarians may have trouble getting enough protein on the trail. You may want to forget it's meat you are eating and just make sure your protein levels are high enough to meet the demands of the trek. As far as vegetarian restaurants, these are few and far between in a culture where meat is still the name of the game, but most menus will offer a vegetarian option.

BUSH TUCKER

Indigenous Australians were superbly adapted to finding sustenance in the arid, seemingly empty vastness of the desert, where their intimate knowledge of the seasons and the secrets of the native plants and animals evolved over thousands of years. The landscape has been likened to a big supermarket for those who knew where to look for game like wallabies, emus, snakes and lizards plus an array of roots, nuts, seeds, ants, honey and grubs. Witchetty grubs are an example of one of the most important insect food sources in the desert. The grubs are the larval stage of the cossid moth. They feed on the roots of the witchetty bush, a familiar plant along many sections of the Larapinta Trail, and were either eaten raw or roasted in the embers of the campfire. The high protein grubs figure prominently in many Dreaming paintings. They are traditionally gathered by women and are said to have a nutty flavour with a "squishy" texture.

INTERNET RESOURCES

There is a wealth of Australia information available on the Internet. Here are a few reliable sites to get you started:

www.parksandwildlife.nt.gov.au/parks/walks/larapinta, is the official Larapinta Trail site, maintained by the Parks and Wildlife Commission, Northern Territory.

www.travelnt.com, is produced by the Northern Territory Tourist Commission.

www.australia.com, the official site of Tourism Australia.

www.centralaustraliantourism.com features a comprehensive guide to Central Australia.

RECOMMENDED READING

A Town Like Alice – Nevil Shute – a very popular novel also made into a film.

A Traveller's History of Australia – John H. Chambers – with good sections on Aboriginal culture.

Alice Springs: Its History and the People Who Made It – Peter Donovan – just what it says.

Australia: A New History of the Great Southern Land – Frank Walsh – a new take on an old story.

Australia: Beyond the Dreamtime – Thomas Keneally, Patsy Adam-Smith, Robyn Davidson – three leading modern Australian writers present their personal view of the country.

Australian Slang Dictionary – John Blackman – a fair dinkum and humorous approach to translation with wonderful illustrations.

Evil Angels – John Bryson – an old story but one that still gets headlines. It recounts the story of Lindy Chamberlain, who claimed her daughter Azaria was taken by a dingo at what was then Ayers Rock. She was eventually charged and convicted of murder but subsequently exonerated.

Going Bush: Adventures Across Indigenous Australia – Catherine Freeman and Deborah Mailman – good insights into Aboriginal culture.

Fatal Shore – Robert Hughes – somewhat dated but still an excellent history of Australia.

In a Sunburned Country – Bill Bryson – Australia as only well-known travel writer Bryson can reveal it.

Larapinta Trail – John and Monica Chapman – the definitive stage-by-stage guide to the trail, filled with plenty of practical and historical information plus details of flora and fauna and excellent maps. Written by two bushwalkers who helped develop the trail, the book includes trail descriptions from east to west and west to east. Available for order online at www.osp.com.au and highly recommended.

Larapinta Trail Package – produced by the Northern Territory Parks and Wildlife Commission, including fact sheets, visitor guide and 12 waterproof, virtually indestructible section maps with detailed notes. Available for order online (see "Internet resources") and highly recommended.

Lonely Planet: Australian Language & Culture – this pocket-sized gem will help you translate Aussie lingo into English. Includes a comprehensive section on indigenous languages.

Lonely Planet: Northern Territory & Central Australia – a comprehensive guide to the region.

Outback – Thomas Keneally – a personal journey providing a fascinating glimpse into the heart of Australia by one of the country's most accomplished authors.

The Australian Outback: The World's Wild Places – Ian Moffitt – a personal journey through the history and natural history of the outback.

The Singing Line – Alice Thompson – the story of the Overland Telegraph, written by the great-great-granddaughter of Charles Todd.

FAUNA FACTS: HOPPING ALONG JUST FINE

In yet another display of perfect environmental adaptation, red kangaroos have come to dominate the arid regions of the outback. Not only do they have a specialized digestive system designed to break down the protective toxins found in desert vegetation, their slow metabolism and ability to seek out plants with higher moisture allows them to limit drinking to about once a week. They pant rather than sweat, allowing them to efficiently lose heat, and their big tails, used as a counterbalance when running, allow for high-efficiency movement. Their reproduction cycle is finely tuned to food supplies. In times of persistent drought, the cycle actually stops and males become sterile, allowing for equilibrium between the living population and what the environment can support.

TOURISM NT

Red kangaroo.

The Songlines – Bruce Chatwin – an account, both real and fictional, of Chatwin's experiences with central Australian Aboriginal people.

Tracks – Robyn Davidson – the classic account of one woman's solo trek across the Australian Outback to the Indian Ocean.

CHAPTER 4 – NEW ZEALAND – FIORDLAND NATIONAL PARK – MILFORD TRACK

{ Milford Track takes its name from the famous Milford Sound, located at the north end of the trail. The sound was originally named Milford Haven by Captain John Grono in 1809 after its Welsh namesake in Pembrokeshire. }

"The Finest Walk in the World"

—*The Spectator* (London), 1908

✱ HIKING RULE 4: Always carry a supply of newspaper in your pack. It works better than a drying room for wet boots.

WHERE IN THE WORLD?

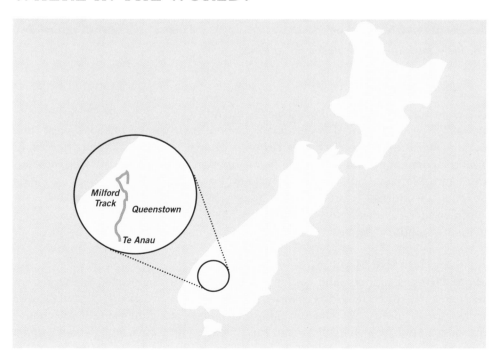

WHAT WILL I SEE?

ULTIMATE HIKES, NEW ZEALAND

The view down the Arthur Valley to Lake Ada.

CLAIM TO FAME

Since the early 1900s the Milford Track has claimed to be "The Finest Walk in the World." The trail is located in Fiordland National Park, part of the Southwest New Zealand World Heritage Area. The region is known to the Ngai Tahu tribe as Te Wahipounamu, the place of greenstone. In addition to Fiordland, the area incorporates Aoraki/Mount Cook, Westland/Tai Poutini and Mount Aspiring National Parks. Covering 2.6 million hectares, or about 10 per cent of New Zealand's land area, it is considered one of the great wilderness regions of the southern hemisphere and a place of exceptional beauty.

HIKE PROFILE

The trail covers approximately 54 km (33.5 mi.) and must be walked one way, from south to north. You can walk as an independent backpacker, carrying all your gear, or with a private outfitter, staying in comfortable lodges along the track. If you choose the lodge option, you will still need to carry a pack with clothes and personal items from lodge to lodge. The trail begins at the north end of Lake Te Anau, climbs to a maximum altitude of 1154 m (3,786 ft.) at the top of Mackinnon Pass and ends at Sandfly Point, close to the entrance to Milford Sound.

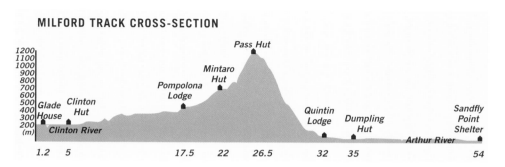

MILFORD TRACK CROSS-SECTION

Hazards

None, unless you are afraid of getting wet. Unlike neighbouring Australia, there aren't even any poisonous snakes or spiders to worry about. Of course, there is always the risk of falling or turning an ankle on rocky or uneven terrain.

The essentials

Getting there: The country is serviced by a number of major airlines or their partners, including Air New Zealand, Air Canada, United Airlines, Qantas, American Airlines, Cathay Pacific, Air China, British Airways and Lufthansa.

Currency: New Zealand dollar, or NZD, or NZ$. NZ$1 = 100 cents. For current exchange rates, check out **www.oanda.com.**

Special gear: Make sure you have good, sturdy, waterproof walking boots. Hiking poles are also highly recommended. Although there is much of the track where you may question why you have them, they will be particularly useful on the day you climb Mackinnon Pass and make the steep descent on the other side. Since this hike is done over four days, you will need a 40-litre backpack if you are hiking from lodge to lodge. If you are going as an independent hiker, plan on a 60-litre pack to carry all your food and utensils in addition to clothes. And of course, a hat, sunscreen and water bottles are essential. But arguably the single most important piece of equipment will be your rain gear. Average annual rainfall along this trail is close to 8 m (26 ft.), so unless you get extremely lucky, you will get wet at some point. (See "The hike" section for a more detailed discussion of gear.)

A note on spelling: Various sources use a confusing array of spellings for personal and place names. I have relied on the spelling conventions in John Hall-Jones's *Milford Sound: An Illustrated History of the Sound, the Track and the Road*. The book was by far the most readable and informative single source on the area that I found.

HIKE OVERVIEW

Just so you know, in New Zealand you are a tramper going on a tramp, not a hiker on a hike.

There are basically two options for doing the hike. You can choose to go as part of a guided walk, with accommodations and meals provided in comfortable lodges, or as an independent walker staying in Department of Conservation (DOC) huts along the route. The guided walk is offered exclusively through Ultimate Hikes. (See "How to do the hike" for more details.) The trail is highly regulated by the New Zealand government, with access limited to 40 independent walkers and 50 guided walkers per day. Bookings are required months in advance to ensure a spot.

The track must be walked from south to north over four days. Because of the booking procedure it is necessary for hikers to keep moving even in extreme weather, which can happen at any time of the year. Adequate gear to handle anything, from snow to strong wind to heavy rain and flooding, is critical. During periods of heavy flooding, DOC evacuations by helicopter may be required.

Access to the trail is via water on both ends, beginning at the north end of Lake Te Anau and ending at Sandfly Point, where you will need to catch the boat across to Milford Sound. The walk basically follows the Clinton River, then climbs Mackinnon Pass, descending into the Arthur Valley and out to Milford Sound along the Arthur River and Lake Ada.

The hike isn't easy, nor is it particularly difficult. Children must be at least 10 years old, while people over 70 may be asked to provide evidence of their health and fitness. There is one long day requiring a climb of close to 500 m (1,640 ft.) up Mackinnon Pass followed by a steep descent into the Arthur Valley of more than 800 m (2,625 ft.) over rocky and uneven terrain.

You need to wrap your head around the possibility that you may have to walk in water up to a metre deep for more than a few steps – so no, you won't be able to keep your boots dry. Once you have done this and are confident you have the gear and fitness to handle it, then try to put this worst-case scenario out of your mind and concentrate on why thousands of trekkers have flocked to this famous trail for well over a century.

As New Zealand poet Blanche Baughan wrote, "To tell the truth, you get so often wet through on the track that you take no notice of it, and the air is so pure and germless that you never take any harm, either." The bottom line is you are going to see some of the most pristine wilderness anywhere in the world, a combination of rain forest, snow-capped peaks, glacier-carved valleys and rivers so pure you can still safely fill your water bottle along the way.

Why would I want to?

In 1908 Blanche Baughan wrote an article for the London *Spectator* that she titled "A Notable Walk." But, as she later explained in the preface to an expanded 1926 book-let version, the responsibility for the title change to "The Finest Walk in the World" rested entirely with the editor. She reasoned that the *Spectator* was a "journal celebrated much more for considered moderation than for any leaping enthusiasms, ... so that I think we of New Zealand may venture to accept the distinction without any fear of boasting." And so the moniker has stuck for over 100 years.

Baughan tends to wax poetic (she was a poet, after all), with the flowery descriptions common to her time, declaring, "this track anyone possessing feet to walk with, eyes to see with, and a love for Nature at her loneliest and fairest, could scarce do better than essay," concluding, "From the variety, the beauty and the scale of the scenes through which it passes, it must certainly be accounted one of the most glorious natural wonders of the world."

Whether the walk is the world's finest or not, it certainly qualifies as one of the world's natural wonders. Expect to see an incredible diversity over the trail's relatively short distance as you pass from magnificent beech forests to the subalpine scrub and tussocks of the pass to the ferns, mosses and lichens common on the Arthur River. Along the way you will be greeted by a rich variety of birds, rugged peaks and the sounds and sights of cascading waterfalls. Maybe Baughan wasn't so over the top after all.

When to go

The track is open from late October to mid-April. Since the yearly average rainfall is close to 8 m (26 ft.) you can expect a lot of rain, even at the height of the summer months. Just prepare to get wet and then enjoy the added beauty of instant waterfalls falling in torrents down the sheer cliffs of the mountains.

What's the story?

The story of the track begins in Milford Sound when a lone Scottish adventurer landed on the shores of the deep fiord on December 1, 1877. Early that morning he had left his camp farther south on Thompson Sound, making the trip of almost 100 km (62 mi.) in ten hours. In his diary he congratulated himself, noting, "I don't want to sound my own trumpet too much, but this is a bully run for a man in an open boat in ten hours."

The man was Donald Sutherland. He came in search of his fortune, convinced the area would yield gold, greenstone (jade), rubies and asbestos. Although he never found any material wealth, he found his roots in this most remarkable place, remaining here for over forty years and eventually earning the name of "the hermit of Milford Sound."

Of course the earliest human history of the area goes back much further, to the Maori, who called the place Piopiotahi after the now extinct thrush-like piopio bird. They came to hunt eel and to collect the rich deposits of greenstone, or takiwai, they found at Anita Bay at the entrance to the sound. The precious stone was transported over what we now know as Mackinnon Pass and then by waterway to Lake Te Anau and beyond. The soft, translucent takiwai was favoured for making fine-quality ornaments and jewellery.

The first European connection was a Welsh sealer named Captain Grono who had worked the Fiordland coast as early as 1809. He gave the sound its original name of Milford Haven after a town close to his home in Wales. By an odd coincidence, he was followed in 1851 by another Welshman who lived close to Milford Haven: Captain John Stokes in HMS *Acheron*. Perhaps Stokes was homesick as he filled his charts with Welsh names for many of the peaks, rivers and points around the sound.

Stokes was charged with surveying the west coast sounds. Of all the inlets they had seen, Commander Sir George Richards declared that Milford, "in remarkable feature and magnificent scenery, far surpasses them all." Its "Alpine features and its narrow entrance," with "stupendous cliffs which rise perpendicular as a wall from the water's edge to a height of

WHAT IS IT?

The early explorers actually got it wrong when they called the inlets along the west coast of New Zealand's South Island "sounds" and not "fiords." Sounds are caused by river erosion, while fiords are gouged out by glaciers.

BREAKING ALL THE RULES

Mitre Peak (named for its resemblance to a bishop's ceremonial headdress), is the centrepiece of the sound. In 1883 Sutherland set out with artist Samuel Moreton in the first attempt to scale its lofty heights. They left "without coats and only one biscuit each" climbing the nearly vertical rock in "stocking soles." In the end they were forced to turn back by a snowstorm, spending the night on the side of the mountain. They finally returned to camp the next day "thoroughly benumbed and drenched through and through," having survived 24 hours on one biscuit each! The peak was finally scaled by Jim Dennistoun in March 1911. Although Dennistoun was successful, he wasn't much better prepared, starting out "with my sandshoes in my pocket and nothing else."

Mitre Peak rises above Milford Sound.

several thousand feet, invest Milford Sound with a character of solemnity and grandeur which description can barely realise."

Little has changed since Richards recorded his first impressions of the sound so long ago. The wild and brooding cliffs still rise in vertical walls from dark waters full of dolphins and seals. When it rains, the entire sound is a magical place of cascading waterfalls plunging down sheer, rocky precipices.

No doubt Commander Richards would be astounded to know this pristine wilderness now draws close to half a million visitors each year, most of them flocking here over the Milford Road during the peak summer months of January and February, while over 14,000 trampers make the trip over the Milford Track. The place is easily one of the country's most famous tourist destinations, and there is a reason it was called the Eighth Wonder of the World for many years.

The sound became a popular stop for cruise ships as early as 1874, but at considerable cost for visitors. The New Zealand government soon realized the tourism potential for the sound if an overland route could be found for trekkers.

Meanwhile, Sutherland had been busy building his "City of Milford," complete with streets, a flag mast and a stone pier. He called his three-roomed hut the

Mount Balloon rises from the mist at Mackinnon Pass.

Esperance Chalet, described by one visitor as "neat and tidy." Sutherland had been joined by John McKay to prospect the area. They knew the government in Queenstown was interested in finding a direct route to Milford Sound, so with £40 cash and six months supplies from the Council, they set off to explore.

In November 1880 the two discovered McKay Falls and the famous three-leap Sutherland Falls, which they claimed were the world's highest. At the upper end of the Arthur Valley they came upon a looming peak they named Mount Balloon "because it was sticking up out of the mist like a balloon."

Once news of the spectacular falls leaked out to the world, Sutherland soon found his "splendid isolation" constantly invaded by cruise ship tourists asking him to guide them up to have a look. Since most of them came from the city and seemed to have some pretty silly questions, Sutherland often called them "ash-felters." He and his wife Elizabeth eventually built a guesthouse called the Chalet, accommodating up to 300 trekkers each season. Known as "The Mother of Milford Sound," Elizabeth stayed on at Milford after her husband's death in 1919, running the Chalet until she sold it to the Tourism Department in 1922.

In 1888 Charles Adams, the chief surveyor of Otago, commissioned Sutherland to cut a track up to the falls (for the grand sum of £50) while Quintin Mackinnon was offered £30 to hack out a trail up the Clinton Valley from the head of Lake Te Anau. Mackinnon had built a log cabin at Garden Point on the western shore of Lake Te Anau in 1885 where he worked at Te Anau Downs Station in the busy months. According to Mrs. Katherine Melland of the Station, "He came to this lovely, beautiful lake to forget and be forgotten."

Mackinnon certainly wasn't forgotten. Not only did he discover the pass to connect the Clinton and Arthur Valleys, but he forged the track up the Clinton Valley in atrocious conditions that would have stopped most men dead in their tracks. On September 7, 1888, Mackinnon and his friend Ernest Mitchell set out on their journey. He described it as "fearful work." Continual rain meant they were unable to light a fire and cook or dry out their tents. As rations ran low they were reduced to one meal a day.

Finally they pushed through to the pass on October 16, eventually making their way to Milford Sound where he wrote in Sutherland's visitors' book, "Found good available track from Te Anau to connect with Sutherland's track. Found Government maps very much out and the Hermit's very much in." Finally, a viable track had been found.

Mackinnon became the track's first guide, famous for his fried scones. On an 1891 guided trip, William McHutcheson described "Mac" as "a stout broad-shouldered Scot, every lineament of whose bronzed and weather-beaten face spoke of determination, endurance and dogged perseverance under difficulties."

Tragically, Quintin Mackinnon's whale boat *Juliet* was found submerged in Lake Te Anau after he was reported missing in 1892. He was presumed drowned but his body was never found. A memorial cross was placed close to the spot where the boat had been discovered and is passed by the ferry on the journey up the lake to Glade Wharf and the beginning of the track he wrenched from the wilderness.

A memorial cross on Lake Te Anau commemorates Quintin Mackinnon's death.

It would take years of building and upgrading to develop the track that exists today. Constantly at the mercy of flooding, wind and avalanche, the track, huts and lodges are a still a challenge to maintain today.

The publication of Baughan's 1908 article in the London *Spectator* prompted even more demand for tourist facilities as walkers flocked to see "The Finest Walk in the World." The opening of the Milford Road in 1953 finally provided vehicle access to the sound, opening the floodgates to tourists from around the world.

Started in the depression years of the late 1920s as an employment project, the road wasn't officially opened until 1954 when the famous Homer Tunnel, under the formidable obstacle of the Homer Saddle was finally completed. Men worked with pickaxes and wheelbarrows to carve out the highway and the 1270 m (4,167 ft.) long tunnel.

The road was built from both ends, with the tunnellers working from the Homer side piercing through to the Milford end in 1940. Construction ceased during the war, and in 1947 the unfinished tunnel was opened to track walkers doing the round trip. This marvel of engineering is now a paved World Heritage highway winding its way through lush forests and rugged mountains from Te Anau to the stunning vistas of Milford Sound.

THE HIKE (A.K.A. THE TRAMP)

As noted in the "Hike overview" section, there are basically two options for completing the tramp. You can choose to join a guided tour with accommodations and meals provided in comfortable lodges or you can walk as an independent hiker staying in designated DOC huts along the route. Camping is not allowed.

The track is highly regulated by the New Zealand government, with access limited to 40 independent walkers and 50 guided ones each day. This may sound like a prescription for disaster, resulting in crowded trails and the potential for a less than optimal hiking experience. But the fact is that the use of one-way travel (the track must be hiked from south to north over four days), and a careful segregation of guided and independent hikers in strategically placed lodges, huts and rest stations

FREEDOM TO WALK

In May 1964, members of the Otago Tramping Club set out to walk the track. They were protesting what they regarded as an excessive fee charged by the Tourist Hotel Corporation that controlled the track at the time. The trampers felt it was every New Zealander's right to walk without charge. Eventually the Fiordland National Park administration agreed to erect the Clinton, Mintaro and Dumpling huts for the "Freedom Walkers," or "Independent Walkers" as they are now called. The huts are well placed along the track to be about a day's hike apart.

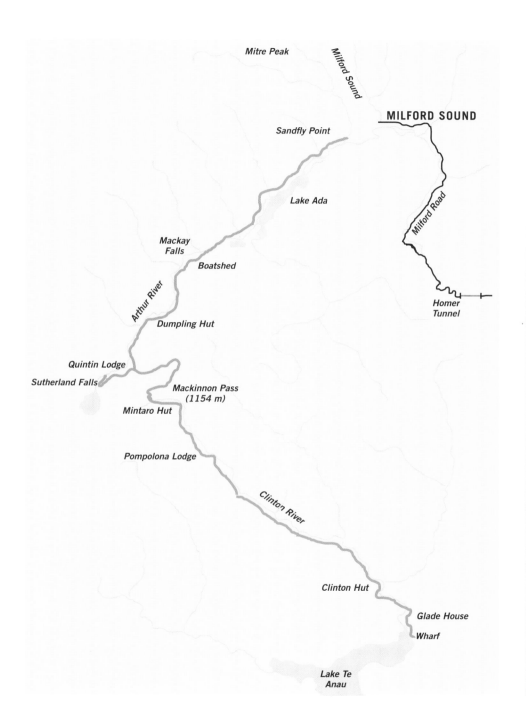

Mitre Peak

Milford Sound

MILFORD SOUND

Sandfly Point

Lake Ada

Milford Road

Mackay
Falls

Boatshed

Homer
Tunnel

Arthur River

Dumpling Hut

Quintin Lodge

Sutherland Falls

Mackinnon Pass
(1154 m)

Mintaro Hut

Pompolona Lodge

Clinton River

Clinton Hut

Glade House

Wharf

Lake Te
Anau

along the way, means the trail can often seem quite deserted. I recall walking in solitary contemplation several times, with not a hiker in sight and only the sound of the river and the bellbirds for company. There was never the slightest hint of congestion anywhere along the trail, even with 90 of us tramping along each day.

I chose to do the guided hike. It is extremely well run, with excellent accommodations and meals provided in each of the lodges. There is no shortage of fresh Kiwi cuisine to keep you fuelled, and each "wilderness" lodge is equipped with comfortable beds, hot showers and some serious drying rooms.

Expect full hot breakfasts and three-course dinners as well as a welcoming afternoon cuppa tea on your arrival off the trail each day. Each morning you will build your own lunch from an enormous selection of options. (Fresh supplies are regularly delivered with military precision by helicopter, so there is never any shortage of food.) Ultimate Hikes also supplies four guides who spread out along the trail and offer excellent commentary on flora and fauna along the way. For added safety, there is always a sweep at the back to make sure no one gets left behind.

SAVE THOSE BOOTS!

Boots and drying rooms don't make a good combination, since the heat affects the glue in the soles and can damage the leather. Ultimate Hikes suggests putting your boots in the drying room close to lights out, since the rooms cool down overnight. But here is a tip I discovered from a fellow hiker after a day of slogging through torrential rain in Scotland. Stuff your boots with old newspaper or paper towels right to the toes. Let the paper sop up the excess moisture, then remove it and restuff your boots with dry material and leave them overnight. In my experience this works far better than a drying room. So newspaper is always in my pack if I know I won't have access to any along the trail.

You will need to carry all your personal clothes and rain gear plus lunch each day. A 40-litre pack is suggested. Ultimate Hikes can supply a backpack plus a heavy-duty raincoat and pack liner if required.

Unlike some backpacking trips in a foreign country, the logistics of doing the walk as an independent tramper are not difficult. In typical Kiwi style, the huts are very well run. Each has gas rings for cooking, coal or gas stoves for heating, tables, basins, bunk rooms with mattresses, flush toilets and a drying room. Hut fees are included in your permit, which you must obtain from the DOC well in advance.

You will still need to carry all your food and cooking utensils in addition to your clothes and rain gear. Plan on a pack capacity of at least 60 litres. If the cost of the guided hike is too rich for your budget, this is certainly a doable option. Just be prepared to miss a few nights sleep due to the inevitable snorers sawing logs next to you.

Please note: Day-to-day descriptions are based on the guided walk option.

Day 1 – Guided – Queenstown to Glade House – 1.2 km (0.8 mi.)

Independent – Te Anau Downs to Clinton Hut – 5.0 km (3.1 mi.)

Guided hikers will join the group in Queenstown for a bus ride to Te Anau Downs and the ferry ride to Glade Wharf at the north end of Lake Te Anau. Independent hikers must make their own way to the boat launch to catch the ferry. (See the "How to do the hike" section below for logistics details.)

Today is an easy introduction to the magnificent scenery that is the trademark of every kilometre of this trail. The sheer mountain peaks and lakes of Fiordland were carved out over two million years by massive glaciers during the last ice age, which ended just 14,000 years ago. The rivers of ice scoured the landscape, forming vertical-sided U-shaped valleys and lakes like Te Anau, the country's second largest.

Hikers disembark at Glade Wharf for an easy stroll through southern beech forest to Glade House. Set in a clearing on the east bank of the Clinton River, the first Glade House was built in 1895 by John and Louisa Garvey. It soon became a place for walkers to stop before beginning the walk.

The Garveys were well known for their hospitality. With their 11 children, they established a tradition of evening entertainment for guests. The original building burned down in 1929 but was rebuilt in 1930. Although the house was linked to Milford with a telephone line, the service was often out of commission from avalanches and wind

YOU WILL GET WET!

The chances of getting clear weather all the way through are virtually zero. With almost 8 m (26 ft.) of rainfall each year, you would have to be extremely lucky to catch four consecutive sunny days. So plan on the worst and hope for the best. There is the potential for snow, heavy flooding and strong winds at any time. (In May 2009, 170 trampers were airlifted from the track after rivers rose 3.8 m (12.5 ft.) in a matter of hours.) You need heavy-duty rain gear that will withstand a downpour, and layers to keep you warm. Locals tend to scoff at Gore-Tex and rain pants, instead recommending heavy-duty slickers and polypropylene long johns under shorts. Apparently these long johns keep the legs warm even if you are fording streams and flooded areas. I have never tried them, but they are certainly the uniform of choice for most Kiwi trampers, so there is obviously something to it. Leave the poncho at home. They are no good in wind. And don't forget to put everything in double plastic bags in your pack with a rain cover over top.

Glade House and the swing bridge across the Clinton River.

damage. The Garveys kept carrier pigeons as well, though, and their "pigeon post" proved quite reliable.

As you walk in, expect to be greeted by a frequent and unwelcome visitor. The pesky sandfly (a.k.a. blackfly) thrives here and unless you keep moving or use a strong repellent, they will be your constant companion over much of the trail.

It seems sandflies are nothing new to the landscape. Maori legend has it that the goddess of the underworld released them to forever keep men from living here, because the land was so beautiful. And as far back as 1773, Captain James Cook remarked on them in his journal during his exploration of the Fiordland coast, noting, "The most mischievous animals here are the small black sandflies, which are very numerous and so troublesome that they exceed everything of the kind I ever met with."

Day 2 – Guided – Glade House to Pompolona Lodge – 16 km (10 mi.)

Independent – Clinton Hut to Mintaro Hut – 16.5 km (10.2 mi.)

The day begins with a walk over the swing bridge that spans the Clinton River. You might be lucky enough to spot black eels and rainbow trout as you cross. The trail heads into lush beech forest along the river, with a chance to spot blue ducks

Lush beech forest along the Milford Track.

and hear the clear, fluid notes of the tui, or parson bird, and the bellbird. Soft, feathery ferns are common, as are fuchsia trees with their purplish-red flowers. A short detour to the Wetland Walk is well worth the time. The boardwalk features interpretive panels as it crosses moss wetland and offers spectacular views up the valley to Mount Sentinel.

For a few kilometres the track follows the old, flat packhorse trail, then heads up along the west branch of the Clinton Valley until it meets the debris from a major avalanche in the 1980s. The rubble blocked the river, forming a lake where dead trees emerge ghostlike from the water. This portion of the track passes through a number of avalanche paths, so be sure to watch for sign posts. According to the DOC, there are 56 such paths along the track, which can cause delays or make the track impassable at any time.

Guided hikers stop for lunch at the Hirere Falls shelter, with a view to the falls across the valley. Not far down the trail, Mackinnon Pass comes into view on the skyline. It looks ominous but in fact the gradient is not much steeper than some you have already climbed.

The track passes Hidden Lake, then heads back into beech forest until it emerges onto the Prairie, a grassy flat with good views of the ice-capped peaks. Guided hikers then head on to Pompolona Lodge. The name comes from "a sort of fried scone" that Quintin Mackinnon often made for his guests. Apparently he sometimes caused dismay when they saw him toss candles into the frying pan to make his famous concoction until people realized the candles were made of mutton fat!

Once the lights are out and quiet descends, you might hear the shrill whistle of the nocturnal and flightless kiwi bird – a two-note call that sounds like *ki-wi*.

Day 3 – Guided – Pompolona Lodge to Quintin Lodge – 15 km (9 mi.)

Independent – Mintaro Hut to Dumpling Hut – 14.0 km (8.7 mi.)

This is the toughest day of the walk, with a climb of close to 500 m (1,640 ft.) to the top of Mackinnon Pass, followed by a steep descent of more than 800 m (2,625 ft.) over rocky, uneven terrain. Although most people worry about the ascent, many agree that coming down is probably the hardest part of the track. It requires concentration and a slow, steady pace. Here is where your poles will pay off big time. Your knees will thank you.

The trail crosses a swing bridge and passes a small, grassy clearing, the remains of a paddock for the packhorses that supplied the huts. Numerous avalanche zones are traversed and hikers should not stop in marked areas. Soon Practice Hill heads up to Lake Mintaro, and the first of the well-graded zigzags (a.k.a. switchbacks) signals the beginning of the climb to the summit. As you follow the 11 zigzags you will pass from a canopy of beech trees to subalpine shrubland to alpine tussock grassland. On a clear day, superb views of Mount Balloon and Nicolas Cirque unfold, but don't forget to watch for the wonders at your feet – like mountain daisies, bluebells and Mount Cook lilies, the world's largest buttercup.

As you near the summit, you will pass the Quintin Mackinnon memorial cairn, honouring the discovery of the pass by Mackinnon and Mitchell in 1888. Now all your effort pays off with spectacular vistas down the Clinton and Arthur valleys and the surrounding ice-covered peaks. Enjoy the view but don't get too close to the infamous 12-second drop. (That's how long it would take you to hit the bottom if you went over the edge.) A series of small tarns or ponds dot the landscape as you head for lunch at Pass Hut and a chance to use the toilet with the best view in Fiordland. From your seat a well-placed window enables you to visually retrace your steps back down the length of the Clinton Valley.

The trail ahead flanks Mount Balloon, then begins the long steep descent to Quintin Lodge. Along the way, stop to admire what are arguably some of the best views the trail has to offer. Hikers will be directed by markers and their guides down the emergency track at times of high avalanche risk – usually spring and early summer. Our group descended via this detour, which is steeper than the main track but shorter. You will know you are close to the end when you glimpse Lindsay Falls and Dudleigh

The Quintin Mackinnon Memorial cairn at the top of Mackinnon Pass.

Pass Hut and the toilet with the best view in Fiordland. Mount Wilmot is on the left and Mount Balloon looms on the right.

Falls. One final steep section brings you to the swing bridge over Roaring Burn (Gaelic for stream or creek) and the welcome prospect of afternoon tea at the lodge.

But you're not done yet! Enjoy the break, and then rally yourself for the 4 km (2.5 mi.) side trip to Sutherland Falls, a pleasant hike through fine silver beech and fuchsia forest. Just a word of warning: there is one steep section to climb, so if your knees are screaming "No," remember there will be a good view of the falls (albeit from a distance) on Day 4 after you leave Quintin Lodge.

ULTIMATE HIKES, NEW ZEALAND

Sutherland Falls.

HIGHEST IN THE WORLD!

When Donald Sutherland and John McKay discovered the three-leap waterfall in November 1880, little did they know they would ignite a push by adventurers for a track or road that would give them access to what had been proclaimed as the highest waterfall in the world. Sutherland initially estimated it at "between 3,000 [and] 4,000 feet high" (914 and 1219 m), later increasing that to "5,700 feet" (1737 m). It is actually 580 m (1,904 ft.). Various sources rate it anywhere from the fifth to the sixty-fifth highest in the world. On that same trip, the pair also discovered another fine waterfall, which purportedly was named McKay Falls on a coin toss. When they later hacked their way to the three-leap falls, apparently it seemed the only fair thing to do was to name it after Sutherland. A young surveyor named William Quill actually climbed the falls three times. John Hall-Jones, in his book *Milford Sound*, recounts Quill's first Sunday climb to the top of the upper leap on March 9, 1890: "But now commenced the real climb. A steady hand and a strong nerve were all that kept me from slipping, where the least slip would send me down the perpendicular rock to be dashed to pieces hundreds of feet below." Certainly an interesting way to spend your day off!

Independent – Dumpling Hut to Sandfly Point – 18 km (11.2 mi.)

This distance is actually longer than Day 3, but the walking is easy with plenty of the spectacular scenery you have come to expect. As you pass the 20 mile peg, be sure to look back for one last glimpse of Sutherland Falls. Soon Racecourse Flats is crossed – a straight section where packhorses once got competitive – then on to the Boatshed Shelter for morning tea. The shelter was used to house the boat used on Lake Ada to ferry passengers and luggage.

Boardwalks and more bridges eventually lead to a short side track to McKay Falls and the curiously eroded Bell Rock. Blanche Baughan's 1926 book *The Finest Walk in the World* sums it up this way: "MacKay Fall [sic]: no Sutherland, but still a glorious outburst of music and bright white light upon a world of green shadowiness and silence ... This is one of the loveliest woodland scenes in the whole walk."

And I would have to agree. The higher rainfall and milder temperatures in the Arthur Valley foster lush vegetation with ferns, mosses and lichens in abundance.

NEW ZEALAND DEPARTMENT OF CONSERVATION

Sandfly Point marks the end of the Milford Track.

Today's trail has some of the best beech forest on the track, along with fine mountain and valley views.

Along Lake Ada you will pass a section blasted out of the sheer rock wall by track builders in 1893, while the broad, easy path at the end is thanks to the "efforts" of a less than enthusiastic crew of 45 prisoners who had arrived in 1890 to "cut the Te Anau road." The project was abandoned as a dismal failure after less than 2 km (1.2 mi.) had been completed in two years.

Sandfly Point marks the end of the track. A shelter here keeps those pesky bugs at bay while you wait for the ferry to take you to Milford. As you wait for your comfortable ride, spare a thought for the early

The "glorious outburst" of McKay Falls.

trekkers. Until the Homer Tunnel was opened to trampers in 1947, people had to turn around and do the whole track in reverse back to Te Anau!

Day 5 – Guided – no walking

Independent – no walking

Guided hikers enjoy a celebratory dinner at Mitre Peak Lodge on the evening of Day 4 before embarking on a cruise of the famous Milford Sound on Day 5 and a bus ride back to Queenstown.

Independent hikers must arrange their own accommodations in Milford and transportation back to Te Anau or Queenstown. (See the "How to do the hike" section for more details.) The cruise prior to departing is highly recommended.

HOW TO DO THE HIKE

Option 1, guided hike: Must be booked through Ultimate Hikes, **www.ultimatehikes .co.nz**. The trip starts and ends in Queenstown. Air New Zealand provides regular air service between Queenstown, Auckland, Wellington and Christchurch. (See the "Consider this" section for more information on Queenstown.)

Option 2, independent walker: Permits must be purchased through the DOC. Booking details are available at **www.doc.govt.nz**. Hikers must catch the ferry across Lake Te Anau to Glade Wharf at the village of Te Anau Downs. There is limited accommodation in the village, but you can use the town of Te Anau as your base. The town is the main starting point for a number of tramps throughout the region, with numerous options for accommodations and tramping supplies. Te Anau does not have an airport, but regular bus service is available from Queenstown, plus shuttle service to the ferry wharf at Te Anau Downs as well as from Milford Sound back to Te Anau or Queenstown at the end of the trek. Check **www.greatwalksnz.com** for bus information and **www.realjourneys.co.nz** for ferry information. The hike ends at Sandfly Point. Hikers must catch the ferry to Milford at designated times and make their own way back to Te Anau or Queenstown.

HOW DO YOU SAY THAT?

There is no denying that Kiwis have a distinct lingo all their own. For example, did you know that if you are going "across the ditch" you are going across the Tasman Sea to Australia, or that you are not cool if you are "daggy"? One particular expression that stumped me for a while was the ubiquitous "sweet as." For the longest time I thought it had an extra "s" tacked on the end, making it somewhat rude. I finally discovered it is an all-purpose term that means "great."

To the untuned North American ear the accent may sound similar to their Australian neighbours, but don't make the mistake of suggesting that to a local.

New Zealand has two official languages – English and Maori – and the latter is enjoying a resurgence as the Maori strive to preserve and promote their culture. You will notice that government departments have been given Maori names and many place names use both the English and Maori versions.

In fact, the use of Maori greetings is becoming more common. Here are a few you might want to try out:

• hello – kia ora (also means good luck or good health)
• goodbye to the person staying – e noho ra
• goodbye to the person leaving – haere ra

CONSIDER THIS: BEFORE OR AFTER THE HIKE

Queenstown tends to be the jumping-off point for anyone planning on tramping the Milford Track. The first white people arrived in the area in the mid-1850s to establish sheep farms. The peace and quiet of the pastoral life was soon shattered in 1862 when two sheep shearers, Thomas Arthur and Harry Redfern, discovered gold on the Shotover River. The discovery triggered a stampede as thousands headed there in search of fortune.

Soon a mining town sprang up on the bay, complete with hotels and all the amenities required to cater to a population that quickly grew to over 8,000. There are several variations on how it was named, all revolving around the statement that it was considered "fit for a queen," hence Queenstown. Although the river yielded record amounts of gold, it had petered out by 1900 and the number of residents dropped to less than 200.

It wasn't until road and air access began to improve in the 1950s that the spot started to become a popular tourist destination. Set on the pristine shores of Lake Wakatipu with the Remarkables mountain range soaring up on its doorstep, the town has become a four-season "Global Adventure Capital." If you can't find anything to do here, you need to seriously reconsider your travel expectations.

AND THE BEAT GOES ON

Lake Wakatipu is a Maori name commonly translated as "the hollow of the sleeping giant." Legend holds the giant was wicked and was set on fire by the hero Matakauri after he rescued the love of his life from the giant's evil clutches. The giant melted until all that was left of him was his heart. The resulting hollow filled with water and became the lake. According to the story, the heart continues to beat, causing the lake to constantly rise and fall as much as 12 cm (5 in.) every five minutes. Of course, there is a less romantic scientific explanation: the rhythmic pulse is caused by variations in atmospheric pressure.

The Remarkables soar above
Queenstown and Lake Wakatipu.

Activities include everything from bungee jumping, jetboating, whitewater rafting, canyoning and paragliding to mountain biking, skiing, snowboarding and zorbing (rolling down a hill inside a transparent plastic ball). You can tramp and climb to your heart's content on nearby trails that rate from easy to challenging, all within a short distance of downtown. If that sounds too exhausting to contemplate after hiking the Milford Track, the town offers many slower-paced alternatives.

One of the most popular choices is the Skyline Gondola, offering a spectacular panorama of Queenstown, the lake and the

PEOPLE PAY TO DO THIS?

Bungee jumping wasn't invented by New Zealander A.J. Hackett, but he started the first commercial operation in 1988 at Kawarau Bridge in Queenstown following a publicity stunt where he jumped from the Eiffel Tower. Hackett was inspired by videos that recorded the jumping antics of the Oxford Dangerous Sports Club in the late 1970s. His gamble paid off. Apparently people will line up to pay for the chance to hurl themselves off a high structure with nothing but a giant elastic band attached to their ankles.

mountains. A number of walking trails can be accessed close to the gondola, or you can pass on the gondola and hike up to the top. I opted for this alternative on a gloriously clear day. From the trailhead on Lomond Crescent, take the upper, left-hand gravel track. The hike is steep in places and takes one to 1.5 hours. Once you've hiked up, you don't need to feel guilty about taking the gondola back down.

ARE YOU READY TO EAT?

You won't have any worries about being limited to mutton and boiled vegetables here. Kiwi cuisine embraces the best of local fresh ingredients, from tender lamb to seafood specialties such as greenshell mussels, clams and scallops to local produce straight from the field. Food styles have been highly influenced by Pacific Rim and Polynesian neighbours, so expect a fusion of tastes and ingredients. New Zealanders like their food, and every little café and restaurant seems to offer a tantalizing array of choices.

Hygiene standards are very high at the lodges on the Milford Track, and in fact there is no cause for concern when eating out anywhere in New Zealand.

Tipping is considered optional. Unlike North America, where workers depend on tips for part of their income, this is not the case in New Zealand. It is entirely up to you if you choose to reward good service.

CHINESE GOOSEBERRIES?

Did you know that kiwi fruit originated in China and are still considered the national fruit there? They weren't introduced to New Zealand until 1906 and were not commercially exported until the late 1950s. Kiwi fruit were commonly called Chinese gooseberries because they resembled gooseberries. The fruit was briefly renamed "melonette," but that was changed to incorporate the Maori word "kiwi" when it was learned there were steep import tariffs on melons.

Vegetarians: There may not be a large number of strictly vegetarian restaurants but most menus will offer a vegetarian option.

INTERNET RESOURCES

There is a wealth of information available on the Internet. Here are some reliable websites to get you started:

www.newzealand.com is the official site for New Zealand tourism.
www.doc.govt.nz, the Department of Conservation site, provides everything you need to know about parks and recreation across New Zealand. Independent walkers will find all the information needed to plan their trip.

www.ultimatehikes.co.nz has everything you need to know about booking the guided track walk.

www.tramper.co.nz features good information for tramping anywhere in New Zealand.

www.destination-nz.com provides excellent website listings.

www.queenstownnz.co.nz is the town's official site.

www.queenstown-vacation.com has good information on everything relating to Queenstown and area.

RECOMMENDED READING

This reading list focuses on the Milford Track and the Milford Sound area only and does not include broader coverage of New Zealand in general.

KIWI Footpaths Track Guide No. 1: The Milford – Gordon and Michelle Hosking and Peter and John Kamp – an excellent waterproof guide that will fit in a pocket. The spiral binding ensures it can be opened to any page and remain perfectly flat, while the two kilometre per page sectional maps provide an easy to follow visual summary of the entire track from Glade Wharf to Sandfly Point. Plus additional information on history, geology, flora and fauna, it is highly recommended. Probably best to look for this when you are in New Zealand.

Lonely Planet: New Zealand – I tend to be partial to the Lonely Planet series if you are looking for a comprehensive guidebook to help plan your trip.

Lonely Planet: Tramping in New Zealand – Jim DuFresne – somewhat dated, this guide provides good information on tramping all over New Zealand, including a section on the Milford Track.

Milford Sound: An Illustrated History of the Sound, the Track and the Road – John Hall-Jones – an excellent source for historical information, maps and photographs, many published here for the first time. Available online through Craigs Design and Print Ltd. at www.craigprint. co.nz. Highly recommended.

The Finest Walk in the World – Blanche Baughan – is still available from used book sellers. I located a copy through www.amazon.ca. Written in the flowery language typical of the early 1900s, it gives a wonderful description of the birds, the plants and the sights along the trail.

The Milford Track Navigator – an excellent waterproof fold-out includes a good map and day to day description of the route. A copy of this is supplied by Ultimate Hikes when you sign up for the guided walk.

Walking the Milford Track – Rosalind Harker – written by a former manager of the Pompolona Hut, the book provides a wealth of information on the birds and the flora along with colour photographs to help with identification. There is a detailed description of the hike as well as a chapter on the history of the famous track. Probably best to look for this when you are in New Zealand.

© FOTOSEARCH.COM

New Zealand kea parrot.

FAUNA FACTS: CHEEKY VANDALS

Milford Track hosts much birdlife along its length, including the blue duck, kaka, weka, kiwi, bellbird and wood pigeon. But the most notorious, and the one you will see for sure, is the cheeky vandal called the kea. This large, rather drab, olive-green parrot has brilliant orange under its wings, a large, curved, grey-brown beak and some serious talons. The birds are fearless when it comes to humans and can make short work of anything left unattended. Keas are notorious for stealing food. They can be quite aggressive, announcing their presence with a raucous "kee-aa" call. You will need to keep a close eye on your gear, since they can destroy boots and backpacks and will vandalize a room if a door is left open for them to sneak in. Their strong beaks can rip tents, sleeping bags and clothing. They have even been known to strip a car bare, right down to the wiring. Keas are almost always at the Pass Hut when you stop for lunch. So don't let them steal your food, because you will need the fuel to make it down the long descent to Quintin Lodge.

CHAPTER 5 – GREAT BRITAIN – ENGLAND – COTSWOLD WAY NATIONAL TRAIL

The Cotswold Way – "Cotswold" from the twelfth century *Codesuualt* or "Cod's-wold," meaning "Cod's high open land," with "Cod" believed to be an Old English personal name; alternatively, "cots," meaning "large sheep enclosures," and "wolds" meaning "hills" – literally "sheep-hills"

The Cotswold country is, as I think, the most beautiful in England ... It is a commonplace to us who know this small country of ours that there is hardly any stretch of twenty miles in it which does not flatter us in the belief that there is no more tender or subtle landscape on earth.

—JOHN DRINKWATER, *Cotswold Characters* (1921)

✳ HIKING RULE 5: On a National Trail there will always be a marker as you pass through a gate or climb over a stile. If you can't find it, you have probably gone the wrong way. When you can't tell for sure which way a marker is pointing, because it is faded or hard to read, just check the other side. The marker for walkers approaching from the other direction will usually solve the mystery.

WHERE IN THE WORLD?

CLAIM TO FAME

Formally designated as a National Trail in May 2007, this superb long-distance footpath runs mainly along the Cotswold escarpment for 164 km (102 mi.), starting at Chipping Campden in the north and ending at the city of Bath, a UNESCO World Heritage Site. Almost the entire trail lies within the Cotswolds Area of Outstanding Natural Beauty, the largest in England and Wales. (AONBs are places of considerable landscape value, chosen to promote conservation and enhancement of their natural beauty.) The Cotswolds AONB was established primarily in recognition of the region's rare limestone grasslands and ancient beech woodlands featuring a rich diversity of flora and fauna. The unique value of the Cotswolds AONB is confirmed by the five European Special Areas of Conservation, three National Nature Reserves and over 80 Sites of Special Scientific Interest that are contained within its boundaries.

WHAT WILL I SEE?

D. LARRAINE ANDREWS

Glorious walking in the "sheep hills" of the Cotswolds.

HIKE PROFILE

The trail begins just above sea level in Chipping Campden, climbing to a maximum elevation of 325 m (1,066 ft.) at Cleeve Hill, eventually descending off the escarpment to Bath. This may not sound very challenging, but never underestimate the English countryside. Over the course of the walk you will encounter countless sharp ups and downs. By the end you will probably have climbed the equivalent of several mountains.

Hazards

As with any walking trail that includes climbs and descents on steep, uneven terrain, the normal cautions regarding twisted ankles and injuries from falling apply here.

There are no natural predators to worry about – only an occasional sheep, squirrel or roe deer that might happen to cross your path.

You will cross innumerable paddocks on this walk. While almost all of them will contain sheep, always be prepared with an exit plan if any of the fields contain a bull or cows with calves. The law states that bulls over ten months of age are not allowed in a field through which a public footpath passes, but there isn't much you can do about it if a farmer has decided to ignore the rules. Stay alert and give any bull, no matter its age, a wide berth. Keep to the edge of the field so you can hop over the fence if you need to. And never take lightly the presence of cows with calves, since they tend to be very protective of their young.

I have found that dogs can sometimes present problems on the trail. But 99 times out of 100 they are with a local out for a walk and are quickly controlled. (The presence of dogs and dog walkers is always a good indication you are getting close to the next village and maybe a welcome cup of tea.)

D. LARRAINE ANDREWS

Curious cows surround a gate at the entrance to a paddock on the trail.

> **Getting there:** The hike is normally done from Chipping Campden in the north to Bath in the south. Both towns are easily accessible by rail from either Heathrow airport (**www.heathrowairport.com**) or Gatwick airport (**www.gatwickairport.com**). These airports would be two of the most common entry points for flights from Canada. The most convenient railway station for Chipping Campden is Moreton-in-Marsh, requiring a short local bus or taxi ride to Chipping Campden. There is frequent rail service from Bath back to London, with easy connections to either airport. Of course, there are many routing options, depending on your own individual travel plans. Websites for both National Express Coaches (**www.nationalexpress.com**) and National Rail (**www.nationalrail.co.uk**) provide excellent starting points.

> **Currency:** pound sterling, or GBP, or GB£. £1 = 100 pence. For current exchange rates, check out **www.oanda.com**.

> **Special gear:** You will need good, sturdy, waterproof hiking boots that are well broken in before you hit the trail. Hiking poles are highly recommended to help maintain balance on uneven or slippery rocks or steps. You will also need to carry rain gear, of course, including gaiters, as well as adequate supplies of food and water. Rain is inevitable. Make sure your pack has a rain cover and that it is also lined with waterproof facing or plastic bags. One particularly indispensable piece of gear for walking in Great Britain is a plastic map pouch. These are wonderful contraptions that you hang around your neck and into which you insert your maps/guidebooks to keep them dry as you walk. Then all you need to do is flip it up to check your location along the trail. I didn't have one of these on my first National Trail walk and ended up with a rain-wrinkled, very weathered guidebook by the end of it.

HIKE OVERVIEW

For much of its 164 km (102 mi.) the Cotswold Way wanders along the limestone escarpment called the Cotswold Edge, climbing and descending countless times as it passes through idyllic, almost picture-perfect villages and some of the finest landscape in the country.

Since almost the entire trail lies within the Cotswolds AONB, it has been designed to encompass some of the very best the area has to offer. The result is a trail that has been described by Kev Reynolds, in his guide *The Cotswold Way: Two-Way Trail Description*, as "a devious route – a switchback, stuttering, to-ing and fro-ing, climbing and falling walk." But one that is superb just the same.

Heading south from the ancient market town of Chipping Campden, with its elegant collection of golden-hued buildings, the walker passes through a stunning landscape of ancient grazing lands and woodland trails filled with beeches, bird-song and amazing wildflowers. Along the way, villages like Stanton, with its iconic Cotswold cottages, seem almost too perfect to be real, while the romantic ruins of Hailes Abbey, the ancient tombs of Belas Knap and the ubiquitous drystone walls clearly show how the famous Cotswold limestone has shaped and defined this country for centuries.

The trail climbs to its highest point on the protected grasslands of Cleeve Common, with fine views back to Winchcombe, then on to the Devil's Chimney on the edge of Leckhampton Hill, with Cheltenham spread out below. Expect more splendid panoramas and fine woodland walking as you head toward the white stone buildings of Painswick. A series of ups and downs leads to rewarding vistas from Haresfield Beacon and Cam Long Down. From here it's down to the old wool town of Dursley, before more climbing to the Tyndale Monument on Nibley Knoll and down to the village of Wotton-under-Edge.

Ahead lies more excellent scarp walking, deep sunken tracks through magical beech forest, quiet country lanes and peaceful vales filled with grazing sheep as you pass villages with intriguing names like Hawkesbury Upton and Old Sodbury. Don't miss a chance to stop for a pot of tea and admire the fine gardens of Dyrham Park and to record your thoughts on the Cotswold Way in the message book by the trail in Dyrham Wood. From here it's not far before the final descent to the elegant streets of Bath. Along the way, be sure to savour the final miles filled with broad panoramas and tranquil country walking before plunging back into "civilization" as you wind your way through the city to the magnificent splendour of Bath Abbey, and the end of this exceptional trail.

Why would I want to?

You may have noticed this book includes two chapters for European walks and both of them are National Trails in Great Britain. I make no apologies for my obvious bias. People often ask me about my favourite hike and although I find that question almost impossible to answer, these are my favourite types of hikes. I have done a number of National Trails and the Cotswold Way ranks close to the top of the list.

Of course, this is entirely my view, but I love the freedom of being able to walk safely on my own, set my own pace and not worry about encountering a bear or a cougar along the trail. I can decide when I want to stop for tea, take a photograph or have a closer look at something. I can decide how far I want to walk each day and where I want to spend a rest day. And best of all, I can do it all with a daypack while someone else takes care of my luggage along the way. (See the "How to do the hike" section for detailed information on logistics.)

When it comes to choosing the Cotswold Way, I suppose the obvious answer is that almost the entire length lies within the largest Area of Outstanding Natural Beauty in England and Wales. It seems John Drinkwater can be forgiven his apparent hyperbole when he calls the Cotswold country the most beautiful in England. Even the official National Trail guide calls it "100 miles of quintessentially English countryside."

At 164 km (102 mi.) in length, the Way gives novice National Trail walkers an outstanding opportunity to sample some of the best the country has to offer without the somewhat daunting challenge of an Offa's Dyke Path (see chapter 6) or other longer alternatives in the extensive National Trail network. Since the Cotswold route passes through numerous villages and towns, walkers have many options when it comes to deciding on where to stop and how far to walk each day. And easy accessibility along the trail means there is always the possibility of hiking just a portion of the path if your time or ambition is limited.

The Way is not difficult, but neither is it a mere stroll. You will climb and descend the escarpment countless times before you reach Bath, but there are no vast open moorlands or lonely mountain tracks to threaten the solitary walker. The land is peaceful, rolling, welcoming. Along the way you will pass through picture-perfect villages where charming thatched cottages and magnificent churches crafted from the famous Cotswold limestone create a veritable "poem in stone." Sheep graze the grasslands as they have for centuries. Orchids and bluebells spring from the rich soil to greet the watchful rambler while a symphony of birdsong fills the ancient beech woodlands. What can I say? The walking is good here.

WHAT IS A NATIONAL TRAIL?

National Trails are long-distance paths for walking, cycling and horse riding that cover some of the finest landscapes in England and Wales. There are 15 designated trails in England and Wales and four in Scotland, where they are called long-distance routes. The first trail, the Pennine Way, was opened in 1965 following a push to protect many of the country's special landscapes. Funded by the national government and other partners, each trail is administered by a National Trail Officer responsible for management and maintenance to meet national standards. Volunteers contribute an enormous amount of time and effort to upkeep, and I salute their dedication in preserving such a superb system of trails. The network includes 4000 km (2,500 mi.) of trails in England and Wales.

When to go

In theory the path can be tackled at any time of the year. The long days of May and June, combined with the superb proliferation of wildflowers and the fact that less rain falls in the spring than at any other time of the year, makes this one of the best times to go. I walked the trail in early June and had only one really bad day of high wind and driving rain. Neither the trail nor the villages were busy, making it an ideal time to walk. Summer is traditional holiday time, with many of the Cotswold villages attracting hordes of visitors throughout July and August. Although most of them aren't there to walk the National Trail, the Cotswold Way is very popular for day trips and loop walks because there is easy access from so many points. This means portions of the trail close to popular destinations such as Chipping Campden or Broadway can be very busy during the summer. Of course, the likelihood of rain is highly unpredictable and ever-present no matter what time of year you choose, with chances slightly higher in the fall and winter. (Having said that, I should also point out that the last major flooding in the area occurred in the summer of 2007, with 2008 a close second.) The brilliant colours in the woodlands and the crisp days make autumn a definite alternative. Winter is not recommended, though. The very short days combined with the possibility of encountering cold winds and driving rain can make for some tough walking conditions.

What's the story?

> ... these walls were still faintly warm and luminous, as if they knew
> the trick of keeping the lost sunlight of centuries glimmering about
> them. This lovely trick is at the heart of the Cotswold mystery.
>
> —J.B. PRIESTLEY, *English Journey* (1934)

Priestley was clearly captivated by the spell of the luminous stone that defines the very essence of the Cotswolds. For centuries, man has captured the magic of the famous limestone in the cottages, the fine churches and the drystone walls that seem an almost natural extension of a landscape that was largely untouched by the Industrial Revolution and hasn't changed for hundreds of years.

Just for a minute you need to put on your geologist's hat to understand what makes this stone, and consequently the Cotswolds, so special. For much of its length, the Cotswold Way follows the Cotswold Edge, a high limestone escarpment formed during the Jurassic period about 150 million years ago. The sedimentary rock emerged out of a warm, shallow sea where the shells of tiny creatures were compressed into a distinctive oolitic (from Greek, "egg stone") limestone that was eventually pushed up and exposed in the undulating cliff of land we see today. The Way follows much of this scarp, providing stunning views over the Malvern Hills and the Severn River as far as Wales on a good day.

According to Anthony Burton, in his *Cotswold Way Official National Trail Guide*, the organic texture of the limestone gives it an unusual ability to "not so much reflect the light as to absorb and throw it back, enriched with a deep, golden glow." The

The "warm and luminous" quality of the Cotswold limestone is captured in this thatched cottage in the village of Stanton.

Belas Knap is a Neolithic long barrow, or tomb.

result is a distinctive honey-coloured stone that is easily worked and considered to be some of the most durable building material in the world. Over the centuries, the easy availability of the rock meant its use was not restricted to grand manors and churches, but graced even the most modest cottages.

The limestone varies in colour as you walk from north to south, gradually changing from the golden-hued buildings of Chipping Campden to the off-white elegance of Painswick and Bath. But the use of this magical stone has never been limited to the towns and villages. Over 4,000 years ago Neolithic people built a communal tomb at Belas Knap incorporating the local limestone into a structure that seems to have hardly changed since then.

When the Romans invaded England in 43 CE they quickly realized the agricultural value of the land in this area, establishing prosperous farming estates in the valleys and building richly decorated stone villas strategically designed to catch the rays of the sun. Ruins can still be seen not far off the trail near Winchcombe and at Witcombe, close to Cooper's Hill. The peaceful prosperity of Roman times came to an end as the legions withdrew in 410 CE and the Anglo-Saxons, with their feudal pattern of farming, advanced into the region. They established small villages clustered around stone manors and churches. But it was the arrival of the Normans, following the invasion in 1066, that saw church-building begin in earnest and the transformation of the high wolds into vast sheep-walks where sheep were said to outnumber people four to one.

By the twelfth century large areas of woodland were being cleared to accommodate even more sheep. As Jane Bingham notes in her book *The Cotswolds: A Cultural History*, it was a situation that would later prompt cleric William Tyndale to complain, "God gave the earth to men to inhabit and not unto sheep." Much of the land was controlled by influential abbots who employed locals to herd and shear the flocks, while a class of powerful middlemen developed to act as wool brokers between the church and the cloth merchants.

By 1586 William Camden was writing in Britannia, "In these woulds there feed in great numbers flockes of sheepe ... whose wool being most fine and soft, is had in passing great account among nations." The best wool in Europe was considered to be English, and the best wool in England was said to be Cotswold. It was produced by a distinctive breed called the Cotswold Lion.

At its height in the fourteenth century, the wool trade was said to account for 50 per cent of England's wealth, a fact that was recognized by "the woolsack," a wool-stuffed cushion originally presented to the Lord Chancellor in the upper house of the British Parliament as a symbol of the prosperity brought by the wool trade.

HILLTOP BEACON

Just south of Winchcombe, right on the Cotswold Way, Belas Knap is one of the finest examples of a Neolithic long barrow, or chambered tomb. The name is thought to mean "hilltop beacon," descriptive of its location on a high hill overlooking the countryside. When it was excavated in the 1860s, a number of skeletal remains were found in its chambers. Writer H.J. Massingham marvelled at the skill exhibited in the construction of the walls, noting they were "built up of thin, close-fitting, superimposed wafers of stone whose perfect workmanship is proven not merely by their appearance but by the fact that parts of the walls have remained without a loose slate to this day ..." He maintained that the building technique in many places was actually superior to more modern versions of the stone walls separating fields throughout the Cotswolds.

The rise of the wealthy wool merchant class left an indelible mark on the countryside, with enormous sums being spent on fine manor houses and grand renovations to existing Norman churches in an exuberant architectural style called Perpendicular Gothic. In the Cotswolds it became known as Woolgothic. One of the finest examples is the parish church of St. James in Chipping Campden, widely recognized as one of the great "wool churches" of the region.

HEAR THEM ROAR?

They may have sounded like regular sheep but they ruled the wool trade with their lustrous, curly "golden fleece." The nickname "lion" came from their large frame and the shaggy "mane" that graced their long necks. They were renowned for their white wool, rapid growth rate and heavy wool clip. The breed eventually went into steady decline as the market faced stiff competition from Spanish merinos and demand grew for woven cloth rather than raw wool. The breed remains in the "at risk" category on the Rare Breeds Survival Trust's "watch list" but are still actively promoted by the Cotswold Sheep Society.

The parish church of St. James in Chipping Campden is a fine example of the Woolgothic style.

William Grevel, who built himself a handsome stone home that still stands on the High Street, was a major benefactor of the church. A memorial brass declares him "the flower of the wool merchants of all England."

As the demand for raw wool exports declined, a prosperous new middle class of textile mill owners emerged, with woollen cloth manufacturing providing yet another source of wealth. They built grand stone houses in Painswick and the Stroud Valley and launched another round of church building. Their mills can still be seen along many of the rivers and streams throughout the Cotswolds, including the grand Stanley Mill at King's Stanley, which included five giant waterwheels. But sharp competition and high tariffs eventually spelled the end of the woollen mills. Many of these lovely stone buildings have since been converted into shops and restaurants to serve the summer tourist hordes.

Despite the huge sheep-walks, there had always been plenty of arable farming land. Eventually the feudal system imposed by the Anglo-Saxons was replaced by a process that saw many villagers become freeholders who owned their own small pieces of land. The imposition of the Enclosure Acts during the eighteenth and nineteenth centuries saw the partition of vast tracts of the wolds into fields, creating the landscape of drystone walls and hedges that still greets modern ramblers along the Way.

A superb example of a drystone wall on the trail to Birdlip.

The Romans understood the agricultural value of the land and the beauty of the stone right from the beginning. It is these elements that continue to sustain the Cotswolds and that give such pleasure to walkers along this extraordinary trail.

"STONE WALL GEORGE"

When writer J.B. Priestley travelled through the Cotswolds in 1933, he met a stonemason named George who was in the process of rebuilding a drystone wall. He recalled a man who touched the stone "at once easily and lovingly, as women handle their babies..." These iconic walls follow the gentle contours of the land in artful undulations that are an integral part of the landscape. There is no intrusion here – they seem to spring as naturally as the bluebells and the sheep-filled grasslands. It is estimated there are as many as 6000 km (3,700 mi.) of walls within the region. They required great skill to construct since the masons used no mortar. Builders fit the stone pieces together like pieces of a jigsaw and then added a "coping," or a row of "toppers" on end along the top of the wall for weight and stability. Priestley describes George's wall as "a delight to the eye and a great contentment to the mind, so weary of shoddy and rubbish. I have never done anything in my life so thoroughly as that old mason did his building."

THE HIKE

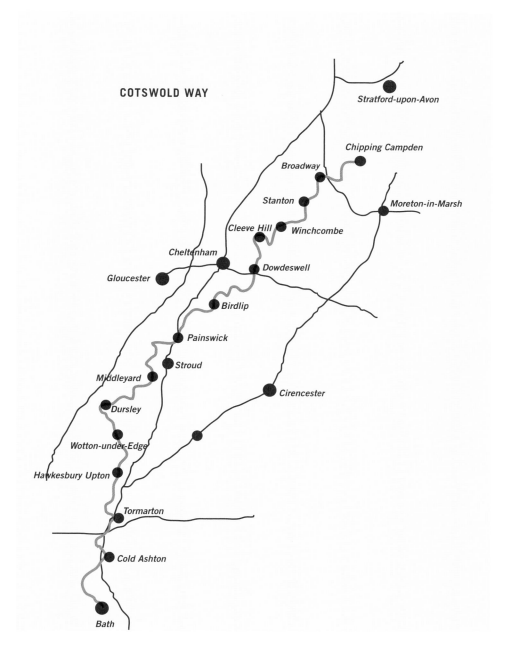

COTSWOLD WAY

Stratford-upon-Avon

Chipping Campden

Broadway

Stanton

Moreton-in-Marsh

Cleeve Hill

Winchcombe

Cheltenham

Gloucester

Dowdeswell

Birdlip

Painswick

Stroud

Middleyard

Cirencester

Dursley

Wotton-under-Edge

Hawkesbury Upton

Tormarton

Cold Ashton

Bath

It is not my intention to provide a detailed, step-by-step account of the trail. There are plenty of excellent guidebooks that do an outstanding job in that department. (See the "Recommended reading" section below.) What follows is an account of the highlights of the Cotswold Way based on stages that allow a walker to cover the trail in a fairly leisurely eight days. The easy accessibility of villages and accommodations along the way means you have many planning options, so you are really only limited by your ambition, your time constraints and your stamina. (I actually did a portion of the Way in reverse in order to incorporate the Cotswold Round into the walk with no backtracking. This routing is discussed in more detail in the "Consider this" section below.)

The issue of which direction to walk always arises. The trail is usually done from north to south. Other than one small portion done in reverse, this is the route I took. There is not much difference in up vs. down no matter which way you travel, and it probably makes sense to walk north with the sun and the prevailing wind at your back. But for many it comes down to the fact that it just seems more fitting to start in the true heart of the Cotswolds and end with a triumphant conclusion in the elegant city of Bath with extra time to savour the remarkable beauty of this UNESCO World Heritage Site. There is also the practical aspect of easy access from Bath, while ending in Chipping Campden can result in missing the last bus out of town if you arrive later than planned. Of course, it is up to you. Either way, you can expect a superb walk.

When it comes to navigating, the waymarking of the path is outstanding. Expect to see a variety of fingerposts, plastic discs and arrows on trees and rocks along with the ever comforting acorn symbol signifying you are on the National Trail. Note that even though Great Britain has adopted the metric system of measurement for everything else, distances are still in miles, on the trail and on the roads as well.

Routing changes are inevitable from season to season as a result of weather events or erosion damage on the trail. Always rely on the waymarking and not your map or your guidebook, since those may not reflect the most recent diversions. And don't feel shy about asking the locals. I have found them more than willing to help. Having said that, I have also found they often know less about the trail than you do. Like locals all over the world, they may not be familiar with the tourist attractions right in their own backyard.

Please note that the distance quotes for each day are based on the official trail route and do not include side trips or off-trail accommodation add-ons.

Day 1 – Chipping Campden to Stanton – 16 km (10 mi.)

Consider arriving a day before your start to tame that jetlag, do a final reorganization on your pack and stock up on lunch provisions for the next few days. (Most of the guidebooks give good information on villages with shops and pubs along the way. See the "Recommended reading" section for detailed listings.)

Chipping Campden certainly qualifies as one of the quintessential market towns of the Cotswolds, so it is worth planning on at least one extra day here to explore all it has to offer. This architectural treasure, with its fine High Street of remarkably preserved, honey-coloured stone buildings, is home to the parish church of St. James, one of the great "wool" churches. The town was also a major centre for the Arts and Crafts movement led by William Morris in late Victorian Britain.

IN SEARCH OF A SIMPLE LIFE – EVEN THEN

The Arts and Crafts movement grew out of the vision of William Morris, a poet and designer-architect. He rejected the shoddy workmanship coming from the factories and believed industrialization stifled creativity, degrading men's souls in the process. Morris and his followers advocated the rights of people to better their lives through the production of beautiful handcrafted objects using traditional materials and methods. Morris only retreated to his Cotswold "heaven on earth" at Kelmscott Manor when he managed to escape his successful design business in London. But some of his followers actually made the move to the country in search of a simpler and better way of life. In 1902 Charles Robert Ashbee moved his Guild and School of Handicrafts to the Old Silk Mill on Sheep Street in the small town of Chipping Campden. Here the skilled craftsmen were allowed the freedom to produce a wide range of beautiful crafts, including jewellery and furniture. Friend and poet laureate John Masefield would later praise Ashbee's creation of a "city of the soul," in one of his poems. Although Ashbee was forced to close the workshops in 1908, the tradition lives on at the Guild Craft Workshops, where descendants of original guild members continue to practise their trades. The Court Barn Museum on Church Street houses a permanent exhibition of some of the finest works produced by Ashbee and other artisans who made the town their home.

The day is a fine introduction to all the Way has to offer, as you climb to the escarpment on Dover's Hill with views over the Vale of Evesham, then on through fields bordered by drystone walls and beech woodlands filled with the scent of wild garlic.

If you are blessed with good weather you can expect many outstanding views along the Way as you climb to the Broadway Tower, descend to the village of Broadway and then ascend to Shenberrow Hill.

Broadway can be thronged with tourists in the summer, but don't let that deter you from taking in the considerable charms of this classic Cotswold town with its magnificent stone buildings and fine topiary displays. As you leave Broadway, don't

The Market Hall in Chipping Campden marks the start of the Cotswold Way.

forget to look back occasionally to catch unexpected vistas opening up behind you. Ahead lies Stanton, often called the perfect Cotswold village. It seems almost too quaint to actually be real – more like a movie set than a place where people live and work. It has managed to escape the commercialism that is rampant in many other Cotswold villages, so be sure to savour the untouched beauty of the place as you pass through.

Day 2 – Stanton to Cleeve Hill – 23.5 km (14.6 mi.)

The initial portion of the route to Winchcombe is a gentle walk through peaceful countryside as grassland gives way to parkland full of horse chestnuts and copper beech trees. There is only one real climb of any significance, from Wood Stanway to Stumps Cross. Along the way you will pass the seventeenth century Jacobean gatehouse to Stanway House (open to the public in the summer). The magnificent gardens boast the tallest gravity fountain in the world, shooting over 91 m (300 ft.). Just down the road

DWILE FLONKING MAKES THE OLIMPICK ROSTER

Dover's Hill marks the site of the "Olimpick Games" initiated by Captain Robert Dover in 1612. The games featured events such as leapfrog, wrestling, shin-kicking and backswords. And of course the ever popular dwile flonking. This skill-testing competition requires two teams, each of which takes a turn dancing around the other as they attempt to avoid a beer-soaked dwile, or cloth, tossed by the non-dancing team. The games are still celebrated each Spring Bank Holiday, concluding with a torchlight procession down the hill to Chipping Campden.

A FOLLY BY ANY OTHER NAME

Follies were generally constructed for no other purpose than extravagance. The fortress-like battlements of Broadway Tower seem to fit the definition perfectly. Perched on Beacon Hill with commanding views of the surrounding countryside, it was built in 1799 by the Sixth Earl of Coventry. Some say it was a gift for his homesick wife so she could see her beloved Worcestershire, some 35 km (22 mi.) away, on a clear day, though it was more likely just to impress the neighbours. During the late 1800s, William Morris spent time there with his family during the summers. His daughter May called it "the most inconvenient and the most delightful place ever seen." Her father and friends apparently took baths on the roof "when the wind didn't blow the soap away."

Broadway Tower is a fine example of a folly.

A picture-perfect cottage in the village of Stanton.

is the lovely thatched cricket pavilion built with money donated by J.M. Barrie, an enthusiastic cricketer and author of *Peter Pan*. A stop at the ruins of Hailes Abbey is highly recommended before you begin the real climbing of the day south of Winchcombe.

Winchcombe is another fine Cotswold town along the Way with much to offer. The parish church of St. Peter is an exceptional example of a "wool" church, famous for its 40 gargoyles – one is said to have been used by Lewis Carroll as a model for the Mad Hatter in *Alice in Wonderland*.

As you leave town, the Way follows Vineyard Street, one of the most beautiful in Winchcombe, with its stone cottages and trellised porches. In the past it was called Duck Street after the ducking stool once set up by the river. Apparently the see-saw-like device was used to dunk malicious town gossipers, presumably to teach them a lesson.

Some of the 40 gargoyles on St. Peter's church in Winchcombe.

South of Winchcombe, the trail begins to climb, first to the ancient long barrow site of Belas Knap and then to the wide open spaces of Cleeve Common. You will be amply rewarded for your efforts with wonderful panoramas back to Winchcombe and Sudeley Castle. One of the finest viewpoints along the Way is from the top of the Common, with Cheltenham spread out below and the Malvern Hills and Brecon Beacons in the distance.

Cleeve Hill is the highest point on the Cotswold Way.

THE BIG LIE

The Cistercian Hailes Abbey was founded by Richard, Earl of Cornwall, in the thirteenth century as the result of a vow to construct a grand structure if he survived a violent storm at sea. When he returned home safely, he made good on his promise. The Abbey's real claim to fame came from a vial said to contain the "Holy Blood" of Christ, brought back from Jerusalem by Richard's son. The holy relic was housed in its own shrine and brought considerable wealth to the Abbey as pilgrims flocked to the site for almost three hundred years to observe the miracle of the non-congealing blood. When the contents were revealed to be honey-coloured saffron and nothing more than a deceitful fraud, the Abbey was ruthlessly destroyed in 1539 on the orders of Henry VIII during the dissolution of the monasteries.

The ruins of Hailes Abbey are worth a stop.

Day 3 – Cleeve Hill to Birdlip – 25 km (15.5 mi.)

Much of the day's walking follows the western edge of the escarpment, skirting the city of Cheltenham below, with many wonderful views. On a clear day you can see as far as the Black Mountains in Wales. Although the Common is criss-crossed with a confusing array of golf and sheep trails, the Way is well marked and easily followed. There is plenty of splendid woodland walking, including the Bill Smylie Nature Reserve, home to more than 30 species of butterfly, and Lineover Wood with its broad-leafed lime trees. Some of the ascents and descents are quite steep, especially the climb up Ravensgate Hill, where a welcome bench at the top gives you a place to enjoy the view and catch your breath. The trail emerges onto the grassland of Hartley Hill and dramatic panoramic views unfold as you follow the scarp along Leckhampton Hill to the rock pinnacle called the Devil's Chimney.

The trail continues over grassland, down country lanes and through woodland with fleeting views of Gloucester opening to a broad panorama before plunging into more splendid beech woods. The track emerges to cross a very dangerous bit of road by the Air Balloon pub. Then it's back to the scarp edge and fine views over the Vale of Gloucester, with the Black Mountains and Brecon Beacons in the distance. The path eventually arrives at the Birdlip road but does not go into the village.

Day 4 – Birdlip to King's Stanley – 26.5 km (16.5 mi.)

The trail to Painswick is one of woodlands interspersed with tantalizing views of Gloucester and the Severn Vale. The Way is generally good

SATAN'S SUNDAY SEAT

This craggy pillar sits just below Leckhampton Hill in an old quarry. Local legend has it that the Devil lobbed stones from here at worshippers going to church on a Sunday. A somewhat more believable version is that it was carved out by quarry workers as a vulgar joke. Over the years it has attracted scramblers eager to beat the record of 13 people on the top at one time. But it is no longer accessible due to concerns that erosion could result in the collapse of the well-known landmark.

D. LARRAINE ANDREWS

The Devil's Chimney is a major landmark along the trail.

underfoot, with welcome shade on a hot day. The riot of birdsong is a constant companion as you make your way through Witcombe Wood, Brockworth Wood, Buckholt Wood and Pope's Wood. Along the way you will make a steep climb to the top of Cooper's Hill with its superb views of Gloucester and the far off Malvern Hills.

The trail eventually leaves the woods to emerge onto the manicured slopes of the Painswick Golf Course, just below the ramparts of Painswick Beacon. A short diversion to the summit of the hill provides good views across the Severn Vale. The Beacon is the site of an Iron Age fort called Kimsbury Camp, which has suffered much damage over the years but still impresses with its extensive double and

DEATH-DEFYING DASH

For some obscure reason, the residents of the nearby village of Brockworth have felt compelled to chase a round of Double Gloucester cheese down the steep slope of Cooper's Hill every Spring Bank Holiday. Take a look over the edge of the hill as you pass by and it becomes evident a person could hardly stay upright just walking down this incline without the added challenge of sprinting after a cheese! The ritual is thought to have its roots in a pagan fertility rite encouraging the fruits of harvest. Not surprisingly, major injuries have resulted over the years to runners as well as spectators hit by wayward cheeses. Whatever the origins, the event has become a victim of its own success as safety concerns and crowd control have forced the cancellation of the contest for the last several years. It is a good spot to stop for lunch and enjoy the view or other pursuits as well – I recall a strong whiff of "the weed" as I neared the top of the climb. Perhaps someone stoking up a bit of courage for the next competition.

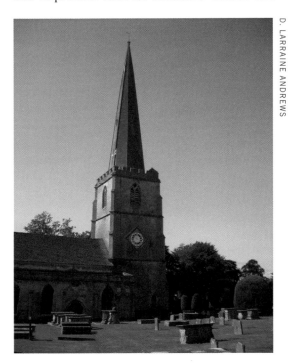

D. LARRAINE ANDREWS

The famous spire and table tombs of St. Mary's church in Painswick.

triple banks and ditches. From here it's mostly downhill to the white stone elegance of Painswick.

Built on the wealth of the woollen textile trade, this old market town is dominated by St. Mary's church with its towering spire (which has suffered two lightning hits over the years). The church is famous for its table tombs, its 99 yew trees (it is said the Devil won't allow 100 to grow), and its annual clipping ritual. The ceremony has nothing to do with clipping the trees, but requires parishioners to join hands and encircle the church in a group hug of "affection and gratitude."

From Painswick, it's open meadows, woodlands and some of the best views along the entire Cotswold Way. The scarp is soon regained, with Painswick clearly visible as you look back from Scottsquar Hill. A milestone confirms you are almost halfway to Bath, with only 55 miles (88.5 km) left! Magnificent vistas over the Severn Vale now open up at the trigonometry point at Haresfield Beacon and the topograph a little further down the trail, followed by the welcome shade of Standish Wood. Field walking and several squeeze stiles eventually lead you across the Stroudwater Canal, past the obsolete Stanley Mill to the small village of King's Stanley. Walkers have the option of taking a longer but more scenic route across Selsley Common, converging with the main trail in Pen Wood. I took the shorter route due to the location of my accommodations for the evening, but have since been advised that the longer route (adding about 2.4 km, or 1.5 mi.) is highly recommended.

Day 5 – King's Stanley to Wotton-under-Edge – 21.5 km (13.4 mi.)

May the weather gods be with you along this section! I walked most of the day in rain and wind, missing the extensive views that are a highlight of this stage. Fortunately, the path includes beautiful sections of woodland walking which offered good shelter from the steady rainfall. It was a good reminder of the need to be prepared with adequate rain gear and accessible snacks, since you are unlikely to stop in such inclement weather to eat properly.

The day brings some fairly strenuous ascents and steep descents as you climb to pass the Nympsfield long barrow and the panoramic views from Coaley Peak. The route eventually follows

© COTSWOLD WAY – NICK TURNER

The view of Cam Long Down from Coaley Peak on a clear day.

a broad track between farms to begin a steep climb to the summit of Cam Long Down.

The ascent was quite treacherous here due to the wet conditions. On a clear day the view includes the Severn River to the west, the curve of the Cotswold escarpment and the old wool market town of Dursley at the bottom of the hill.

I am forever grateful to the staff and patrons of the Old Spot pub who welcomed me in my sodden gear and gladly served me on a busy afternoon. The pub lies directly on the route and is a good place to stop for a break (even when it isn't raining) before heading up the next challenging climb through woodland to the golf course on Stinchcombe Hill. Here you have the choice of cutting straight across the end of the course to meet up with the main trail that follows a circuitous and much longer route around the edge of the golf course. The shortcut eliminates almost 4 km (2.5 mi.) and is highly recommended in bad weather since the views from the escarpment are obviously lost. If you opt for the longer route when conditions are good, you will be rewarded with views all the way.

The trail continues through woodland and across open fields through the village of North Nibley and up another climb to the escarpment by the Tyndale Monument on Nibley Knoll. The climb is quite steep but there are good stairs with a handrail. The trail emerges at the base of the monument.

From here the trail follows a welcome section of level grassland and more woodland before emerging at the Jubilee Plantation on Wotton Hill with more grand views. (The plantation initially celebrated the English victory at the Battle of Waterloo. The trees were replanted to recognize the golden jubilee of Queen Victoria after they had been burned earlier to mark the end of the Crimean War.) Then it's downhill all the way to the village of Wotton-under-Edge.

MONUMENT FOR A MARTYR

The monument was erected in 1866 in honour of locally born William Tyndale, a leading figure in the Protestant Reformation. His English translation of the Bible was the first to draw from Hebrew and Greek texts. For his efforts he was jailed in Brussels, where he was convicted of heresy, executed by strangulation and his body burnt at the stake in 1536.

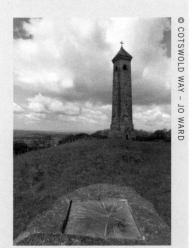

© COTSWOLD WAY – JO WARD

The Tyndale Monument on Nibley Knoll.

Day 6 – Wotton-under-Edge to Old Sodbury – 20 km (12.4 mi.)

A combination of country lanes, gentle valleys, woodlands and airy views along the scarp greet the walker along this stage. And of course, a few steep climbs along the way. As you follow the track through woodland to the edge of Wortley village, you will pass down a deep sunken lane.

If it is springtime, expect a profusion of wood violets and primroses to line the banks as the lane dips ever lower before emerging into open farmland. Soon the trail passes the small hamlet of Alderley and then follows the edge of meadows stretching into the Kilcott Valley.

Along the way you will pass an impressive stand of very large larch trees and eventually head up to the Somerset monument. This rather oriental-looking landmark commemorates the services of General Lord Robert Somerset, who served under Wellington at the Battle of Waterloo.

At Wortley, the trail follows a sunken lane through woodland.

A red beech tree on the trail between Alderley and Lower Kilcott.

The trail bypasses the town of Hawkesbury Upton, but maybe that is a good thing, since the sign at the entrance to the town declares "You'll never leave." The track passes an old drovers' pond and then heads out along country lanes, through woodland and across fields with good views along the way. As you approach Little Sodbury keep your eye open for the waymark by the church. I completely missed it and went several miles out of my way before I realized my error. It was covered by the leaves of a large tree. I should have known I had gone too far without seeing another waymark, but fortunately it was a beautiful day and good walking, although it made for a long trek. The trail follows through Sodbury Camp, a very well-preserved Iron Age hill fort with excellent views, before heading down to the village of Old Sodbury.

Day 7 – Old Sodbury to Cold Ashton – 14.5 km (9 mi.)

This is a short but beautiful stage with delightful walking and several highlights despite the need to cross a few large roadways during the day. The path follows open parkland through Dodington Park before crossing the busy A46 highway, and into the village of Tormarton, where the lovely little church boasts a massive Norman tower and table tombs. Once across the ugly slash of the M4 motorway, the track follows beside a series of huge cultivated fields, then skirts the edge of Dyrham Park (famous for its elusive deer) along a drystone wall that is one of the best examples seen along the trail. The walking is superb along this section, with wonderful views and out-standing examples of ancient strip lynchets plowed into the terraced hillsides.

It seems all too soon when the path descends into the town of Dyrham and past the gate of Dyrham House. The house and its magnificent grounds were featured in the film *The Remains of the Day* and are well worth a visit. Don't miss a chance to leave your thoughts on the Cotswold Way in the message box as you pass through Dyrham Wood, then continue on through the fields to the village of Cold Ashton, with its broad, sweeping views over the valley.

Strip lynchets are ridges formed on a hillside by long-repeated plowing.

D. LARRAINE ANDREWS

Day 8 – Cold Ashton to Bath – 17 km (10.5 mi.)

Sadly, the end of this wonderful walk approaches, but not before a final day of brilliant walking capped off with far-reaching panoramas before the final descent to the magnificent city of Bath. The path follows quiet country lanes and sheep-filled paddocks across a gently rolling landscape before climbing to follow a series of metal standards

Don't forget to leave a message in the box along the trail through Dyrham Wood.

The magnificent Bath Abbey marks the end of the Cotswold Way.

marking the Civil War battlefield of Lansdown Hill with its fine view to the southeast. Soon the scarp edge is regained with more fine vistas the reward. The trail winds past a golf course to the Bath Racecourse, then along the scarp to a well-known lookout called Prospect Stile (though there is actually no stile there) and your first view of Bath in the valley below. From here it's a steady downhill to the elegant winding streets of Bath. The trail ends at the doors to the magnificent Bath Abbey, a grand finale to a superb walk.

HOW TO DO THE HIKE

This is a superb long-distance walk that can easily be done safely on your own or with a walking group. It is also possible to do parts of it if the full distance seems overwhelming or if time constraints limit your ability to complete the whole path at one go.

Over the years, I have used the services of Contours Walking Holidays (**www.contours.co.uk**) for a number of National Trail hikes and would highly recommend them. They book your accommodations, arrange your luggage transfers and supply you with all the guidebooks and maps you need to complete the route. The trip is prepaid, avoiding the need to worry about carrying cash for small B&Bs that do not accept credit cards. Many other companies supply similar services for self-guided trips or fully guided options. For a list of other reputable companies, check the Trailblazer guide described in the "Recommended reading" section below.

There is also the option of booking your own accommodations, but this can be a slow and frustrating process, requiring the need to communicate with many establishments, only to have to change your plans as you find out they don't have room on the days you want to stay. The official trail website at **www.nationaltrail.co.uk/Cotswold** provides a whole planning section if you want to tackle it yourself. If you choose this alternative, you can also decide whether you want to carry all your clothes etc. or instead arrange for luggage transfers. For anyone considering camping, be advised that official campsites are few and far between, while wild camping is not allowed anywhere along the Cotswold Way. It may be possible to camp in a field, but definitely not without the explicit permission of the owner.

HOW DO YOU SAY THAT?

In theory, English-speaking visitors shouldn't have too many problems understanding the locals. That is the theory, anyway. What follows are a few interesting translations of place names you will encounter along the trail.

- Alderley – "the clearing in the alders"
- Belas Knap – "hilltop beacon"
- Broadway – refers to the wide main street built to accommodate stagecoaches stopping here en route to London

- Chipping Campden – "chipping" means market; "campden" is from the Saxon "campa denu," meaning "a valley with cultivated fields ringed by unfenced hill pastures"
- Dyrham – from the Saxon "deor hamm," meaning "enclosed valley frequented by deer"
- Stanton – or Stan Tun, meaning "stony farm"
- Tormarton – or Tower Marton, from the very large Norman tower of the church
- Tump – the local name for a long barrow or communal burial ground
- Winchcombe – means "valley with a bend." The High Street bends with the combe or valley.
- Wotton-under-Edge – from the Saxon meaning "the farm in the wood." The village lies tucked directly under the Cotswold Edge.

CONSIDER THIS: BEFORE OR AFTER THE HIKE

Glorious Bath!

Oh, who can ever be tired of Bath?

—Catherine Morland in Jane Austen's *Northanger Abbey* (1817)

An aerial view of the Royal Crescent and the Circus.

Bath Abbey towers over the Roman baths.

The Royal Crescent.

It is a sentiment I would echo. But apparently Jane herself wasn't particularly happy during the time she spent in the elegant Georgian city that had become a popular eighteenth century destination for the prominent social, political and cultural leaders of the day. Dubbed the "busiest idle place in the world," Bath saw people flocking there in droves to indulge in every leisure and business pursuit the city had to offer and to partake of the famous hot springs. "Taking the waters" became a fashionable activity after a visit by Queen Anne seeking a remedy for dropsy. One doctor claimed the springs could cure "rheumatic, gouty and paralytic afflictions, in all those disorders originating from indigestion and acidity of the stomach, bilious and glandular obstructions, hypochondriac and hysterical afflictions." (Little wonder that the term "aquatic doctor" is the origin of the slang term "quack doctor.")

The hot springs had been recognized for their curative powers as far back as 863 BCE when legend maintains they miraculously cured the young Prince Bladud of leprosy. They reached their zenith under the Romans, who developed a religious sanctuary and spa honouring Sulis Minerva. The name combined Sul, the Celtic goddess of the waters, and Minerva, the Roman goddess of wisdom and healing. The Roman baths at Aquae Sulis ("waters of Sul"), became renowned across Europe.

The usual superlatives just don't seem to do the city justice. You could easily spend a week here and still have plenty left on your list of things to see and do. Designated a UNESCO World Heritage Site in 1987, the city reflects some of the finest examples of two great eras in human history – the Roman and the Georgian. Not only have the ancient Roman baths been restored, but the extraordinary Georgian buildings, which suffered extensive bomb damage during the Second World War, were eventually reconstructed to their former glory.

The architectural genius of John Wood the Elder (1704–1754) and his vision of a "New Rome" is reflected in his masterpieces of The Circus, Queen Square and much else in Bath. Following his death, his work was continued by his son, John Wood the Younger, who completed The Circus and went on to build the dramatic Royal Crescent, with its 30 terraced houses connected with giant Ionic columns.

Built from the light-coloured Cotswold stone quarried from nearby Coombe Down, Bath is, in the words of UNESCO, "a demonstration par excellence of the integration of architecture, urban design and landscape setting, and the deliberate creation of a beautiful city." Make sure you plan to spend some time here before you head home.

The Cotswold Round

For anyone interested in adding more miles of walking in the Cotswold countryside, it is possible to easily incorporate the Cotswold Round into the Cotswold Way without any backtracking. As the name suggests, the Round basically takes you in a circle and can be started from any of the villages along it. The path covers a distance of about 82 km (51 mi.), including approximately 29 km (18 mi.) of the Cotswold Way, from Chipping Campden to Winchcombe. I started my walk in Winchcombe, heading north on the Cotswold Way to Broadway and Chipping Campden, then on to Moreton-in-Marsh, Stow-on-the-Wold, Bourton-on-the-Water and back to Winchcombe. From there I headed south on the Cotswold Way to Bath.

The Round combines sections of several well marked trails, including the Monarch's Way, Windrush Way, Wardens' Way and the Cotswold Way. Expect more superb walking and a chance to see some of the region's most iconic Cotswold villages not visited on the National Trail. I used the services of Contours Walking Holidays, who custom-designed the itinerary for me, booked all the accommodations and luggage transfers and provided detailed trail notes. (See the "How to do the hike" section for more information.)

ARE YOU READY TO EAT?

Eating options along the trail vary. Your accommodation will provide the traditional cooked breakfast to get you started in the morning. This seems to last me well past noon, so I generally rely on picnic-type food such as fruit, cheese, crackers and energy bars to snack on along the trail during the day. Most towns and villages will have a shop or full-sized grocery where you can stock up. Many B&Bs will make your lunch for the next day for an additional charge and supply an evening meal if you are stopping in a village with few other options. Or you can always self-cater. I find most establishments are quite happy to supply you with a plate and utensils and let you eat your own meal if you are so inclined.

Bath offers the weary walker an extensive choice of restaurants and pubs for a celebratory dinner, but don't miss the chance to sample some of the specialties specifically associated with the city.

The Bath Chap is the salted and smoked lower half of a pig's cheek and can be found at the Guildhall covered market. Bath Oliver biscuits, the Georgian equivalent of a slimming aid and antidote for rich food, are still available. They were invented by Dr. William Oliver, who opened the Bath General Hospital (now called the Royal Mineral Water Hospital) in the mid-eighteenth century and was a well-known anti-obesity campaigner even then. Oliver is also said to have invented the Bath bun, a sweet roll that was a favourite of Jane Austen when she lived in the town. These should not be confused with the famous Sally Lunn bun, which claims to be the original Bath bun. Described as "a rich, round and generous brioche bun," it is still prepared from a closely guarded secret recipe and served at Sally Lunn's, a popular café located in the oldest house in Bath.

Hygiene standards are generally high and there should be no concerns about most food establishments.

Tipping is expected. Normally 10 to 15 per cent of the bill would be considered reasonable.

Vegetarians: Although strictly vegetarian restaurants may be few and far between along the trail, many will provide some vegetarian options, including pubs. Most B&Bs are happy to cater to vegetarian concerns. Just ask.

INTERNET RESOURCES

There is an enormous amount of information available on the Internet relating to the Cotswolds and the Way. The following websites provide excellent sources and related links to help get you started. Many of the larger villages and towns along the Way also have their own websites, providing more detailed local information.

www.nationaltrail.co.uk/Cotswold is the official National Trail website for the Cotswold Way.

www.cotswolds.com is the official website of the Cotswolds.

www.cotswoldsaonb.com is the official website for the Cotswolds Conservation Board.

www.ChippingCampden.co.uk has information on Chipping Campden and the surrounding area.

www.beautifulbroadway.com contains information on Broadway and the surrounding area.

www.winchcombe.co.uk features information on Winchcombe and the surrounding area.

www.visitbath.co.uk is the official website for the city of Bath.

RECOMMENDED READING

There are several excellent guidebooks to the trail. Those listed here are the ones I used and would highly recommend. Also included in the list are some books of historical and cultural interest relating to the Cotswolds.

Bath Valley of the Sacred Spring – Kim Green – stories of Bath including photographs.

Cotswold Characters – John Drinkwater – prose sketches of five Cotsaller characters, including a mason, a fisherman, a foreigner, a footballer and a thatcher. Available at www.archive.org.

Cotswold Way: Chipping Campden to Bath – Tricia and Bob Hayne – the Trailblazer series are some of my favourite guidebooks for the National Trails. They offer comprehensive information on towns and places along the trail, flora and fauna, together with exceptionally detailed, easy to follow maps.

Cotswold Way: Official National Trail Guide – Anthony Burton – this official trail guide provides

© FOTOSEARCH.COM

Hedgehogs are common in English hedgerows.

FAUNA FACTS: HIDING IN THE HEDGEROWS

For chocolate addicts, the word may conjure up visions of the odd-shaped treats made famous by Purdy's, but real hedgehogs are common in English hedgerows, where they feed on a diet of insects, worms, snails, mice and snakes. The descriptive name refers to the fact that they emit a pig-like grunt as they poke through hedges in search of food sources. If threatened, hedgehogs curl up into a ball, using their protective coat of sharp spines for defence. Although the spines are not barbed or poisonous, they tend to deter most predators. Hedgehogs are popular as pets because they feed on common garden pests. Since they are nocturnal, you are not too likely to spot any as you walk, although they are often victims of cars as they attempt to cross roadways at night. Believe it or not, a hedgehog-flavoured crisp (potato chip) was introduced in Britain in the 1980s, though apparently they did not actually contain any hedgehog bits.

excellent trail descriptions and maps along with practical information on planning your walk and good historical background. This is the guide I carried with me every day.

Did You Know? Bath: A Miscellany – Julia Skinner – fascinating trivia along with an outstanding collection of archival photographs.

Lonely Planet England – a good starting point to plan your trip to England.

Stories of Bath: A Selective History in Eleven Episodes – Diana White – not your standard history, this collection of eleven stories provides a fascinating insight into this extraordinary city.

The Cotswolds: A Cultural History – Jane Bingham – an excellent introduction to the history and unique culture of the Cotswolds including an outstanding section of further reading.

The Cotswold Way: Two-Way Trail Description – Kev Reynolds – this Cicerone guide provides the trail description from Chipping Campden to Bath as well as in reverse from Bath to Chipping Campden. These are excellent guides with good trail descriptions and maps along with great historical information interspersed throughout the text.

The Little Book of the Cotswolds – Gillian Broomhall – a wonderful collection of facts and miscellany about the Cotswolds. Includes a good list of further reading.

CHAPTER 6 – GREAT BRITAIN – ENGLAND/WALES – OFFA'S DYKE PATH NATIONAL TRAIL

Offa's Dyke Path, or Llwybr Clawdd Offa (Welsh)

There was in Mercia in fairly recent times a certain vigorous king called Offa,
who terrified all the neighbouring kings and provinces around him,
and who had a great dyke built between Wales and Mercia from sea to sea …
—BISHOP ASSER, *Life of King Alfred* (893 CE)

✳ HIKING RULE 6: If you are walking on a National Trail in Great Britain and you see a hill ahead of you, the trail will inevitably go up the hill.

WHERE IN THE WORLD?

SCOTLAND

ENGLAND

WALES *Offa's Dyke Path*

London

CLAIM TO FAME

One of Britain's longest National Trails, Offa's Dyke Path (or as the Welsh say, Llwybr Clawdd Offa) is a magnificent long-distance walk that meanders for 285 km (177 mi.) along the English–Welsh border. Starting at the marker stone at Sedbury Cliffs near Chepstow and ending at the seafront monument at Prestatyn, it passes through three Areas of Outstanding Natural Beauty (the Wye Valley, the Shropshire Hills and the Clwydian Hills) as well as Brecon Beacons National Park, crossing the border more than 20 times. Along the way, it follows portions of the 1200-year-old earthwork known as Offa's Dyke, Britain's longest ancient monument, crossing over a UNESCO World Heritage Cultural Site at the Pontcysyllte Aqueduct. The dyke has actually become part of the language of Wales – the outside world is called "beyond Offa's Dyke," while tourists are said to come "from the other side of Offa's Dyke." The convention is common even for Welsh from west Wales who often have never seen the earthwork.

WHAT WILL I SEE?

The path follows Offa's Dyke as it snakes across the countryside north of Llanfair Hill.

HIKE PROFILE

The trail begins near sea level at the Sedbury Cliffs overlooking the Severn Estuary by Chepstow, climbs to its highest point of 700 m (2,300 ft.) on the Hatterrall Ridge in the Black Mountains of Brecon Beacons National Park, and eventually descends to sea level at Prestatyn on the shore of the Irish Sea. This may sound fairly benign for anyone accustomed to mountain hiking, but don't be fooled. Over the course of this superb walk you climb and descend multitudes of "hill-waves," gaining and losing literally thousands of metres over the course of the hike.

Hazards

As with any walking trail that includes climbs and descents on steep, uneven terrain, the normal cautions regarding twisted ankles and injuries from falling apply here.

There are no natural predators to worry about – only an occasional sheep, squirrel or deer that might happen to cross your path.

Having said that, always be prepared for the possibility of an unpleasant encounter with a bull protecting his cow harem. You will pass through many, many paddocks on this walk, and although the majority will have sheep in them, you will also find some with cows or bullocks (the English equivalent of steers) and the occasional scary bull.

Dogs sometimes present problems on the trail, but 99 times out of 100 they are with a local who is out for a walk and they are quickly controlled. (The presence of dogs and walkers is always a good indication you are getting close to the next village and maybe a welcome cup of tea.)

Although you might think of Great Britain as a fairly gentle landscape with few natural hazards, never underestimate the ability of the weather to turn and put you in a bad situation. There are several parts of this hike that pass through fairly wild country, particularly in the Black Mountains and the Clwydian Hills, where the weather can change very quickly as fog and rain roll in unexpectedly. Always be prepared with extra clothes, water and food to avoid the possibility of hypothermia, which is a potentially dangerous condition that occurs when your body can't generate sufficient heat to maintain its core temperature.

BULL IN FIELD!

Theoretically, the law says bulls over ten months of age are not allowed in a field through which a public footpath passes, but there isn't much you can do about it if a farmer has decided to ignore the rule. Always stay alert and give any bull, no matter its age, a wide berth. Some farmers will put out a warning sign that actually says "Bull in Field." But I think sometimes they do this out of a sadistic sense of humour just to scare walkers. Whenever I have encountered such a sign, there hasn't been a bull or cow in sight, but maybe I just got lucky. It certainly makes you move faster to the next paddock. If you do spot one, keep to the edge of the field so you can hop over the fence if you need to. Just be careful and have an exit plan.

I recall one memorable meeting with a bull that definitely didn't meet the age restriction. Unfortunately, he was standing directly on the path between two fenced areas and he wasn't planning on moving anytime soon. It meant clambering over some extra barbed wire to go around him and many backward glances to ensure he wasn't in pursuit! Bulls are always a concern, but don't turn your back on cows with calves, since they tend to be very protective of their young.

Getting there: The hike is normally done from Chepstow in the south to Prestatyn in the north, both of which are located in Wales. Chepstow is easily accessible by bus or rail from either Heathrow Airport (**www.heathrowairport.com**) or Gatwick Airport (**www.gatwickairport.com**). Prestatyn is easily accessible from either airport by rail. These airports would be two of the most common entry points for flights from Canada. Of course, there are many routing options, depending on your own individual travel plans. Websites for both National Express Coaches (**www.nationalexpress.com**) and National Rail (**www.nationalrail.co.uk**) provide excellent starting points to plan your journey.

Currency: pound sterling, or GBP, or GB£. £1 = 100 pence. For current exchange rates, check out **www.oanda.com**.

Special gear: You will need good, sturdy, waterproof hiking boots that are well broken in before you hit the trail. Hiking poles are highly recommended to help maintain balance on uneven or slippery rocks or steps. You will also need to carry rain gear, of course, including gaiters, as well as adequate supplies of food and water. Rain is inevitable. Make sure your pack has a rain cover and that it is also lined with water-proof facing or plastic bags. One particularly indispensable piece of gear for walking in Great Britain is a plastic map pouch. These are wonderful contraptions that you hang around your neck and into which you insert your maps/guidebooks to keep them dry as you walk. Then all you need to do is flip it up to check your location along the trail. I didn't have one of these on my first National Trail walk and ended up with a rain-wrinkled, very weathered guidebook by the end of it.

HIKE OVERVIEW

Offa's Dyke Path, or ODP, is a National Trail opened in July 1971. Curiously, although it has been around for over 40 years, you will find different "official" mileage quotes along its entire length. (Even though Great Britain has adopted the metric system of measurement for everything else, distances are still in miles, on trails as well as roads.) The official website, **www.nationaltrail.co.uk/OffasDyke**, quotes 177 mi. (285 km), while the marker stone on the Sedbury Cliffs shows 168 mi. (270 km) and the fingerpost at the end of the hike in Prestatyn shows 182 mi. (293 km).

Suffice it to say you should expect to cover close to 322 km (200 mi.) by the time you are finished. This is because there are several places where you will need to leave the trail to reach your accommodation and then return the next morning to resume the walk, plus a few diversions that are not to be missed.

The path takes its name from Offa's Dyke, a 1200-year-old earthen barrier built by King Offa of Mercia in the eighth century to mark the western boundary of his kingdom and protect it from the wild Welshmen on the other side. (Please note the path is referred to as the ODP throughout this chapter, while references to the dyke itself will clearly state that fact.) Although the ODP follows some of the most spectacular portions of the dyke, practicalities of access combined with the need to choose the most scenic route mean you will not see the dyke along its whole length. In fact, it is now generally agreed it simply does not exist along many parts of the border.

D. LARRAINE ANDREWS

The fingerpost at the end of the trail, in Prestatyn.

Beginning at the Sedbury Cliffs overlooking the Severn Estuary, the walk makes its way through woodlands and paddocks full of sheep and past romantic ruins such as Tintern Abbey. Following ancient drover's tracks and quiet country lanes it winds its way through historic villages, sometimes in England, sometimes in Wales, climbing to the dramatic, windswept and remote high point on Hatterrall Ridge in the Black Mountains, then down Hay Bluff to a book lover's paradise at Hay-on-Wye, a good spot for a rest day.

Some of the finest sections of the dyke greet the walker near Knighton. Prepare yourself for the "hill-waves" of the South Shropshire Hills, and some of the best walking on the entire path. Then on to a not-to-be-missed diversion along the canal path to Welshpool and the terraced gardens of Powis Castle. Take a breather as you follow the Severn River, then prepare for the dizzying walk over Telford's famous aqueduct. Soon the limestone cliffs of Trevor Rocks loom, and then it's on to the ominously named World's End and more splendid ridge walking in the Clwydian Range. With any luck you'll catch some views of the mountains of Snowdonia as you make your way into the seaside resort of Prestatyn and the end of the trail.

Why would I want to?

The Reverend Lord Sandford (admittedly he was a long-time member of the Offa's Dyke Association) declared at one of their meetings: "It's not the longest, nor the oldest but it's certainly the best footpath in Britain." And who could argue with a Lord?

You may have noticed this book includes two chapters for European walks and both of them are National Trails in Great Britain. I make no apologies for my obvious bias. People often ask me about my favourite hike and although I find that question almost impossible to answer, these are my favourite types of hikes. I have done a number of National Trails in Great Britain and the ODP is definitely at or near the top of the list.

Of course, this is entirely my view, but I love the freedom of being able to walk safely on my own, set my own pace and not worry about encountering a bear or cougar along the trail. I can decide when I want to stop for tea, take a photograph or have a closer look at something. I can decide how far I want to walk each day and where I want to spend a rest day. And best of all, I can do it all with a daypack while someone else takes care of my luggage along the way. (See the "How to do the hike" section for detailed information on logistics.)

There is no doubt the ODP is challenging. Not only is its length somewhat daunting, it traverses some remote and wild areas where you must be prepared for sudden and potentially dangerous changes in the weather. But the sheer physical and mental pleasure of meeting the challenge is extremely satisfying. Combine this with the chance to follow some of the best bits of Britain's largest archaeological monument, to experience an incredible diversity of terrain and revel in absolutely brilliant scenery (as the British would say), and I'd have to agree with Lord Sandford that there are few long-distance paths in Britain or anywhere else that will match it.

When to go

In theory the path can be tackled at any time of the year. The long days of May and June, combined with the superb proliferation of wildflowers and the fact that less rain falls in the spring than at any other time of year, makes this an ideal time to go. I did the path in mid-May and the bluebells were breathtaking. Although summer is traditional holiday time, the trail is generally not filled with masses of walkers other than at a few popular spots. Long days and usually more predictable weather make this a good time to head out. Rainfall increases in the fall and days are shorter, but the autumn colours in the woodlands and the crisp days make this a definite alternative. Winter is not recommended, given the short hours of daylight and the high chance of heavy rainfall.

What's the story?

> It was customary for the English to cut off the ears of every Welshman
> who was found to the east of the dyke, and for the Welsh to hang
> every Englishman whom they found to the west of it.
>
> —George Borrow, *Wild Wales* (1862)

Borrow's comments make for good storytelling. Unfortunately there is no general agreement among archaeological experts about the purpose or the true extent of

Bluebells and birdsong greet spring hikers.

the dyke. But the sheer immensity of the project certainly speaks to the power of the man who ordered and oversaw the completion of this great earthwork. His name was Offa and he was a ruthless and aggressive leader who was king of Mercia and Emperor of Britain from 757 to 796 CE.

Ever since 893 CE, when Bishop Asser wrote of a "great dyke" extending from "sea to sea," there has been considerable debate about the where and the why of the famous earthwork. In an 1857 article entitled "Offa's Dyke in the Neighbourhood of Knighton," historian John Earle spoke of the difficulty in determining the "use and efficiency" of such "vast undertakings," noting, "They partake on the one hand of the character of a fence, on the other of a fortification, and yet it is difficult to suppose them to have been either the one or the other. For a mere fence, ... the work is too considerable; as a fortification they are far too extensive to allow of the idea that the petty nations they divided were powerful enough to keep them manned."

It was not until 1925 that actual archaeological fieldwork on the dyke was begun by Sir Cyril Fox, who took Asser's comment about "sea to sea" literally, observing that obvious gaps could be explained by the existence of natural barriers such as rivers or dense forests. He concluded, "it was not a military boundary" but "... a boundary defined by treaty or agreement between the men of the hills and the men of the lowlands."

"KING OF THE ENGLISH"

Even though he became one of the most powerful rulers of one of the most powerful kingdoms in Britain, little is known about the man who gave his name to the famous dyke. As David Hill and Margaret Worthington point out in their definitive work *Offa's Dyke: History & Guide,* "We might imagine Offa as grim; no man who overthrew his predecessor and reigned over a kingdom that he successfully expanded during 40 years in a harsh age, did so by a love of poetry and the visual arts." Although written records are scant, Offa didn't confine his activities to Britain. His influence extended well beyond national boundaries to the European stage, where the great Charlemagne called him "dearest brother," and his silver penny coins, intended for use in foreign trade, referred to him as Rex Anglorum – "King of the English."

DIG AND STACK: A SIMPLE CONCEPT

The dyke itself is an earthen bank with a ditch to the west allowing fine views into Wales from the Mercian side. Even now, after 1200 years, there are places where it rises to heights of up to 6 m (20 ft.), while in other spots it is nothing more than a rounded bump on the landscape.

Once the route had been settled (by using beacons to get the correct alignment), the actual construction required the digging of the ditch and the piling of the excavated turf and soil to create the barrier. These weren't difficult building concepts, and experts believe the task could have been easily tackled with the tools of the day. But who did the digging and stacking? In typical English fashion, records show there was already a well-organized tax system in place. In lieu of money, each village would receive a "tax assessment" in men. Each man travelled with his own implements and food to his assigned section of the dyke. Hill and Worthington suggest men worked in teams of four, each assigned about 1.3 m (4 ft.). When they completed their allotted portion, the men had effectively "paid" their taxes and were free to go home. A simple system that would have got the job done!

Since the early 1970s, David Hill and Margaret Worthington of the University of Manchester have conducted extensive research into the mysteries of the giant earthwork through the Offa's Dyke Project. Their excellent book mentioned earlier, *Offa's Dyke: History & Guide,* takes issue with Fox's theories. Their mile-by-mile analysis has resulted in new interpretations about the extent and purpose of the dyke, clearly demonstrating there is little evidence that it stretched from "sea to sea." They make the case that Asser's statement was merely trying to give the impression of great length and the expression was "no more than a literary device ..."

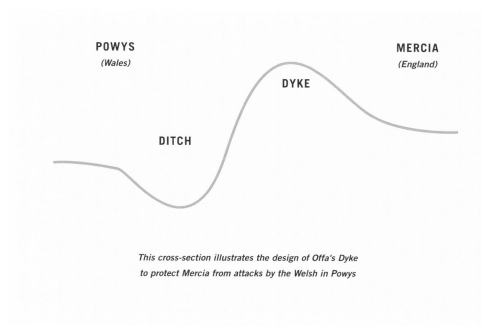

POWYS
(Wales)

MERCIA
(England)

DYKE

DITCH

This cross-section illustrates the design of Offa's Dyke
to protect Mercia from attacks by the Welsh in Powys

D. LARRAINE ANDREWS

The path winds along beside the grass-
covered hump of Offa's Dyke.

Although the research is ongoing, they conclude that conflict between Mercia and the "virile" Welsh kingdom of Powys, at the beginning of Offa's reign, provides strong evidence of a military incentive for the dyke's construction; and that it runs for 103 km (64 mi.) from Rushock Hill near Kington to Treuddyn near Mold. The sidebar on page 174 describes how a relatively simple agrarian society may have had the ability to build such a massive structure.

Fortunately for us, the ODP follows some of the best sections of the dyke as it crosses the hills from Knighton to the Clun Valley and on to the Kerry Ridgeway. As you pause to admire Offa's handiwork, it becomes obvious that the Mercians knew exactly what they were doing, as they designed the dyke to take advantage of hill contours and natural watercourses to give the best views to the west and those nasty Welshmen.

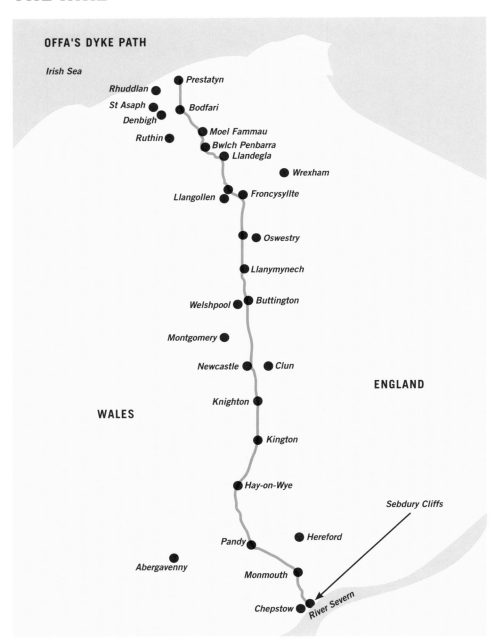

OFFA'S DYKE PATH

Irish Sea

Prestatyn
Rhuddlan
St Asaph
Bodfari
Denbigh
Moel Fammau
Ruthin
Bwlch Penbarra
Llandegla
Wrexham
Llangollen
Froncysyllte
Oswestry
Llanymynech
Buttington
Welshpool
Montgomery
Newcastle
Clun
ENGLAND
Knighton
WALES
Kington
Hay-on-Wye
Sebdury Cliffs
Hereford
Pandy
Abergavenny
Monmouth
Chepstow
River Severn

It is not my intention to provide a detailed step-by-step account of the trail. There are plenty of excellent guidebooks that do an outstanding job in that department. (See the "Recommended reading" section below.) What follows is an account of the highlights of the ODP based on the stages I chose to hike over a period of 14 walking days (an average of about 22.5 km (14 mi.) per day, including diversions). The trail offers a large selection of accommodation in the many villages located on or close to the path, so you are really only limited by your ambition, your time and your stamina. (See the "How to do the hike" section below for trip planning.)

I walked the ODP from south to north. This is the usual direction based on the fact that the sun and the prevailing winds are at your back. But it is entirely up to you if you choose to be a renegade. When it comes to navigating, the waymarking on the path is outstanding. Expect to see a variety of fingerposts, plastic discs and arrows on trees and rocks along with the ever comforting acorn symbol signifying you are on the National Trail. Please note that the distance quotes for each day are based on the official trail route and do not include side trips or off-trail accommodation add-ons.

Routing changes are inevitable from season to season as a result of weather or erosion on the trail. Always rely on the waymarking and not your map or guidebook, since they may not reflect the most recent diversions. And don't feel shy about asking the locals. I have found them more than willing to help. Having said that, I have also found they often know less about the trail than you do. Like locals all over the world, they may not be familiar with the tourist attractions right in their own backyard.

The ODP officially begins at the marker stone on Sedbury Cliffs above the Severn Estuary, 2.4 km (1.5 mi.) from the junction with the trail from Chepstow.

It is worth arriving a day before your start, to tame that jetlag, do a final reorganization on your pack and stock up on lunch provisions for the next few days. If you are staying in Chepstow the night before you begin the walk, and it important to you to cover every mile, plan to head out to the marker the night before. This avoids the need to hike out to the Cliffs the first day and then backtrack again to where the trail intersects the route from Chepstow. Local lore maintains there is a horse

This stone on Sedbury Cliffs marks the official start of the trail near Chepstow.

buried underneath the marker stone, which is a sedimentary conglomerate called puddingstone.

Chepstow Castle dominates the town from its perch on the tall cliffs overlooking the Wye River. The foundations of this massive structure were begun in 1067 by William Fitz Osbern. Don't miss a chance to have a closer look at the castle and the museum if you have time.

Day 1 – Chepstow to Redbrook-on-Wye – 21 km (13 mi.)

Wintour's Leap overlooking the Wye River.

The day offers excellent walking following the lower Wye valley through beech and oak woodlands full of bird song, bluebells and the pungent odour of wild garlic. As you leave Chepstow you will cross John Rennie's ornate 1816 cast iron bridge with a fine view of the castle. The bridge marks the boundary between Wales and England, just one of many border crossings you will make over the course of your journey.

Tintern Abbey as seen from the Devil's Pulpit.

Don't miss the river view from Wintour's Leap a short distance down the trail. During a Civil War skirmish, Sir John Wintour is said to have jumped off the sheer 100 m (330 ft.) cliff with his horse and survived to tell the tale.

Soon after you reach the Devil's Pulpit, you will come to the 1.6 km (1 mi.) diversion to the ruins of Tintern Abbey. The Pulpit offers a distant and tantalizing view of the impressive ruins resting peacefully by the river below. It is said the devil himself preached from the Pulpit in an effort to lead the monks down the path of evil. The side trip is highly recommended.

From the Abbey diversion, the path continues along the river, through woodlands bursting with bluebells and on into Redbrook-on-Wye.

Day 2 – Redbrook-on-Wye to Llantilio Crossenny – 21 km (13 mi.)

Expect another day of fine walking over a gently rolling landscape, through many sheep-filled paddocks and woodlands, combined with a few good ascents up to excellent views. The trail passes through the National Trust's Kymin property, with commanding views of the ancient border town of Monmouth and the surrounding countryside before descending past more bluebells to cross the famous Monnow Bridge with its historic gatehouse.

The turreted Round House at the top of the Kymin was built by some of the well-heeled local gentlemen in the late 1700s for use as a dining house where they could enjoy the view.

There is little doubt you are in Wales here. Along the way I stopped for a break at

ROMANCING THE STONE

Established in 1131, Tintern Abbey was the first Cistercian monastery in Wales, the second in all of Britain. The monks devoted their lives to poverty and prayer, siting their abbeys far away from any contact with towns and villages. Following the dissolution of the monasteries by Henry VIII in 1536, the Abbey was abandoned until it was "rediscovered" by tourists, artists and poets. During a visit in 1798, William Wordsworth was inspired to write his famous "Lines Composed a Few Miles above Tintern Abbey." The abbey soon became a popular destination for followers of the "picturesque" movement, who were captivated by the romantic vision of the isolated, ivy-covered ruins.

ROB DINGLE, OFFA'S DYKE PATH NATIONAL TRAIL OFFICER

The Monnow Bridge and gatehouse at Monmouth.

St. Michael's Church in Llanfihangel Ystum Llywern, a Welsh tongue twister for sure.

Day 3 – Llantilio Crossenny to Longtown – 21.5 km (13.4 mi.)

Some walkers may choose to make the long walk over the Black Mountains from Pandy to Hay-on-Wye in one day. This covers a distance of almost 27 km (17 mi.) making it a very long and tiring day, with the added risk of doing a large portion of it in less than ideal conditions due to the potential for bad weather. I planned the length of the preceding days so I could break up this part of the journey with an off-trail stop in Longtown. This required descending off the ridge for the evening and climbing back up the next day to resume the walk.

The trail from Llantilio Crossenny to Pandy is mainly across agricultural land with plenty of sheep paddocks and quiet country lanes. In the process you will pass the entrance to the White Castle, so called for the white plaster on the outer wall that remains visible in spots. It is open to the public and worth a look if time permits. Soon the town of Pandy can be seen in the valley with fine views of the Black Mountains and Hatterrall Ridge beyond.

Once you reach Pandy, the serious climbing begins up to the ridge past an Iron Age hill fort. Ahead you will see the track running over the ridge. Now it is simply a matter of keeping to the undulating path, and if you are blessed with good weather, enjoying the wide vistas as they unfold before you. To the east are the fields of Herefordshire with the Malvern Hills and Cotswolds beyond. To the west, layers of mountain ridges fill the distance.

Walkers who have chosen to break their trek along the ridge have two choices. They can descend off the west

> **DID YOU KNOW?**
>
> A local boy made good, Henry V was born in Monmouth, where his decisive victory at Agincourt is commemorated in Agincourt Square. In Shakespeare's *Henry V* he proudly proclaims, "For I am Welsh, you know ..." while Captain Fluellen declares, "All the water in the Wye cannot wash your majesty's Welsh blood out of your body."

ROB DINGLE, OFFA'S DYKE PATH NATIONAL TRAIL OFFICER

The view from Hatterrall Ridge.

Llanthony Priory as seen from Hatterrall Ridge.

side to Llanthony Priory or off the east side to Longtown. The turnoff for Longtown lies between the first and second triangulation points and is clearly marked.

I chose the diversion to Longtown because there were more options for accommodation. The Priory alternative offers a chance to explore the ruins of the twelfth century Cistercian monastery.

In theory, walkers going to Longtown can head across the fields into town, but there are no clearly marked footpaths (that I found) and I was concerned about crossing paddocks where I might not have a right of way. So I followed the trail down to the road and into town. This was a very long walk of probably close to 4 km (2.5 mi.) at the end of a long day. I eventually walked into a bed and breakfast along the way and paid the

REBEL MONKS

The monks who built the Llanthony Priory were serious about their vows to live a simple life. They refused to wear underwear or to dye their tunics black as was the usual custom. They considered these practices self-indulgent and became known as the White Monks because of their undyed clothing.

owner to drive me into town. The town's castle ruins are worth a look if you have the time and the energy.

Day 4 – Longtown to Hay-on-Wye – 21 km (13 mi.)

Fortunately the cook at the inn where I stayed drove me back to a different starting point after breakfast, so I was able to avoid the long walk back. She assured me it was well marked, but of course she had never walked it herself. There was one way-mark and then a plethora of sheep trails heading every direction up to the ridge. I couldn't believe my luck when a Dutch couple I had met several times along the trail on previous days came along with their Global Positioning System device. We eventually found the correct trail and I headed out along the ridge to Hay Bluff, leaving them behind. The weather had moved in, so the entire ridge walk required slogging through rain, sleet, fog and strong wind. I admit it was an eerie experience walking through the rolling mist with not a walker in sight (except two crazy joggers I met who were running in shorts!).

These are exactly the kind of conditions you must be prepared for with adequate clothing and food supplies. I made sure my pockets were stocked with easily accessible snack food to eat as I walked. In weather like this you need fuel against the cold but you aren't likely to stop and open your pack for lunch. The trail is well marked but I was exceedingly glad to reach Hay Bluff, a clearing sky and good views.

From the bluff it is more or less downhill into Hay-on-Wye, with lovely walking through fields and along country lanes. On the way you will follow Dulas Brook, the boundary between Wales and England. Legend says the stream ran red with blood for three days following a battle in 1093, but the reddish soil in the area may have provided a more mundane explanation. Known as the Town of Books, Hay-on-Wye is a good spot to consider as a rest day. (See the "Consider this" section for more information.)

ROB DINGLE, OFFA'S DYKE PATH NATIONAL TRAIL OFFICER

Hay Bluff as seen from the north side looking south.

Day 5 – Hay-on-Wye to Kington – 24 km (15 mi.)

The day begins with delightful walking along the Wye River then passes through the woodland of Bettws Dingle to follow country lanes to the tiny village of Newchurch.

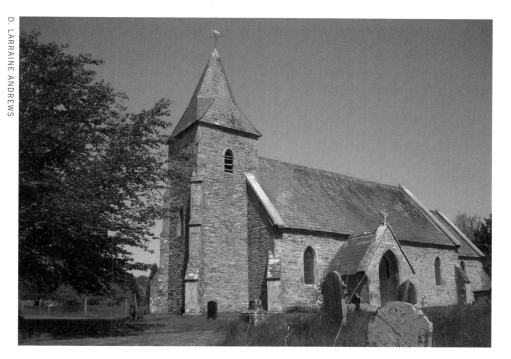

St. Mary's in Newchurch welcomes walkers with everything required to enjoy tea or coffee and a biscuit.

Be sure to stop in at St. Mary's church, where you will find a picnic table for walkers, and inside, a table stocked with biscuits and facilities for thirsty walkers to make tea or coffee. There is no charge but donations are welcome. Expect a series of long, steady climbs as you ascend Disgwylfa Hill and Hergest Ridge. Your efforts will be rewarded with fine views to the village of Gladestry and Hatterrall Ridge on the Black Mountains.

LIVING FENCES

Throughout the ODP you will see prickly hawthorn hedges marking field boundaries. These quick-growing plants were used to mark out fields created as a result of a series of Enclosure Acts that were introduced in various parts of the country, beginning in the seventeenth century. Not only do they make an effective living barrier for people and livestock, but they fill the countryside with the scent of their sweet-smelling blossoms every spring.

The village of Gladestry from Hergest Ridge.

Finally the path crosses the ellipse of an abandoned race course to descend into the old English border town of Kington.

Day 6 – Kington to Knighton – 21.5 km (13.4 mi.)

Expect another wonderful day of hill climbing with good views of the dyke and very pleasant walking through woodlands and open fields and along country lanes. Portions of the trail are actually on top of the dyke near Burfa. The view of the dyke near Discoed is popular in many photographs of the area.

The path eventually descends steeply into Knighton, "the town on the dyke" located in Wales with its train station in England. Congratulations! You've covered almost half of the ODP. The Offa's Dyke Association is headquartered in the information centre, where you will find interpretive displays about the dyke. The clock tower on Broad Street was built in 1872 and is the focal point of the town, which actually sits astride the dyke. Thursdays are market day when farmers come to town to buy and sell livestock.

Day 7 – Knighton to Brompton Crossroads – 24 km (15 mi.)

This turned into my longest trail day, partly because I had to go some distance off

The path follows Offa's Dyke near Discoed.

the path at Cwm to my accommodation and partly because I got lost trying to find it. My notes say that despite being a hard day of ups and downs, it was one of my most enjoyable walking days, with superb views of the dyke and the countryside.

Sheep and walkers share the trail.

My notes are also full of references to steep climbs and steep descents. The dyke and the path head inexorably north, across valleys and ridges running west to east, making for several stiff climbs and earning the section from Knighton to Montgomery the nickname of "the Switchback."

Leaving Knighton, the trail passes by the information centre, following the Teme River for a short distance. Then whammo, the climbing begins! Make sure you have plenty of water (I almost ran out) and just enjoy the day and the spectacular views. Along the way you will ascend Llanfair Hill, the highest point on the dyke at about 431 m (1,414 ft.) then on to Cwm-sanaham Hill for more great views.

The quiet little church at Churchtown is a good spot to regroup, then on to bisect the Kerry Ridgeway. The road is called Wales's oldest. It has been in use for at least 4,000 years, first by Bronze Age traders, then for over 800 years by Welsh drovers taking their sheep and cattle to the English markets.

Day 8 – Brompton Crossroads to Buttington Bridge – 19 km (12 mi.)

D. LARRAINE ANDREWS

The Montgomery Canal towpath provides a pleasant walk into Welshpool.

Good news! This is a pleasant day of walking over field paths, quiet lanes and woodland, with some climbing but nothing compared to the day before. Your efforts will be rewarded with wonderful views over the valley of the Severn River and good walking close to or on the dyke. The track actually passes through the yard of Rownal farm, where the lady of the house kindly asked if I needed water. I was impressed, considering the number of walkers she must see over the course of the season. After leaving Leighton Woods, the path ascends to Beacon Ring, a spooky Iron Age hill fort at the summit of the Long Mountain, with good views across to Welshpool and Powis Castle.

At Buttington Bridge the

path shares the span with an extremely busy road, making for a very dangerous crossing. It could take a while to get across here, but make sure to wait for a safe opening in the traffic, because the drivers have no room to go around you. Walkers can continue along the Montgomery Canal at this point, or take the 3.2 km (2 mi.) detour to Welshpool. I chose to break my journey here for a rest day and to have a look at the famous Powis Castle, a diversion I highly recommend. (See the "Consider this" section for more information.) The trail winds along the Montgomery Canal towpath, making for some excellent walking into the centre of town.

Day 9 – Buttington Bridge to Llanymynech – 16.5 km (10.3 mi.)

Thankfully, there is no bridge crossing required! Expect a very pleasant day of almost level walking following the canal towpath, then field after field along the flood banks of the Severn River. The path passes by the door of the Golden Lion pub at Four Crosses, a good place for a pot of tea, or perhaps a pint if you prefer, then rejoins the towpath for another delightful stretch of walking into Llanymynech. The name may be Welsh, but the border actually runs along the main street.

Day 10 – Llanymynech to Castle Mill – 20 km (12.4 mi.)

The day brings good walking over undulating countryside with some good climbs as the path winds its way through paddocks and woodlands, down quiet lanes and even across a golf course. There is much evidence of quarrying as you leave Llanymynech and ascend to the tiny village of Nantmawr, clinging to the hillside. Walkers are greeted with splendid 360-degree views from the grassy summit of Moelydd before descending steeply to the valley of the River Morda and on to the double-headed horse sculpture at the Oswestry Old Racecourse. But no need to worry about dodging any horses here; the last race took place in 1848.

The path follows the dyke off and on most of the day, then leaves it for good before you cross the River Ceiriog and arrive at Castle Mill. Castle Mill is a dot on the map, but bus service is readily available into the town of Chirk or you can safely walk along the verge of the highway to divert to overnight accommodations.

As you work your way north you are no doubt becoming an experienced stile crosser.

FLOATING THE STONE

The Montgomery Canal was first opened in 1796 to allow narrow, horse-drawn boats to transport limestone and other types of cargo. The limestone was quarried at Llanymynech and either used for building or crushed and burned to make mortar for bricks and plaster. The canal is currently undergoing a large restoration and offers wonderful walking along the pathway which is lined with wildflowers and home to much wildlife.

Hopefully you have worked out the most efficient system for getting over them. There is a particularly good one along the dyke south of Chirk.

A wooden stile on the dyke south of Chirk.

Day 11 – Castle Mill to Trevor Rocks (for Llangollen) – 14.5 km (9 mi.)

The day offers a short but spectacular walk with lots of up and down and several options. From Castle Mill, walkers have summertime access on a diversion to Chirk Castle, a National Trust property open to the public. It was originally built around 1300 by Roger Mortimer, who helped Edward I defeat Llywelyn the Last, Prince of Wales. The official route swings to the west of the estate, with views of the castle on a clear day. Woodlands full of the pungent

QUAINT, BUT ONLY FOR A WHILE!

Over the course of the walk, you will probably clamber over a few hundred of these quaint contraptions. They allow walkers a convenient method of crossing from field to field while ensuring livestock cannot escape. At first they are a novelty, but this soon wears off! They tend to break your stride and by the end of a long day, any notion of appealing quaintness is long gone. Fortunately, you will find that most of the stiles along the southern portion of the trail have been replaced by wonderful self-latching metal gates, or "kissing" gates. (I was disappointed to find the name has nothing to do with a design to promote kissing by people. Actually the name reflects the fact that the gate "kisses" either side of the fence opening and does not need to be securely latched.) Unfortunately, as you head north, many of the older, wooden stiles remain. So you will definitely be a stile expert before the end of the walk!

scent of ramsons, or wild garlic, and more pleasant walking along the Llangollen Canal lead to a decision point at the swing bridge at Froncysyllte. The official route crosses the River Dee via a narrow stone bridge, providing stunning views of the famous Pontcysyllte Aqueduct, where walkers and boats appear to glide across the

TELFORD'S TRIUMPH

Designated a UNESCO World Heritage Site in 2009, the Pontcysyllte Aqueduct was begun in 1795 and took ten years to complete. Travelogue author George Barrow noted that his guide proclaimed it to be the "finest bridge in the world, and no wonder, if what the common people say be true, namely that every stone cost a golden sovereign." The aqueduct stretches for 307 m (1,007 ft.) across the River Dee, allowing boats and walkers a very narrow clearance but providing superb views if you can manage to look up to see them. (As Borrow wrote of his crossing of the aqueduct in the 1860s, "… the height was awful.") UNESCO describes the elegant structure as "a pioneering masterpiece of engineering and monumental metal archi-

tecture, conceived by the celebrated civil engineer Thomas Telford." Believe it or not, when canal maintenance is required, they actually unplug the troughs and let the water fall into the river below.

The Pontcysyllte Aqueduct towers above the River Dee. Note walkers crossing along the top.

ROB DINGLE, OFFA'S DYKE PATH NATIONAL TRAIL OFFICER

sky far above you. If you are at all challenged by heights or vertigo, the official route is recommended. (I admit, this is the one I chose.) Otherwise, you can continue along the towpath to follow the canal across the River Dee on the aqueduct and meet up with the official route on the other side.

Once past the aqueduct, you can choose to follow the towpath into Llangollen or take the official route over the Panorama Walk. The official route is highly recommended unless you are running out of time and energy. If you take the canal path you won't miss the wonderful views from Castell Dinas Brân the next day, but I still think the official route is preferred.

The name "Panorama" offers a hint, but the remainder of the walk entails some steady climbing through woodland eventually opening up to reveal fine views of the ruins of Castell Dinas Brân sitting ominously on top of the conical hill ahead of you and the limestone bluffs of Trevor Rocks to the right. The hill looks daunting but the climb only took me about 15 minutes. Admire the panorama and then head down a series of switchbacks and a well-marked pathway to the town of Llangollen. (The ODP does not officially include the diversion to Llangollen, but this is the most logical stopping place on this portion of the trail and is a lovely spot to spend some time.)

CROW CASTLE?

The dark, brooding ruins perched atop the steep hill seem to have emerged directly from some Arthurian legend. Indeed, many myths are associated with the spot. One such legend centres on a mace-wielding giant called Gogmagog who terrorized the area and was eventually killed by a brave Norman knight named Payn Peveril. The dying giant tells a tantalizing tale of a huge golden ox buried there, but of course he does not reveal the location. The current castle is thought to have been started in the 1260s on the site of an Iron Age hill fort built around 600 BCE. Much has been written about the origins of the name, which is said to identify a place where crows live. George Borrow says it may mean "the castle of Bran or Brennus, or the castle above the Bran, a brook which flows at its foot."

Castell Dinas Brân sits brooding atop the conical hill, with Trevor Rocks to the right.

ROB DINGLE, OFFA'S DYKE PATH NATIONAL TRAIL OFFICER

Boardwalk crosses marshes and barren moors just north of World's End.

Day 12 – Trevor Rocks (via Llangollen) to Clwyd Gate – 21.5 km (13.4 mi.)

The day offers much variety as you cross scree slopes to World's End, then head out over open heather-covered moorland and through dense, dark forest to meet the challenges of the Clwydian Range. Walkers have the choice of following the single-track road beneath the cliffs of Trevor Rocks or taking to the steep limestone scree slopes along the western scarp of Eglwyseg Mountain. Many consider this one of the highlights of the ODP, but I must admit I took the road. I am not good on narrow scree trails and was warned that some parts are not much more than boot-width. Both trails meet at World's End, and assuming the world hasn't actually ended, the way continues across a very barren and exposed section of moorland before plunging into Llandegla Forest.

Heavy rain forced me to stop at the tiny village of Llandegla, where I was fortunate

WERE THEY OR WEREN'T THEY?

The delightful Welsh market town of Llangollen became famous as the residence of the "most celebrated virgins in Europe," Lady Eleanor Butler and Miss Sarah Ponsonby. The two had "eloped" there from Ireland in the 1770s, disguised as men. For close to 50 years they lived in their home of Plas Newydd, which today is open to the public. The home is full of unique gifts brought to the ladies by their array of famous and inquisitive visitors, including the Duke of Wellington, Lord Byron, William Wordsworth and Sir Walter Scott, to name but a few. The unorthodox liaison of the Ladies of Llangollen scandalized and fascinated their contemporaries, leading to much speculation about the true nature of their relationship.

to find a local bus service that took me right to Clwyd Gate. The remainder of the day's walk, according to the guidebook, heads across paddocks and follows country lanes before beginning the climb into the hills of the Clwydians. (For the uninitiated, "Clwyd" is pronounced "Cly-dee." The Welsh may smile inwardly at your attempts to get it right, but in my experience they won't correct you. As for any of the other Welsh names you will encounter, all I can say is good luck. This is probably the easiest one along the whole route.)

Day 13 – Clwyd Gate to Bodfari – 18.5 km (11.5 mi.)

Just a word of warning: all my notes for this day refer to many steep ascents and descents, with one comment that asks, "When will these hills end?" Some walkers consider the portion of the ODP over the Clwydians to be the most challenging of the entire trail. The path is not particularly difficult, but it is relentless as it climbs and descends its way across the heather-covered hills with little opportunity for shelter. The weather gods smiled on me this day – it was cool and threatening rain, but only spit a few times. Take your time across here. Enjoy the magnificent views and the wonderful walking, but be careful to assess the weather. The hills are exposed and definitely not a good place to be if rain and wind move in. There are some escape routes along the track, so have a plan in mind if weather forces you off the path.

The trail climbs to the top of Moel Famau and the ruins of the Jubilee Tower.

ROB DINGLE, OFFA'S DYKE PATH NATIONAL TRAIL OFFICER

Day 14 – Bodfari to Prestatyn – 19 km (12 mi.)

With any luck the final day will finish up with fine views of the Irish Sea and Snowdonia from the cliffs overlooking the seaside resort of Prestatyn.

Along the way there is much navigating of fields and the inevitable stiles, combined with quiet country lanes. And of course there are a few good climbs before you finally make the steep descent through the Prestatyn Hillside Nature Reserve into town. Be sure to follow the trail all the way to the seafront and the sculpture on the promenade. Titled "Dechrau a Diwedd" – "Beginning and End" – it signifies the beginning or end of your journey along the ODP. Then give yourself a big pat on the back and go put your feet up for a while!

HOW TO DO THE HIKE

This is a superb long-distance walk that can easily be done safely on your own or with a walking group. It is also possible to do sections of it if the full distance seems overwhelming or if time constraints limit your ability to complete the whole path in one go.

Over the years, I have used the services of Contours Walking Holidays (**www.contours.co.uk**) for many National Trail hikes and would highly recommend them. They book all the accommodations, arrange the luggage transfers and supply you with all the guidebooks and maps you'll need to complete the route. The trip is all prepaid, avoiding the need to worry about carrying cash for small B&Bs that do not accept credit cards. Many other companies also supply similar services for self-guided trips as well as offering fully guided options. For a list of other reputable

THE MOTHER MOUNTAIN

The highest point of the range is reached at Moel Famau, "the mother mountain." Rising to 555 m (1,820 ft.) it offers views all the way to Liverpool on a clear day. Perched on top of the hill are the remains of the Jubilee Tower, built to celebrate 50 years of the reign of King George III. Completed in 1812, it collapsed 50 years later as a result of a fierce wind storm. (The remaining stump provides a convincing reminder of the need for an exit plan if the weather turns on you.)

D. LARRAINE ANDREWS

"Dechrau a Diwedd," on the seafront at Prestatyn, marks the beginning and the end of the trail.

companies, check the Trailblazer guide described in the "Recommended reading" section below.

There is also the option of booking your own accommodations, but this can be a slow and frustrating process, requiring the need to communicate with many establishments, only to have to change your plans as you find out they don't have room on the days you want to stay. The official trail website at **www.nationaltrail.co.uk/OffasDyke** provides a whole planning section if you want to tackle it yourself. If you choose this option, you can also decide whether you want to carry all your clothes etc. or arrange for luggage transfers. In general, camping opportunities are more limited but it is also possible to do the whole trail using this alternative.

HOW DO YOU SAY THAT?

Despite the common use of Welsh in Wales, there is no need to speak the language along the ODP. And that's a good thing, since the unusual combinations of vowels and consonants can be somewhat intimidating to say the least. If you want to take on the challenge of learning some basic Welsh words and phrases, check out Lonely Planet's guidebook on Wales or their phrasebook called *British Language & Culture*. Here is a small sampling of words you will encounter in place names along the trail that describe a feature of the countryside:

- afon – river
- bryn – hillside
- clawdd – dyke
- cwm – valley
- dinas – hill fortress
- dingle – deep, wooded valley
- llan – church
- moel – bare hill
- mynydd – mountain
- pandy – fulling mill (fulling is part of the process of making woollen cloth which involves first scouring the wool to remove oil and dirt, then milling or thickening it by matting the fibres together)

CONSIDER THIS: BEFORE OR AFTER THE HIKE

In each of the other chapters this section provides ideas for places to see and things to do before or after you finish the main hike that aren't actually part of the hike. But this chapter departs from the normal format to include a couple of outstanding, not-to-be-missed highlights that can be included as part of the walk itself. This is because the ODP is so long that you will certainly need to plan for a rest day or two along the

Just one of the many bookstores in Hay, the Town of Books.

way if you walk its entire length and these suggestions seem to fit well. Of course, these selections are entirely based on my opinion.

Hay-on-Wye, the Town of Books is the home of the internationally acclaimed Hay Festival that runs each spring and regularly attracts 85,000 visitors from all over the world. Former US president Bill Clinton famously called the annual celebration of literature and culture a "Woodstock of the mind." For over 25 years the festival has attracted high-profile celebrities of the book and political worlds, including such luminaries as Ian McEwan, Bill Bryson, Gordon Brown and Al Gore. Unless you reserve far in advance, don't plan on arriving during

KING RICHARD, COEUR DE LIVRE

Hay owes its stunning metamorphosis, from failing agricultural border town to world capital of used books, to the brilliant machinations of Richard Booth, the self-proclaimed King of Hay. In 1962 Booth bought his first bookshop in Church Street. Thanks mainly to his ingenuity and tenacity, the town went on to become the largest trading centre for second-hand and out-of-print books in the world. On April Fools Day in 1977, in a brilliant display of publicity savvy, Booth declared himself ruler of the independent Kingdom of Hay. Newspapers and television stations provided all the hype he could have hoped for as he arrived on his horse Caligula, which he named the new prime minister.

Powis Castle, with its terraced gardens, is a short walk from the town of Welshpool.

the festival, because there won't be a room to be had anywhere. But it's not just the festival that brings visitors. Long before the annual celebration, Hay-on-Wye was already a destination for book lovers, mainly due to the prodigious efforts of the King of Hay. Even if you don't have time to stop an extra day, give yourself a few hours to browse through the impressive selection of bookshops to be found in this town of barely 1,500 souls.

Welshpool isn't on the official trail but is well situated for a rest day and a chance to visit Powis Castle and its famous terraced gardens. Be sure to take the 2 km (1.3 mi.) footpath from town through the stunning parkland surrounding the castle. The Welsh name, Castell Coch, means the "red castle" and you will quickly see why. The castle itself sits on high ground above the Severn River, offering commanding views of the valley and the Long Mountain. Don't miss a chance to tour the Clive Museum, an extensive collection of artifacts collected by Robert Clive – Clive of India – during his time there in the 1700s.

ARE YOU READY TO EAT?

Dining options vary along the trail. Your accommodation will provide the traditional cooked breakfast to get you started in the morning. This seems to last me well past noon, so I generally rely on picnic-type food such as fruit, cheese, crackers and energy bars to snack on along the trail during the day. Most towns and villages will have a shop or full-sized grocery where you can stock up. Many B&Bs will make your lunch for the next day for an additional charge and supply an evening meal if you are stopping in a village with few other options. Or you can always self-cater. I find most establishments are quite happy to supply you with a plate and utensils and let you eat your own meal if you are so inclined.

Although Welsh food was typically viewed as lacklustre and plain in the past, there has been a revolution on the food scene inspired by fresh, local produce and cooks eager to offer new twists on traditional fare. A good example is laverbread, a high-protein staple of Welsh miners in the 1700s and 1800s that has recently been reborn as a delicacy served with seafood dishes. It's boiled seaweed rolled in oatmeal and fried in bacon fat, traditionally served with breakfast.

Hygiene standards are generally high and there should be no concerns about most food establishments.

Tipping is expected. Normally 10 to 15 per cent of the bill would be considered reasonable.

Vegetarians: Although strictly vegetarian restaurants may be few and far between along the trail, many will provide some vegetarian options, including pubs. Most B&Bs are happy to cater to vegetarian concerns – just ask.

INTERNET RESOURCES

For websites related to the ODP, check out:
www.nationaltrail.co.uk/OffasDyke, the official site for the ODP; and
www.offasdyke.demon.co.uk, the official site of the Offa's Dyke Association.

For general information on Wales, visit:
www.visitwales.co.uk, the official Wales site for tourist information;
www.hay-on-wye.com, the town's official website, with good information on the Hay Festival; and
www.welshpool.com, which includes good links to other Welsh towns in the area.

RECOMMENDED READING

There are several excellent guidebooks to the trail. Those listed here are the ones I used and would highly recommend. Also included in the list are some books of historical and cultural interest relating to Wales in general and the Dyke in particular.

Favourite Welsh Recipes, Traditional Welsh Fare – a small collection of local recipes available in many bookstores in Wales.

Kilvert's Diary – edited by William Plomer – available online at www.archive.org. The local curate lived and wrote of his life near Hay-on-Wye in Victorian times.

Ladies of Llangollen – Elizabeth Mavor – an interesting account of the famous friends who attracted some of the most celebrated figures of the early 1800s to their home.

Lonely Planet: Wales – a good starting place to plan your trip to Wales.

Offa's Dyke History & Guide – David Hill and Margaret Worthington – written by the two primary researchers on the Offa's Dyke Project, provides some fascinating history together with the how and why of the dyke without the need to get lost in the technical mile-by-mile analysis.

Offa's Dyke: A Journey in Words and Pictures – Jim Saunders – this gem follows the trail in all its glory with fabulous pictures and plenty of information on the history, the flora and the fauna along the way. It is the companion book to the BBC series on the dyke and is highly recommended.

Offa's Dyke Path: Prestatyn to Chepstow – Keith Carter – the Trailblazer series are some of my favourite guidebooks for the National Trails. They offer comprehensive information on towns and places along the trail, flora and fauna, together with exceptionally detailed, easy to follow maps. This guide goes from north to south, which can cause confusion if you are walking the other direction. I still recommend it for the wealth of town by town information it contains.

The Book of Hay – Kate Clarke – Everything you ever wanted to know about Hay-on-Wye.

The Offa's Dyke Path: Walking Guide to the National Trail – David Hunter – is the guide I carried with me every day. The trail descriptions are excellent and the historical information is outstanding.

The Matter of Wales: Epic Views of a Small Country – Jan Morris – the well-known travel writer is from Wales so she has her own perspective on her native country.

Welsh Traditions and Traits – Chris Stephens – a fascinating collection of tales about all things Welsh.

Wild Wales – George Borrow – an account of his visit to Wales in the mid-1800s, available online at www.visionofbritain.org.uk.

© FOTOSEARCH.COM

Hares are common along the path.

FAUNA FACTS: HARE BEFORE, TROUBLE BEHIND!

It is not uncommon to see a hare loping along the trail. But beware. According to English folklore, if a hare crosses your path in the morning, it means trouble ahead. An old remedy suggests you can avoid any problems by spitting over your left shoulder and saying, "Hare before, trouble behind: Change ye, Cross, and free me." Another charm suggests all you need to do is touch each shoulder with your forefinger while declaring, "Hare, hare, God send thee care." Folklore and myths associated with hares are common throughout the world, as far back as the ancient Egyptians, who regarded hares as androgynous, able to switch their gender. Hares are even associated with madness, but this clearly comes from the wild antics of the males, which leap and box each other to establish dominance during the spring mating season. This is the origin of the common expression "mad as a March hare." Hares, which are larger than rabbits, have long, black-tipped ears and are capable of running long distances to evade predators.

CHAPTER 7 – CANADA – WATERTON LAKES NATIONAL PARK – CARTHEW–ALDERSON TRAIL

{ Waterton Lakes National Park was named in 1858 for the eccentric British scientist, ornithologist and naturalist Charles Waterton by Lieutenant Thomas Blakiston during his explorations in the area as a member of the British North American Exploring Expedition, or Palliser Expedition. The Blackfoot name of the place was *Pukto-na-sikimi*, meaning "inside lake," because the lakes are inside the first range of the Rocky Mountains. }

I had settled long years before that when the day for squatting came I would come back to this spot and so in 1877 I built a cabin between the Middle and Lower Lakes …

—JOHN GEORGE "KOOTENAI" BROWN,
first superintendent of the park

✳ HIKING RULE 7: This is grizzly country. The best way to avoid a bear encounter is to avoid the bear. Make noise, travel in a group and watch for signs of recent activity such as fresh scat or diggings. If you do encounter a bear, do not run! Stay calm and back away slowly, talking in a firm measured voice. Avoid direct eye contact, which can be interpreted as aggression. Leave the area as quickly as possible.

WHERE IN THE WORLD?

WHAT WILL I SEE?

The view south to Upper Waterton Lake.

CLAIM TO FAME

In 1932 the park was combined with Glacier National Park in Montana to form Waterton–Glacier International Peace Park, the first of its kind in the world, to recognize the "peace, goodwill and cooperation" between Canada and the United States. In 1979 Waterton was designated part of the UNESCO Waterton Biosphere Reserve, the first in Canada with a national park at its core. The park includes two National Historic Sites: the Prince of Wales Hotel and the Lineham Discovery Well. And in 1995, as part of the International Peace Park, it was recognized as a UNESCO World Heritage Site. In addition to the park's spectacular mountain scenery and distinctive glacial landforms, the designation recognizes its key location on the "Crown of the Continent" which has resulted in the development of "plant communities and ecological complexes" not found anywhere else in the world.

An embarrassment of riches sums up this extraordinary gem tucked away in the southwest corner of Alberta. Parks Canada provides some of the remarkable statistics. At 505 km² (195 sq. mi.), it is the smallest national park in the Canadian Rockies. But within its boundaries it contains 45 different habitat types that sustain an astonishing variety of plants, many of which are rare or threatened. More than half of Alberta's plant species are found in Waterton. Of the more than 1,000 species of vascular plants, 179 are considered rare in Alberta, 22 of which are unique to the park. And with over 600 different kinds of wildflowers, it is described as a "botanic motherlode" by the Parks Canada wildflower guide. The incredible plant variety also fosters animal diversity, with more than 60 species of mammals and over 250 species of birds calling this place home.

UNESCO cites five distinct ecoregions located here: alpine tundra, subalpine forest, montane forest, aspen parkland and fescue grassland. One of the park's most distinctive features is the almost complete absence of foothills. This creates a sudden and dramatic transition from prairies to mountains that contributes to the exceptional diversity of plants and animals living within such a small area.

As if all this uniqueness weren't enough, the park also sits on the edge of two major bird migration routes, resulting in an incredible variety of species in marsh and lake areas, including bald eagles, peregrine falcons, nesting ospreys and rare trumpeter swans.

HIKE PROFILE

The Carthew–Alderson Trail is a one-way hike that requires a shuttle to the trailhead at Cameron Lake, located at the end of the Akamina Parkway. The trail begins at an elevation of 1660 m (5,446 ft.) and climbs to 2311 m (7,582 ft.) at the Carthew Summit, for an elevation gain of 651 m (2,136 ft.). It then descends steadily via Alderson Lake

"CROWN OF THE CONTINENT"

In 1901 the well-known conservationist George Bird Grinnell coined the term for the hydrological apex from which the headwaters of the continent flow into three separate drainages – the Pacific Ocean, the Atlantic via the Gulf of Mexico and Hudson Bay. According to the Crown of the Continent Geotourism Council, this region is centred more or less at the spot where Alberta, Montana and British Columbia meet and is considered "one of the most diverse and intact ecosystems in the temperate zones of the world." Blakiston didn't have such a catchy phrase for it, but he recognized the significance of the area, describing it as "the culminating point of North America." Long before either Grinnell or Blakiston, however, First Nations tribes already understood the special nature of the region, calling it the "Backbone of the World." Parks Canada notes that since it is also one of the narrowest areas in the Rocky Mountain chain, it represents a key pinch point for wildlife moving along the north–south corridor.

NATHAN ANDREWS

The mountains meet the prairies in a dramatic transition just north of Waterton Park.

WHERE THE MOUNTAINS MEET THE PRAIRIES

Unlike the Rocky Mountains north of the Crowsnest Pass, there is no gradual transition from prairies to foothills to mountains here. For some unexplained reason, the mountain-building process, which normally involved the movement of a series of overlapping thrust sheets to create the familiar crumpled aspect of foothills and mountain ranges, didn't happen in Waterton. As explained by Graeme Pole in his *Canadian Rockies Explorer*, the mountains here were formed by one single, massive wedge of rock, estimated to have been up to 30 km (19 mi.) thick and 110 km (68 mi.) wide, that gradually moved about 100 km (62 mi.) northeastward onto the prairies. When it finally stopped it had created one of the most distinctive landscapes anywhere along the eastern slopes of the Canadian Rockies. Known as the Lewis Overthrust (after Meriwether Lewis of the US Lewis and Clark Expedition), the older rocks of the thrust sheet plowed right over the younger shales of the prairies, earning the peaks of Waterton the moniker of "upside down mountains." One of the best places to view the abrupt transition from prairies to mountains is from the viewpoint on Highway 6, just north of the park.

to follow the Carthew Valley between Buchanan Ridge and Bertha Peak to emerge by the Watertown townsite at 1290 m (4,232 ft.), for an elevation loss of 1021 m (3,350 ft.) and a total hiking distance of 20.1 km (12.5 mi.).

CARTHEW-ALDERSON TRAIL

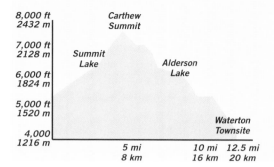

Hazards

As with any hiking on steep or uneven terrain, the normal cautions regarding twisted ankles and injuries from falling apply here. However, the biggest threats in Waterton tend to be weather related. The park is the wettest and windiest spot in the province. Weather patterns are unpredictable and can change frequently, without warning. Don't rely on the morning forecast – always watch the sky for approaching storms and take evasive action if required.

Sudden, dramatic decreases in temperature can occur as storms move in, creating the very real possibility of hypothermia. This is a dangerous condition where the

HANG ON TO YOUR HAT!

Why is Waterton so wet and windy? Location and topography are the biggest factors. The park is strongly influenced by persistent Pacific Maritime weather systems that bring warm, moist air across the Coast Mountains and Columbia Plateau. When they are forced up by Arctic air, they dump plenty of snow and rain, making Waterton the wettest place in Alberta. According to Parks Canada, the average annual precipitation is 1072 mm (42 in.), most of which falls as snow. The park's location at one of the lowest spots on the Continental Divide, plus the fact that the valleys trend west to east, causes the wind to funnel through this lower mountain gap. This magnifies its velocity, making the park the windiest place in Alberta after the Crowsnest Pass to the north. Speeds of 100 km/h (62 m.p.h.) are not uncommon, while gusts of over 160 km/h (100 m.p.h.) have been recorded. The warmer air makes it one of Alberta's warmest winter spots, even though temperatures can still dip to −40°C (−40°F). Also, given that the persistent southwest winds bring seeds from areas more commonly found west of the Continental Divide, Waterton is an unexpected hot spot for an incredible diversity of plants normally associated with regions to the south and west.

body begins losing heat from its core, especially if you get wet and cold. Signs include uncontrolled shivering and mental confusion. If anyone in your group is exhibiting these symptoms, it is essential to stop, warm up and refuel before continuing. This is particularly applicable to the Carthew–Alderson trail, which climbs to a totally exposed crest on Carthew Summit before dipping down to more protected terrain.

Lightning on the exposed ridge is also a risk in a thunderstorm, while wind can reach extreme velocities that have the potential to actually blow you off. Once over the top of Carthew Summit, the hike descends steadily into an alpine valley that offers good shelter if required.

The park is home to grizzly and black bears as well as cougars. Always check for current trail alerts from Parks Canada and take them seriously. Travelling in groups and making noise are your best bet for avoiding problems on the trail. (Bear bells are not loud enough to make any difference.) Cougars are generally very elusive, solitary animals. But if you encounter one on the trail, pick up any small children you may have with you, face the animal and back up slowly. Don't run! You'll just look like prey if you do. Unlike with bears, you should try to look aggressive with a cougar, waving your arms or a stick to scare it off. If either a bear or a cougar does attack, fight back.

Deer may seem friendly but they can be very dangerous. Recent years have seen an increasing number of deer attacks on people in the townsite. Unfortunately, they have become habituated to the lawns available for grazing, the food offered by tourists and the protection offered from natural predators. Deer have extremely sharp hooves and can become very aggressive, especially if you have given them food and then stop once you've taken a picture. Never feed them (or any other wild animals). All it does is foster dependency on an easy food source. Deer may also eat discarded food wrappers or bags that smell like food, causing havoc with their digestive systems and even death. Elk commonly roam the townsite as well. They should never be approached, especially females with young, or males protecting their harem during the mating season.

D. LARRAINE ANDREWS

The exposed crest on Carthew Summit can be a dangerous place during a wind or lightning storm.

The essentials

HIKE OVERVIEW

The Carthew–Alderson Trail is a one-way hike rated as moderately strenuous, with an elevation gain of 651 m (2,136 ft.) to the Carthew Summit, and an elevation loss of 1021 m (3,350 ft.) from the summit to the Waterton townsite. Beginning at the trailhead by Cameron Lake, the trail ascends through lush forest to Summit Lake and then climbs steadily to the barren ridge of Carthew Summit with its wide expansive views into the mountains of Glacier National Park to the south and west. From the summit it descends steeply past the three Carthew Lakes to Alderson Lake, then follows a forest trail along the Carthew Valley to emerge at the townsite, about 50 m (164 ft.) south of Cameron Falls.

© BERNIE MCMAHON

Cameron Falls, at the end of the Carthew–Alderson hike, is a popular spot for photographs.

OLDER THAN DIRT!

A popular spot for photographs and squirrel watching, Cameron Falls (along with the creek and the lake) were named after Donald Cameron, the head of the British section of the 1872–76 International Boundary Survey. The falls tumble over limestone outcroppings that are 1.5 billion years old, some of the oldest visible sedimentary rock in Alberta. Follow the stairs up the north side for a good vantage point.

Why would I want to?

The Carthew–Alderson Trail is consistently rated as one of the best in the park by many Waterton veterans. In fact, in their hiking "bible" (otherwise known as the *Canadian Rockies Trail Guide*), authors Brian Patton and Bart Robinson call it "the most popular one-way hike in the Canadian Rockies." At this point I must disclose that I am in no way unbiased when it comes to Waterton. Since I was born about a two-hour drive from here, I have had the good fortune to have visited the park most summers since I was a child and have hiked this trail a number of times. After all these years and all the places I have been in the world, Waterton still ranks close to the top of my list for sheer, unsurpassed beauty. There isn't much that can beat it, in my opinion.

But don't take my word for it. When it comes to the trail, consider this: you will see nine alpine lakes and walk along the shores of four of them. You will pass through lush subalpine forest and, if you are lucky, meadows full of showy beargrass, then rise above treeline to stand on one of the highest trail-accessible lookouts in the entire Waterton–Glacier International Peace Park. From here the endless views to the south and west are simply spectacular. On a clear, blue-sky day there are few superlatives that can truly do it justice. The descent brings more lakes and the promise of wildflowers as you pass through forest and valley to emerge at the cool waters of Cameron Falls and the end of a truly remarkable introduction to a truly remarkable place called Waterton.

When to go

Waterton is the wettest place in Alberta, with an average annual precipitation of 1072 mm (42 in.). However, because the majority of this falls as snow, it is not unusual for the snowpack at higher altitudes to linger well into July, limiting access to the backcountry, including the Carthew–Alderson Trail. Spring brings a profusion of wildflowers, but depending on the snowpack, "spring" wildflowers can be found anytime from June to September as the snow gradually retreats at higher elevations and blooms suddenly emerge in the warm sunshine. (The annual Waterton Wildflower Festival runs for ten days every June.)

August is generally the most dependable month for hiking, when the weather is usually the warmest and driest and there is almost always plenty of blue sky. Late summer and fall also bring good wildlife viewing opportunities, including ungulates such as deer, elk and bighorn sheep, while the annual autumn migration offers spectacular birdwatching. Snow can come to the higher elevations anytime, but it is not uncommon for it to arrive by late August or early September. One year, I had a group hike organized for the Carthew–Alderson Trail during the first week in September, when a snow dump of almost 610 mm (24 in.) abruptly ended everyone's hiking season.

What's the story?

The scenery here is grand and picturesque ... game is abundant, including Grizzly bears ... and we obtained both fresh meat and fish.

—Thomas Blakiston (September 1858)

Thomas Blakiston, a member of the famous British North American Exploring Expedition,

BEST OF SHOW

Beargrass is almost always described as "showy," sometimes "sensuous," and if you are lucky enough to see a patch of blooms in all their glory you will understand why. The species is the unofficial floral emblem of Waterton–Glacier International Peace Park and is not a grass at all, but a member of the lily family. The plants are often spotted in meadows throughout the park, but you can't always count on seeing them in large bunches because individual plants bloom only once every five to seven years. In years when the flower gods are coordinated, beargrass can appear in broad swaths on open hillsides – an unforgettable spectacle.

D. LARRAINE ANDREWS

Showy beargrass blooms are the unofficial floral emblem of Waterton Park.

COLLEEN F. BAINS

Chief Mountain. The Blackfoot name, Nínaiistáko, means "mountain that stands apart."

THE KING

There is much confusion over the original names of the Waterton Lakes, but it is now generally agreed that Chief Mountain Lakes probably referred to the Upper and Lower St. Mary's Lakes in Glacier National Park. Chief Mountain, referred to as "The King" on early maps of the region, has been a landmark for travellers for centuries. It is a sacred site to the Blackfoot, who call it Nínaiistáko, or "mountain that stands apart." Located just south of the international border in Montana, it is an unmistakable example of the Lewis Overthrust as it rises from the prairies in solitary splendour. On a clear day the mountain is often visible for incredible distances, but you can see it up close as you approach or leave the park on Highway 5 or on Chief Mountain International Highway.

commonly called the Palliser Expedition after its leader John Palliser, was probably the first white man to see the magnificent mountains and lakes of what we now know as Waterton Lakes National Park. He promptly named the lakes for Charles Waterton, a fellow ornithologist, conservationist and explorer who travelled extensively but never came anywhere near his namesake. Waterton is often described as an "eccentric" who in the early 1800s established one of the world's first bird sanctuaries, at Walton Hall, his family home in England. The concept of protecting wildlife was totally foreign at the time and often met with hostility. Not only did he contribute to the practice of anesthesia through his research on curare, a by-product of certain South American plants, but he apparently climbed to the top of St. Peter's Cathedral in Rome, where he left his gloves on the lightning rod to prove it.

Waterton may have been an interesting fellow, but the choice of name wasn't popular with many of the locals. Cardston Anglican clergyman Canon S.H. Middleton, a tireless advocate for the park, called the word Waterton "weak, insipid," without "the appeal of romance. The mystic background of the Indian is ignored and tradition is not sustained." Over the years, the lakes were variously referred to as Chief Mountain or Kootenay after the tribe long associated with it.

The Blackfoot knew the lakes by several names, including "big water." But in the end, Waterton stuck. Perhaps it isn't entirely inappropriate that a conservationist, who championed such progressive concepts of wildlife preservation well before they were generally accepted, should lend his name to this wondrous place.

Seven years after Blakiston's journey of discovery through the area, another white man had his first glimpse of the prairies stretching out from the foot of what the First Nations called the "Shining Mountains." It was 1865 and not only had the fearsome reputation of the Blackfoot Confederacy managed to keep the land virtually empty of settlers, the country was still home to immense herds of bison. As recounted in William Rodney's *Kootenai Brown: His Life and Times 1839–1916*, John George "Kootenai" Brown later recalled the unforgettable sight:

> Emerging from the South Kootenay Pass we hit the foothills near the mouth of Pass Creek and climbed to the top of one of the lower mountains. The prairie as far as we could see east, north and west was one living mass of buffalo … As we rode through…, the great beasts just moved off slowly. We made a lane of only about one hundred yards and they paid little attention.

It would be 1877 before Brown would return, with his family, to take up residence at a spot between the Middle and Lower Lakes. Not quite 20 years later, in 1895, a small, protected reserve called Waterton Lakes Forest Park would be established, and in 1911 Brown would become the first superintendent of it.

Incredibly, by the time Brown arrived to settle by the lakes little more than a decade after his first visit, the enormous North American bison herds had been devastated, reduced from an estimated 60 to 70 million animals in the late 1700s to less than 1,000 on the entire continent. They had been almost annihilated by an uncontrolled commercial slaughter fed by the tremendous appetite for hides and leather used for industrial belting. The process was hastened by a systematic government policy in the United States aimed at wiping out the bison as a method of subduing Native Indian tribes who relied on the huge beasts for every aspect of their livelihood. Combined with an uncontrolled liquor trade and diseases such as smallpox and measles, to which indigenous peoples had no resistance, the mighty Blackfoot Confederacy was brought to its knees, on both sides of the border. In September 1877, Treaty Seven was signed by members of the confederacy at Blackfoot Crossing southeast of Calgary, and the First Nations were moved onto reserves.

With First Nations issues taken care of, the Canadian government began a concerted effort to promote European settlement on the vast plains in an effort to avert any territorial claims by the Americans. Extremely favourable grazing leases were

GLENBOW ARCHIVES NA-678-1

John George "Kootenai" Brown.

LEGEND OF THE WILD WEST

To say Brown became something of a legend is probably an understatement. In his book *60 Years in an Old Cow Town*, Pincher Creek businessman A.L. Freebairn recounted the first time he saw Brown noting, "... he sure was a picturesque-looking old fellow; long hair down over his shoulders, buckskin shirt, moccasins and all the frills." It was a mountain-man image Brown liked to foster. Stories about his life of danger and adventure seemed to include every conceivable escapade that one person could possibly pack into a single lifetime. Brown's reputation for a certain amount of embellishment hasn't helped when it comes to sorting out fact from fiction. From soldier in the British Army in India to gold seeker in the Cariboo to pony express rider in the Dakota Territory, including his capture and subsequent escape from Sitting Bull's warriors, his life was apparently a series of bold, adventurous exploits.

We do know he was a soldier, a buffalo hunter, a whisky trader, a scout, a policeman and a prospector. He even claimed to have known General George Custer and to have declined an invitation to act as a guide for Custer on his ill-fated trek to the Little Bighorn. Following his release from a Montana jail, on a charge of murdering a fellow wolfer, Brown finally headed north to settle by the lakes he called Kootenay Lakes. He eventually became a tireless advocate for the establishment of the park and the protection of its wildlife, working as a fishery officer and ranger and later, in 1911, becoming the park's first superintendent. He took his job seriously, too: at the age of 74 he was still making his rounds on snowshoes, travelling up to 32 km (20 mi.) in −36°C (−33°F) weather. You can visit his gravesite along the west side of Lower Waterton Lake.

offered to encourage ranchers to take up to 100,000 acres at a cost of one cent per acre per year. The unique climate and topography of the area made the Waterton country particularly attractive because the famous chinook winds could generally be counted on to keep the rangelands relatively free of snow each winter. This allowed for cheap, year-round grazing of large cattle herds.

Once the railway arrived at Pincher Creek, farmers inevitably followed. But ranching and farming weren't the only things the land was good for. Would-be settlers and entrepreneurs in search of a quick buck soon learned the region had considerable potential for natural resources such as coal, oil and gas, lumber and even minerals like gold, silver and copper. The Forest Park designation in 1895 provided no protection from exploitation of these resources. Under the 1884 Dominion Lands Act Amendment, such reserves were "without special supervision or protection." They were essentially viewed only as sources of fish and game. (Fish were certainly plentiful. In 1861, British surveyor Charles Wilson recalled a catch of nine dozen fish in the space of four hours!)

The lack of protection resulted in a brief oil boom in 1902 when Rocky Mountain Development Company drilled the first oil well in Western Canada at Oil City near Cameron Lake. (You will pass the marker for this National Historic Site when you drive up the Akamina Parkway to the lake.) Drilling even occurred by Cameron Falls. Thankfully, these ventures had fizzled by 1908.

But that wasn't the end of the threats. In the early 1900s the Waterton Mills set up lumber operations on the northern edge

A WELCOME BLAST OF SPRING IN THE DEPTHS OF WINTER

A chinook is a westerly wind from the Pacific. It scoops up warm, moist air carrying it across the mountains, dropping the moisture, much of it in the form of snow, as it rises and cools. Once over the mountains, the now dry air plunges to the prairies, warming at a rate of about 1°C for every 100 metres of descent. As it blasts out across the plains it melts the snow in its path. The wind tends to funnel through the mountains near Waterton at a higher intensity because of their lower elevation and because the valleys trend from east to west.

On a frigid day in February 1875, Dr. Richard Nevitt, the first surgeon with the North-West Mounted Police in Fort Macleod, 105 km (65 mi.) northeast of Waterton, made this notation in his diary: "Still cold and the snow on the ground about six inches deep. At about 4:30 a strong wind from the west sprang up and in nine minutes the thermometer had risen 32 degrees! From +8°F to +40°F." Two days later he wrote, "You never saw such a change in your life. A few days ago, so white and cold and hard, now so black and brown and wet ..." It is no surprise the First Nations people called the warm wind "snow eater."

of Maskinonge Lake, and mines were also briefly worked in hopes of unearthing a fortune. These schemes too were short-lived. The last big challenge came in 1919, when government engineers raised the spectre of building an irrigation dam across the narrows between the Middle and Upper Waterton Lakes to relieve the severe drought that had plagued the area for several years. Fortunately, public outcry and several wet summers stopped the project that would have forever altered the incredible beauty of the entire region.

Although development pursuits had been effectively stopped, wildlife remained under tremendous pressure. In fact, as late as the 1920s a policy of predator eradication was still being actively pursued. It's hard to believe now, but according to Graham MacDonald in *Where the Mountains Meet the Prairies: A History of Waterton Country*, the list included "puma, wolf, coyote, lynx, bear (if nuisances), eagle, hawk, woodpecker and blue heron (for eating geese eggs)." Not until 1930 would the concept of conservation and the protection of special places such as Waterton be codified by legislation in the National Parks Act. The law recognized the need to set aside parks to "be maintained and made use of so as to leave them unimpaired for the use of future generations." It was a vision that had already been pioneered by Charles Waterton over a century before.

THE HIKE

This one-way hike, which is rated moderately strenuous, is generally done from the trailhead at Cameron Lake eastward to the Waterton townsite. It is possible to do it in reverse, but that converts what would normally be a descent of 1021 m (3,350 ft.) from the Carthew summit to the townsite into a strenuous slog up to the summit from the townsite.

You should plan on being at the summit by late morning or early afternoon. Since thunderstorms tend to roll in later in the day, this should allow you to be over the top and dropping into the sheltered part of the hike if storms threaten. Starting the trek at Cameron Lake makes it easier to reach the summit early and beat any potential weather. The full force of the wind often doesn't develop until later in the morning. Although the wind can be fierce at the top, I have seen days when it is completely calm. Since the summit is entirely exposed, you should never attempt the hike if there are signs of an impending storm. It may become almost impossible to find the trail in fog or snow, so turn back if it looks like you may get caught at the top.

Cameron Lake is at the end of the Akamina Parkway, 16 km (10 mi.) from town. Unless you have access to two vehicles, you will need to organize a shuttle to the lake. Reliable, daily services are offered by Waterton Outdoor Adventures and can be booked in advance. Check **www.hikewaterton.com** for information.

The trail begins on the east side of the lake by the bridge over Cameron Creek. But

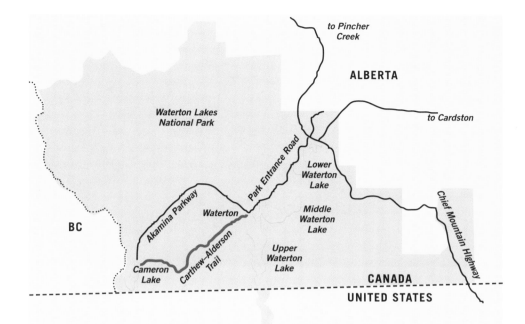

to Pincher
Creek

ALBERTA

Waterton Lakes
National Park

to Cardston

Park Entrance Road

Lower
Waterton
Lake

Akamina Parkway

Waterton

Middle
Waterton
Lake

Chief Mountain Highway

BC

Carthew–Alderson Trail

Upper
Waterton
Lake

Cameron
Lake

CANADA

UNITED STATES

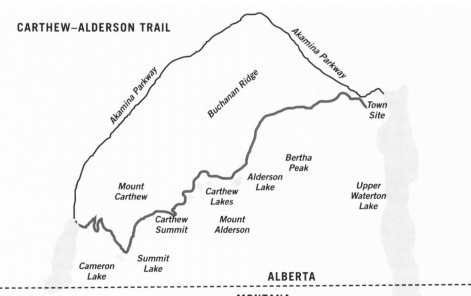

CARTHEW–ALDERSON TRAIL

Akamina Parkway

Akamina Parkway

Buchanan Ridge

Town
Site

Bertha
Peak

Mount
Carthew

Alderson
Lake

Carthew
Lakes

Upper
Waterton
Lake

Carthew
Summit

Mount
Alderson

Cameron
Lake

Summit
Lake

ALBERTA

MONTANA

Cameron Lake reflects the snowy headwall of Mount Custer.

before you head out, be sure to take in the view across the lake to the snowy head-wall of Mount Custer. The mountain was not named after the famous general, but for Henry Custer, a topographer on the United States Northwest Boundary Survey (1857–59). It is actually located in Glacier National Park. In fact, Cameron Lake is one of three in Waterton Lakes National Park that straddle the international boundary. The other two are Crypt Lake and Upper Waterton Lake.

Chapman Peak and Mount Custer rise on the far side of Summit Lake.

Don't miss a chance to try the fancy flush toilets by the inter-pretive kiosk and then cross the bridge to enter the forest. The trail soon begins climbing a series of gradual switchbacks through a lush forest of old-growth subal-pine fir, some of the largest trees in the park. Along the way you will catch brief glimpses of Forum Peak to the west and Mount Custer to the south. After about 3 km (1.9 mi.) the trail tends to level out as it heads through open bits of parkland before reaching the

The view from Carthew Summit, with Lake Wurdeman and Chapman Peak on the left, Lake Nooney and Mount Custer on the far right and Thunderbird Mountain in the distance.

Snow lingers most of the year at the head of the three Carthew Lakes.

shore of tiny Summit Lake. It's a good place to catch your breath before the next ascent and to take in the impressive views of Chapman Peak and Mount Custer rising on the far side. Stunning displays of wildflowers, and if you are lucky, showy beargrass often fill the meadows here.

From Summit Lake the trail forks left to begin the ascent up Carthew Pass to the summit. The trail is a steep traverse where the trees become more stunted, gradually giving way to a barren, wind-swept ridge and red scree slopes. (The distinctive red hue is from the broken argillites of the Kintla Formation.) A series of steep, exposed switchbacks bring you to the top of Carthew Summit where a glorious sea of peaks spreads out in every direction. To the south the brilliant blue of Lake Wurdeman and Lake Nooney sparkle on the flanks of the Hudson Glacier, while Thunderbird Mountain rises in the distance.

Take in the spectacle, but don't linger if there are any signs of storm clouds. From the summit, the trail continues east, descending over more steep scree slopes to reach a glacial basin and the first of the three Carthew Lakes. The startling red of the argillite is very pronounced here, with the barren jagged peaks of Mount Carthew on your left and Mount Alderson on your right. On a clear day, the view beyond the three tiny cirque lakes stretches out in an almost endless vista across the Alberta prairies, far in the distance. Snow commonly lingers by the lakes all year and care must be taken when crossing the snowfields. Proceed slowly, with measured steps,

D. LARRAINE ANDREWS

D. LARRAINE ANDREWS

Chapter 7 – Canada – Waterton Lakes National Park – Carthew–Alderson Trail {215}

D. LARRAINE ANDREWS

The startling red argillite is quite pronounced on the barren peaks of Mount Alderson.

DID YOU KNOW?

Mount Carthew, Carthew Lakes and Carthew Creek were named after William Carthew, a participant in the boundary survey between Alberta and British Columbia in 1913. He was killed in action in the First World War at the Battle of Ypres in 1916. Mount Alderson and Alderson Lake honour Lieutenant General E.A.H. Alderson, commander of the Canadian Expeditionary Force in France during the same war.

Alderson Lake sits at the foot of Mount Alderson and the back side of Bertha Peak.

D. LARRAINE ANDREWS

using your hiking poles for balance and control, or you could easily end up sliding into the frigid lake.

The mountain views tend to capitalize your attention, but don't miss the tiny wildflowers at your feet, clinging bravely to the scree slopes. Keep a lookout for yellow alpine buttercups, snow cinquefoil and the aptly named stinky Jacob's ladder, and try not to step on them! From the summit the trail descends in earnest, skirting the three lakes past an amazing array of wildflowers tucked into the protective nooks and crannies of the rock. Along the way you will also see the stunted, scrubby evergreens called kruppelholz, German for "crippled wood." The trees have been shaped and bent by the extreme wind and weather here. There is a good place to stop for lunch close to the waterfall and out of the wind.

From here the trail drops out of the basin into an alpine valley, descending steeply to Alderson Lake, a turquoise gem at the foot of the sheer cliffs of Mount Alderson.

A short spur goes into the campground by the lake. Otherwise, stay left and follow the trail through the welcome shade of the pine, spruce and Douglas fir of the forested valley in a steady descent between Buchanan Ridge and Bertha Peak. Depending on the season, you may be lucky enough to spot lady's slipper orchids and trailing purple clematis in the forest undergrowth. Views of Upper Waterton Lake and Vimy Peak are revealed as you continue along the trail, which ends a few steps south of Cameron Falls. Watch for scratch posts placed strategically along portions of the trail. The posts are there because the area is frequented by bears, so be sure to make some noise and remain vigilant.

YOU CAN SCRATCH YOUR OWN BACK!

Along many of the trails you will see trees with barbed wire attached to them. These are scratch posts frequented by bears in the park. The hair captured on the wire is analyzed for DNA to estimate the bear population in the Waterton region. We saw many scratch posts with hair on them, but thankfully no bears!

D. LARRAINE ANDREWS

Scratch posts capture bear hair for DNA analysis.

HOW TO DO THE HIKE

Since the Carthew–Alderson Trail is a one-way hike beginning at Cameron Lake and ending at the Waterton townsite, you will require transportation to the trailhead unless you have access to two vehicles. Reliable, regular daily shuttles are available through Waterton Outdoor Adventures and should be booked in advance during the peak summer season. (See details below.)

If you would like to join an organized day hike, complete with the services of an interpretive guide, check out Waterton Outdoor Adventures at **www.hikewaterton.com**. Located in the Tamarack Outdoor Outfitters store on Mount View Road, they offer the Carthew–Alderson Trail as well as other full- and half-day options throughout the park. Or they will customize a trip for you. The company, which is one of the largest independent outdoor retailers in Alberta, is run by the Baker family. Now in their sixth generation, they have been a continuous and respected part of the business community in Waterton for over 90 years. The service here is outstanding, with very knowledgeable, friendly guides, many of whom have grown up hiking in the park and know it intimately. I routinely use their services to hike on my own with a guide, especially when I want the freedom of being able to stop for good photo shoots without holding up a larger group, but still have the security of hiking with a reliable buddy.

Waterton is very hiker-friendly with almost 225 km (140 mi.) of well-marked, established trails. If you have your own group and want to make your own plans, the best starting place for information is the Parks Canada website, at **www.pc.gc.ca/waterton**.

There are few independent tour operators who offer hiking in the park. Because of Waterton's small size and relatively remote location, most focus their attention on the much larger Glacier National Park to the south.

Timberline Adventures, **www.timbertours.com**, is a highly reputable operator that offers a combination hiking tour of both parks. Although I have not taken this particular trip with Timberline, I have travelled all over the United States with this company and have never been disappointed. They have been in business for over 30 years, which speaks volumes about how they do business. The trips are all-inclusive, with a high standard of accommodation, safety and personal service. All hikes include two knowledgeable guides. Their six-day Glacier–Waterton trips take in three Waterton hikes, including Carthew–Alderson, before heading back to Glacier for the remainder of the trip.

QUITE A LADY

Bertha Peak, Lake and Falls are the only park features named after a woman – Ruby Ridge is named for its colour. Bertha's last name was never recorded but stories abound about who she was and the nature of her profession. She is claimed to have been everything from a bootlegger to a counterfeiter to the niece of a Pincher Creek postmaster.

HOW DO YOU SAY THAT?

Glacially formed landscapes are often described with a confusing array of terms. Although there are no longer any glaciers in Waterton, their slow, grinding movements over countless millennia have helped sculpt many of the distinctive landforms that make the national park such a visual feast. Here are a few obvious examples:

- alluvial fans – are deposits of gravel and silt from glacial meltwater, formed over thousands of years. There are two such fans in the park. The site of the town is actually a fan formed by deposits from Cameron Creek. The Blakiston Fan, created by Blakiston Creek, is the largest in the park. It has grown to the point where it bisects what was once one large lake, to form the Lower and Middle Waterton Lakes. Both fans are clearly obvious from the viewpoint on Bear's Hump. (See more information on this hike in the "Consider this" section below.)
- arête – a sharp mountain ridge formed where two adjacent glacial valleys meet. Citadel Peaks, which dominate almost any view of Upper Waterton Lake, are a superb illustration of this formation.
- cirque – a bowl-shaped hollow carved by a glacier, often visible at the head of a valley or on a mountainside. A good example is Cameron Lake, located at the trailhead for the Carthew–Alderson hike.
- col – a pass between two mountain peaks, such as that between Mount Carthew and Mount Alderson.
- esker – a ridge of glacial debris formed by deposits left by a stream running beneath a former glacier or ice sheet. The bison paddock, to the north of the park entrance, provides a fine example.
- hanging valley – a side valley, gouged by the action of a smaller glacier, joining a main glacially carved valley at a high level. The valley at Upper Rowe Lake is a good example.
- kame – the Prince of Wales Hotel sits on a kame, which is a hill comprised of sand and gravel left by a glacier.
- moraine – a ridge of rock debris deposited by a glacier. Such a ridge actually forms a natural dam that holds Alderson Lake.
- tarn – a mountain lake or pool formed in a cirque that has been excavated by a glacier. Tarns are often formed in a descending string of bowls, such as the three Carthew lakes. Such formations are sometimes called paternoster lakes because they resemble rosary beads.
- U-shaped valley – a vale gouged out by a glacier moving downhill, such as the Upper Waterton valley. In fact, the scouring motion of the glacier made Upper Waterton Lake the deepest in the Canadian Rockies, at 148 m (486 ft.).

CONSIDER THIS: BEFORE OR AFTER THE HIKE

The compact size of Waterton Park makes it relatively easy to see many of the highlights in a fairly short time frame. Here are some I would include in the "don't miss" category.

Additional hikes

Bear's Hump: At 1.4 km (0.9 mi.) one way, this is the shortest and most popular hike in the park. It is also rated as one of the steepest short hikes in the Canadian Rockies. (The locals called it the Pimple before the trail was built to the top.) You will be amply rewarded for your efforts with sweeping views south down Upper Waterton Lake. At your feet the alluvial fan on which the townsite sits is clearly visible.

Don't forget to turn around – the Prince of Wales Hotel perches on the hill above the narrow strait called the Bosporus connecting Middle and Upper Waterton Lakes, while one of the best examples of the transition of mountains to prairies stretches to the north.

The trailhead starts directly behind the Waterton Visitor Centre, located on the park entrance road. The wind can be extreme up here, so be cautious and don't venture out if it's blowing too strong. Gusts can easily carry you over the edge.

The view south from Bear's Hump.

PAT HUGHES

The view north from Bear's Hump, where the mountains meet the prairies.

Upper Rowe Lakes via Rowe Meadows: At 6.3 km (3.9 mi.) one way, this route to the upper lakes is rated a strenuous climb, with an elevation gain of 622 m (2,040 ft.). If you time it right, the meadows are a veritable mecca of wildflowers, some of the best

in the park. But you can almost always expect to encounter fine displays in the many small, sunlit, grassy areas you will pass throughout the hike. The trail briefly follows Rowe Creek before climbing through lodgepole pines to an avalanche slope with good views of Mount Rowe and Mount Lineham. Be sure to take the short spur trail to Lower Rowe Lake, and then continue on to cross the grassy bowl of the meadows.

Rowe Meadows with Mount Lineham in the background.

Upper Rowe Lake with Mount Rowe on the left.

From here it's a sharp climb up a series of switchbacks to Upper Rowe Lake and its wonderful subalpine larch. Watch for showy exhibitions of beargrass all the way. The trailhead starts at the pullout located 10.7 km (6.6 mi.) up the Akamina Parkway from the townsite.

International Peace Park Hike: This route leaves from the Bertha Lake trailhead, south of Cameron Falls. The hikes are run jointly during the summer by a Glacier Park

THE GRAND LADY OF THE LAKE

The *Lethbridge Herald* called her "… without doubt, the finest in the West." First launched in June 1928, MV *International* was the brainchild of Louis Hill, head of the Great Northern Railway. Hill saw her as the perfect complement to the magnificent Prince of Wales Hotel, which had opened the year before. Now hotel patrons could enjoy boating excursions along Upper Waterton Lake in comfort while taking in the stunning scenery. Suitable attire was expected – women wore dresses, hats and gloves, while the men sported suits and ties – although the rules were relaxed for guests boarding at Goat Haunt after a trail ride of several days. A trip on the Grand Lady of the Lake remains a Waterton tradition, but thankfully you can now leave the dress, gloves, suit and tie at home.

MV International.

ranger and a Waterton Park interpreter and are limited to 35 people. The free hike follows the trail along the shores of Upper Waterton Lake to Goat Haunt, Montana, in Glacier National Park, for a distance of 13 km (8 mi.). Hikers then return to Waterton by boat. Since you are crossing the international boundary during the hike, you will need official government-issued photo identification such as a passport. Even if you don't take the hike, the boat trip is definitely a highlight of any trip to Waterton.

Scenic drives

Red Rock Parkway follows the Blakiston Valley and part of the ancient buffalo trail used by First Nations on their hunting forays into the region. The road runs for 15 km (9 mi.) over rolling prairie to Red Rock Canyon and offers an excellent visual example of "where the mountains meet the prairie." Visitors can take the loop trail or walk to the falls to see the striking red and green argillite rocks that are clearly visible along the canyon walls. (The red rocks contain oxidized iron, while the iron in the green rocks has not oxidized.)

COLLEEN F. BAINS

The stunning red argillite rocks of Red Rock Canyon.

Buffalo Paddock Drive, just north of the park entrance. In addition to the chance to see a small herd of bison, this circle route through the paddock offers outstanding views of Waterton's glacial landscape. But don't get out of your car!

ARE YOU READY TO EAT?

For such a small place, the quality of the eating establishments here is generally quite high. The short season tends to push the prices up, but you can usually count on a decent meal that isn't your typical fast-food fare. In fact, other than the ubiquitous Subway, there are no fast-food joints in the park – just a first-rate selection of mainly family owned businesses serving good food. Consider taking the short drive north of the park on Highway 6 to the tiny hamlet of Twin Butte (the road separates the two

The iconic Prince of Wales Hotel reflected in the waters of Emerald Bay.

WALTER DANYLAK

PRINCE OF THE PARK

Designated a National Historic Site in 1993 in recognition of its unique architectural style and its contribution to mountain tourism, the Prince of Wales Hotel is actually a little piece of American real estate in the middle of a Canadian national park. Constructed during one of the windiest and snowiest winters on record, the hotel was established by the Great Northern Railway of the US as part of their network of chalets and grand tourist hotels in Glacier National Park in Montana. The Canadian contractors, Doug Oland and James Scott, faced monumental construction challenges during the winter of 1926 to 1927. Not only was there 4.2 m (14 ft.) of snow, but hurricane-force winds actually shifted the partially completed east and west wings almost 8 cm (3 in.) out of plumb during one particularly memorable storm in December. Horse-powered winches were used to pull them back into line. Oland later recalled finding the floor of his office covered with stones that had been "shot" through the windows like bullets from the force of the wind. Little wonder the hotel earned the nickname "Prince of Gales."

The mastermind for the unlikely project was Louis Hill, chairman of the Great Northern, who selected the site in 1913 as he stood on the windy knoll overlooking Upper Waterton Lake. Hill understood immediately the draw of the dramatic scenery. But the real draw at the time was the fact that tourists could drink legally in Alberta while Prohibition in the United States had effectively shut down the liquor trade since 1919. For the tidy sum of $1,000 (about $13,000 today), tourists could see the Rocky Mountain wilderness in luxury, arriving in East or West Glacier by train and travelling by boat, bus and horse between hotels. Once the Prince of Wales opened in 1927 and MV *International* began shuttling patrons arriving on horseback at Goat Haunt up the Lake to Waterton in 1928, well-heeled travellers could tour in style all the way to the princely hotel on the hill. Ironically, the hotel was opened in 1927 but effectively became outdated in 1933 with the repeal of Prohibition in the United States. Despite this setback, along with fires, floods and closures during the Great Depression and the Second World War, the hotel has managed to survive as one of the icons of the park.

buttes that give the place its name) and the Twin Butte Country General Store and Restaurant. You will have to compete with the locals for a table (usually a good sign), but the food is well worth the wait and the place is usually hopping with live entertainment during the summer months.

The Bayshore Inn Resort & Spa, located on the shores of Upper Waterton Lake, offers elegant dining with fine lake views, but one of the most famous vistas of the park is framed by the floor to ceiling windows of the iconic Prince of Wales Hotel.

Perched high on the hill overlooking the town and the lake, you can enjoy fine dining with what is arguably one of the most spectacular mountain views anywhere in the world. Dinner here will set you back a fair sum, but there is always the option of stopping in for the traditional English afternoon tea in the lobby, where you can linger over your finger sandwiches and dainties, taking in the view with the added bonus of no wind.

Hygiene standards are high and there should be no concerns about food establishments in the park.

Tipping is expected. Normally at least 15 per cent of the bill would be considered reasonable.

Vegetarians: Although there are no strictly vegetarian restaurants in the park, most will offer several options.

INTERNET RESOURCES

www.pc.gc.ca/waterton is the official Parks Canada website for Waterton Lakes National Park.

www.hikewaterton.com lists everything you need to know about hiking and shuttle services in Waterton with Waterton Outdoor Adventures.

www.mywaterton.ca provides extensive impartial information about the park, including accommodations and events.

www.watertonwildflowers.com is the official website for the annual ten-day Waterton Wildflower Festival.

www.wnha.ca, by the Waterton Natural History Association, includes good information on books, events and camping reservations at the Association's campground east of the park.

www.chinookcountry.com, the official website of the Chinook Country Tourist Association, provides good information on the southwest region of Alberta.

www.nps.gov/glac is the National Park Service website for Glacier National Park in Montana, part of the Waterton–Glacier International Peace Park.

www.glacierparkinc.com is the concessionaire for Glacier National Park, with information on accommodations, hiking and transportation in the park, including the interpark shuttle service.

RECOMMENDED READING

60 Years in an Old Cow Town – A.L. Freebairn – stories and recollections of the Pincher Creek area written by an authentic old timer.

Charles Waterton, Traveller and Conservationist – Julia Blackburn – one of several biographies of the unusual man whose name graces this famous park.

© FOTOSEARCH.COM

Plains bison have a distinctive shoulder hump.

FAUNA FACTS: BISON AREN'T BUFFALO

North American bison are not buffalo. Unfortunately the name stuck after early explorers began using it. The plains bison found here have a unique shoulder hump that distinguishes them from buffalo that are native to Africa and Asia. To the First Nations they were the equivalent of a "walking Walmart." Not only were the flesh, fat and bone marrow major sources of food, the bones were fashioned into tools or bows, while the hides were used for everything from blankets to caps, moccasins and leggings. Hides were also used to cover tipis and lodges or stretched across a wooden frame and fashioned into ceremonial drums. The carcass provided material for a long list of things such as whistles, ropes and glue. Little wonder the bison were regarded with reverence, playing a major role in the mythology, art and songs of prairie First Nations culture.

Grizzly Country – Andy Russell – by a lifelong resident, rancher, guide, conservationist and prolific author (also by Russell, *Trails of a Wilderness Wanderer* and *Memoirs of a Mountain Man*).

High on a Windy Hill: The Story of the Prince of Wales Hotel – Ray Djuff – a fascinating history of the hotel written by a former employee; includes a good bibliography.

Hiking Glacier and Waterton Lakes National Parks: a Falcon Guide – Erik Molvar – a very comprehensive guide to both parks with excellent maps and hike descriptions.

Kootenai Brown: His Life and Times – William Rodney – the definitive and highly readable story of the park's colourful first superintendent, including a good bibliography.

MV International – Chris Morrison and Ray Djuff – the story of the "grand lady" of Waterton Lakes.

Place Names of Glacier National Park – Jack Holterman – the stories behind 663 geographic names in Glacier National Park and Waterton Lakes National Park.

The Palliser Expedition: An Account of John Palliser's British North American Exploring Expedition 1857–1860 – Irene M. Spry – a detailed account of the expedition, based on the original journals.

Waterton and Glacier in a Snap: Fast Facts and Titillating Trivia – Ray Djuff and Chris Morrison – exactly what it says, full of interesting tidbits and facts about both parks.

Where the Mountains Meet the Prairies: A History of Waterton Country – Graham A. MacDonald – written by an historian for Parks Canada, with good maps, archival photographs and a comprehensive bibliography.

CHAPTER 8 – CANADA/UNITED STATES – KLONDIKE GOLD RUSH INTERNATIONAL HISTORICAL PARK – CHILKOOT TRAIL

{ *Chilkoot after the First Nations tribe of the same name. The Chilkoot Pass was called "Kwatese" by the Tagish, meaning "over the mountain."* }

I have roughed it for the past 15 years in Siberia, in Borneo and in Chinese Tartary, but I can safely describe that climb over the Chilkoot as the severest physical experience of my life.

—HARRY DEWINDT, 1896

* HIKING RULE 8: Always carry a roll of duct tape. In a pinch, it will fix practically anything.

WHERE IN THE WORLD?

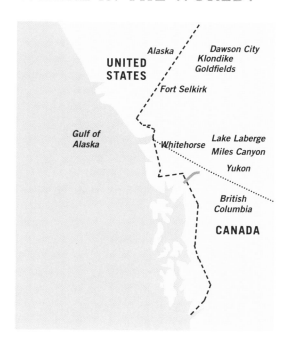

CLAIM TO FAME

The Chilkoot Trail retraces the route followed by the stampeders of the Klondike Gold Rush as they struggled over the Chilkoot Pass in the depths of the winter of 1897 to 1898. They were driven by dreams of fabulous wealth reported to be coming from the gold fields around Dawson City, Yukon. (Once over the pass, stampeders faced another 805 km (500 mi.) of rivers and lakes to navigate before they reached Dawson City.) Even though the trail was only used for one winter, it has given us iconic images of the gold rush that continue to capture the imagination. The historical significance of the trail was recognized by the United States in 1976 with the establishment of the Klondike Gold Rush National Historical Park and by the Canadian government in 1993 as the Chilkoot Trail National Historic Site. Since 1998 both countries have officially designated the Chilkoot Trail as part of the Klondike Gold Rush International Historical Park. The trail is jointly operated by Parks Canada and the US National Parks Service.

WHAT WILL I SEE?

SYLVIA FOWLER

Coastal rainforest on the American side of the summit.

Alpine tundra at Crater Lake on the Canadian side of the summit. Note artifacts left on the trail by the stampeders during the Klondike Gold Rush.

BOBBIE-LYNNE BROCK

HIKE PROFILE

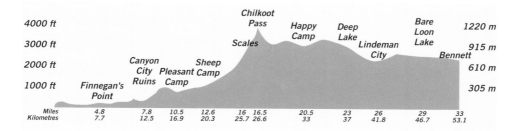

The trail covers a distance of 53 km (33 mi.) rising 1080 m (3,543 ft.) from the ocean at the Dyea, Alaska, trailhead through coastal rainforest, high alpine tundra and boreal forest. Much of the climb occurs on the "pass day" between Sheep Camp and the summit, where the trail rises close to 800 m (about 2,625 ft.) over a distance of about 6 km (3.7 mi.). Hikers cross into Canada at the summit. From the pass, the trail descends to an altitude of just over 610 m (2,000 ft.) at Bennett Lake, British Columbia.

Hazards

This is a physically challenging route that should not be undertaken unless you are a fit and experienced hiker and backpacker. You must be prepared to deal with steep, rocky, uneven terrain and the potential for walking in deep mud, snow, fog and severe wind or rain, even in the middle of summer. Avalanche hazard continues until mid-July. Hypothermia, especially at the top of the pass, is a distinct possibility if you are not properly equipped with adequate clothing and food. This is a potentially life-threatening condition where the body begins losing heat from its core if you get too wet and cold. Signs include uncontrolled shivering and confusion. If anyone in your group exhibits these symptoms, it is essential to stop, warm up and refuel before continuing. The trail is also home to black and grizzly bears. Bear caches and bear poles for stowing food and other attractants such as toothpaste are provided at the campgrounds, but you will need to bring your own rope (9 m, or 30 ft.) to use the bear poles.

The essentials

Getting there: The majority of outfitters leave from Whitehorse, Yukon. The city is serviced with regular flights from Vancouver, Calgary and Edmonton by Air Canada and Air North. If you are planning the hike on your own, you will need to arrange your own transport to the trailhead at Dyea, Alaska, and from the end of the trail at Bennett Lake in British Columbia. The trailhead is accessible through Skagway, Alaska, which can be reached by road from Whitehorse via personal or rented vehicle or summer bus service. Ferry and air connections to Skagway are also available. From Bennett Lake the only alternatives are via floatplane to Whitehorse or by train to Carcross, Yukon; Fraser, BC; or Skagway. (See more-detailed information in the "How to do the hike" section.)

Currency: United States dollar, or USD, or US$. US$1 = 100 cents. Canadian dollar, or CAD, or C$. C$1 = 100 cents. For current exchange rates, check out **www.oanda.com.**

Special gear: Make sure you have good, sturdy, waterproof hiking boots that are well broken in. Hiking poles are highly recommended, although Parks Canada suggests poles be used only on snowfields or where you need them for safety reasons, in order to reduce erosion on the trail. The hike can only be done by backpacking, which means you will need to carry all your clothing as well as food, cooking utensils, water filtration equipment, tent and sleeping bag. Several reputable outfitters do organized trips on the Chilkoot Trail, so you will be able to rely on their expertise when it comes to gear lists. Outfitters will normally supply all the food, cooking gear, tents and other equipment, while you will be responsible for providing your own clothing, eating bowl, sleeping pad and sleeping bag. You will need a backpack with a minimum capacity of 60 litres, and be prepared to carry a weight of at least 16 kg (35 lb.). Food and tents will normally be split among group members, so you can usually figure on carrying at least 4.5 kg (10 lb.) of shared supplies in addition to your personal gear.

If you are planning on arranging the hike with your own group, the entire logistics of the expedition are then your responsibility. You should be an experienced backpacker to undertake this trip on your own. It is a demanding hike through backcountry wilderness that will test your mettle. You must be equipped with appropriate emergency first aid training and supplies, since you will not have access to immediate assistance on most portions of the trail. Anyone attempting the hike in early June must be prepared with winter travel equipment such as snowshoes, crampons and an ice axe. (See the "Recommended reading" and "Internet resources" sections for more detailed information sources on undertaking the hike with your own group.)

PROPRIETY TRUMPS COMMON SENSE

Ladies, as we hike in our quick-dry, moisture-wicking, lightweight, high-tech gear, spare a thought for the women who crossed the trail during the gold rush. No matter the conditions they faced, they were still expected to maintain the proprieties of the day – trousers were out of the question. Consider the "outing costume" worn by Martha Purdy on her climb over the pass. Imagine what it must have weighed! She describes it as follows: "It was made of heavily ribbed … corduroy velvet with a skirt of shockingly immodest length (it actually showed my ankles), with five yards around the bottom … It had a Norfolk jacket with many pleats, a blouse with a high, stiff collar almost to my ears, and a pair of voluminous brown silk bloomers, which came below the knee. As the day advanced the trail became steeper, the air warmer and footholds without support impossible. I cursed my hot, high … collar, my tight, heavily boned corsets, my long corduroy skirt, my full bloomers which I had to hitch up with every step." Martha, whose first marriage had disintegrated on the trip north, was actually pregnant when she did that climb but didn't know it yet. She later married George Black. He was a prominent lawyer who served as territorial commissioner and member of Parliament, a position she assumed when George became ill. She lived in the Yukon until her death in 1957 at the age of 91.

HIKE OVERVIEW

Almost all hikers travel south to north, from Dyea, Alaska, to Bennett Lake, British Columbia, following the original route of the stampeders on their way to the Klondike gold fields near Dawson City. Since most weather systems blow in from the coast, hiking in this direction means driving rain and strong wind will tend to be at your back. It also avoids the need to descend from the pass to the scales, a section that is extremely treacherous and steep. There is much greater threat of injury if you are descending rather than climbing this section. That said, our group encountered two runners who not only completed the entire trail in a day but also did it in reverse, from north to south. So much for the warnings!

From the trailhead at Dyea to Sheep Camp, the trail passes through lush coastal rainforest filled with western hemlock, western red cedar, Sitka spruce and abundant mosses and lichens. Along the way, expect breathtaking breakout views (on clear days) and the chance to visit the ruins at Canyon City, with its collection of gold rush artifacts. From Sheep Camp, hikers face the challenging scramble over the Chilkoot Pass, beginning with the climb up the Long Hill to the Scales. From here it is a hard slog up the boulders of the Golden Stairs to the summit. Ahead lies rocky, undulating terrain to Happy Camp. The trail enters the boreal forest zone, passing several lakes and more outstanding scenery as it gradually descends to the end of the trek at Bennett Lake.

Access to the track is highly regulated, with a total of 50 hikers per day permitted to cross the border into Canada on the Chilkoot Trail. A daily total of 42 reservations is taken, leaving eight spots for walk-ins. The popularity of the trail makes it essential to book well in advance. "US only" hikers are allowed to use the trail for day or overnight hiking, but overnight hikers must register in order to ensure a spot at a designated campground. Hikers found without the proper permit are subject to fines and may be turned back.

Camping is allowed only in official campgrounds, and open fires are prohibited. Both the US and the Canadian parts of the trail follow a strict "leave-no-trace" policy, requiring you to pack out everything you pack in. Each jurisdiction takes a slightly different approach to the disposal of grey wastewater. On the US side it may be disposed of in the fastest part of the river, while Canadian regulations require the use of the grey-water disposal pits provided in the campgrounds.

Drinking and cooking water needs to be purified. Toilets are provided at the campgrounds, and the Canadians (bless them) even provide toilet paper.

While some parts of the hike are rated easy to moderate, don't fool yourself. This is a demanding hike and you need to be prepared mentally and physically for everything the weather can throw at you and then some. The possibility of encountering severe conditions, including snow, sleet, hail, driving rain, high winds and heavy fog at any time of the summer, especially above treeline, cannot be discounted.

BOBBIE-LYNNE BROCK

All the comforts of home at the Canadian summit, including toilet paper!

SYLVIA FOWLER

Grey-water disposal pits must be used on the Canadian portion of the trail.

Expect snow, fog and cold on the climb to the summit.

On pass day, it is not uncommon for hikers to take 12 hours to climb the summit from Sheep Camp and descend to Happy Camp, a distance of only 12.7 km (7.9 mi.).

Why would I want to?

A fair question, based on those previous comments! I admit I waffled about doing this hike for a couple of years before I finally took the plunge. Many years ago I had read *Klondike*, Pierre Berton's definitive history of the gold rush. I was always intrigued by the possibility of actually hiking in the footsteps of the stampeders, with the chance to see the physical remnants of their hopes and dreams abandoned on the trail as they faced the gruelling reality of the 45 degree climb to the summit. (These artifacts are now protected by law and disturbing them is a crime on both sides of the border.)

The enormity of the task that was confronted and met by thousands of men and women in their headlong quest for wealth and a better life becomes very real as you struggle against the forces of gravity from the Scales up the Golden Stairs to the top of the pass. This is real, living history, recreated with every step.

Artifacts on the trail to Lindeman Lake.

But the unique history is only part of the story. In a mere 53 km (33 mi.) hikers pass from coastal rainforest to high alpine tundra to boreal forest, crossing an area of spectacular natural beauty and diversity. Add to that the sense of personal accomplishment in successfully meeting the physical and mental challenges of the trail and it becomes obvious why hikers from around the world travel here each year.

In the end I decided that if a pregnant Martha Purdy could climb that pass in the middle of winter, in her velvet skirt, silk bloomers and boned corsets, then I could certainly do it in the middle of the summer with all my lightweight, high-tech gear!

When to go

In theory, the trail can be hiked from early June to late September, but the peak season is generally from mid-July to mid-August, when the trail can be snow free and the daylight hours are long. (Our group crossed at the beginning of August and encountered large snow patches at the top.) Significant snow conditions and avalanche hazard can persist into mid-July. The trail is generally snow free later in August and into September, but daylight is shorter and the weather wetter. Patrol staff on both sides of the pass leave the trail in early September, so you are on your own after that.

What's the story?

> *At 3 o'clock this morning the steamship* Portland, *from St. Michael for*
> *Seattle, passed up the sound with more than a ton of solid gold on board*
> *and 68 passengers. In the captain's office are three chests and a large safe*
> *filled with precious nuggets … from the size of a pea to a guinea egg.*

—The Seattle *Post-Intelligencer*, July 19, 1897

A few days earlier the *Excelsior* had docked in San Francisco, disgorging a scruffy collection of thin, dishevelled miners, their luggage filled to the bursting, not with clothes, but with gold. Within days, according to Pierre Berton, who has written extensively about the Klondike gold rush, "a kind of mass lunacy had seized the continent."

As the news spread like wildfire around the world, people of every description left their jobs, their homes and their families in search of the promise of fabulous wealth somewhere in the mythical place called the Klondike. Many had no clear idea of where that was or how to get there, but the lure of gold was irresistible. They certainly had no idea at all of the extreme hardships they would face on their journey to the fabled gold fields.

By a fluke of history, the wild stories of discovery came in the midst of a period of severe economic depression, when despair and a sense of brooding hopelessness about the future was suddenly turned on its head by the prospect of striking it rich. This odd coincidence of timing meant the story was never just about experienced miners. The frenzy soon spread to the common person desperate to share the wealth. And so it is estimated that as many as one million people made plans to go to the Klondike. Of these, about 100,000 actually headed north, with an estimated 30,000 making the gruelling trek over the Chilkoot Pass.

Miners had been crossing the Coast Mountains in search of gold well before the big find that started the frenzy. On August 16, 1896, a native Tagish/Tlingit named James "Skookum Jim" Mason, his brother-in-law George Carmack and his nephew Dawson Charlie had discovered gold on a tributary of the Yukon River that would become known as Bonanza Creek. (One version credits Carmack's wife, Kate, who supposedly found gold while doing George's washing.)

Geographic isolation meant the news didn't reach the mainstream media until the arrival of the gold-laden ships in San Francisco and Seattle in July 1897, almost a year later. What the reports failed to say was that the entire creek and its neighbouring tributaries had all been staked within months of the original discovery.

But why let a few minor details stand in the way of a good story? The prospect of "mining the miners" was just too good to be true as people lined up to spend their money. By February 1898 the North-West Mounted Police was requiring everyone to bring enough provisions to last a year before they could enter Canada (at the top of the pass). This equated to about a ton of goods that merchants happily supplied to Klondike hopefuls.

Thanks to heavy promotion by the Seattle Chamber of Commerce, almost 75 per cent of the stampeders came through that city on their way north, creating a bonanza for merchants. But many other port cities also shared in the lucrative trade, including Vancouver and Victoria, Portland and San Francisco.

No scheme seemed too lunatic, says Berton, to part willing believers from their money. One enterprising promoter claimed to have trained gophers to dig for the elusive treasure, while others said they would be able to find the golden treasure by consulting crystal balls. One group of 500 hopeful widows actually chartered a steamer to head north in search of rich husbands. Leaving from New York, they rounded the Horn and made it to Seattle before they ran out of money and were forced to abandon their dreams.

No matter that winter was fast approaching. That fall every vessel capable of floating to Alaska was filled to the brim with stampeders. Ships headed to the towns of Skagway or Dyea, which had sprung up almost overnight on the end of the Lynn Canal. Here the travellers had two choices. From Skagway they could cross the lower but longer trail over White Pass, or from Dyea the steeper but shorter Chilkoot Trail.

The majority of stampeders opted for the shorter Chilkoot route. But imagine their dismay when they reached the tidal flats at Dyea only to discover there was no wharf on which to unload their supplies. Wilson Mizner described the chaos in December 1897 as arrivals were "almost pushed off into waiting scows, rafts and rowboats. Horses,

DEAD HORSE TRAIL

At first, many stampeders opted for the White Pass Trail. They started out with packhorses, but it soon became evident that this plan wasn't a good one. The White Pass Trail was far more rugged and by September had become an impassable quagmire of mud and sinkholes, forcing it to be closed down for repairs. Horses were pushed unmercifully by their owners until they dropped in their tracks and were "trampled into porridge." Jack London, who made his fortune writing about the Klondike, describes it this way in his short story, "Which Make Men Remember":

As many as 3,000 horses died on the trail like mosquitoes in the first frost, and from Skagway to Bennett they rotted in heaps … men shot them, worked them to death, and when they were gone, went back to the beach and bought more … Their hearts turned to stone – those which did not break – and they became beasts, the men on the Dead Horse Trail.

The harbour and freight yards at Dyea, Alaska, about 1898.

cattle and dogs were run or pitched overboard to swim for shore, and vast amounts of freight … was [sic] eventually piled on a beach already crowded with the possessions of other arrivals."

Those who could not afford to pay someone to move their goods were forced to race against the incoming tide. For many it marked an early end to the adventure as the sea destroyed their dry supplies of flour, sugar, baking soda and oatmeal. One man recounts, "We saw grown men sit down and cry when they failed to beat the tide."

Before the flood of Klondikers arrived on the shore of Dyea, the native coastal Tlingit had established an extensive and lucrative fur trading network with tribes in the interior. They jealously guarded access to their trade routes, including the Chilkoot Trail. By 1880 the Tlingit agreed to allow miners through as long as they did not to interfere with the fur trade and paid Tlingit guides a fee for packing their gear over the pass. But the monopoly could not withstand the juggernaut of the gold rush and they eventually lost control of the pass and the packing business as enterprising businessmen moved in to build tramways and railroads to move the huge amounts of freight. By May 1898 there were five tramways operating on the trail.

For those who managed to safely unload their goods and head up the trail, the awful reality of what lay ahead soon began to sink in. Along the trail, trekkers before them had abandoned anything not essential for survival. Not only did they face steep, snow-filled canyons and rivers of mud, but they were in constant danger of avalanche. On Palm Sunday, April 3, 1898, a massive snowslide swept down, killing close to 70 stampeders. Even today, the risk of avalanche remains one of the most dangerous threats to hikers on the trail each spring.

But it had all been a cakewalk compared to what came next as they gathered at the Scales to make the final 45 degree climb up the Golden Stairs – 1,500 steps carved out of the ice, with a single rope to grab to keep from slipping back. Each person was required to have enough supplies to last a year, or about a ton (907 kg). This meant they didn't just make the trip once, but close to 40 times, hauling at least 23 kg (50 lb.) each time! Depending on the weather, it could take up to three months for one man to get his supplies to the top.

The winter of 1897 to 1898 saw 21 m (70 ft.) of snowfall at the summit. It meant supplies were constantly buried beneath mountains of snow, forcing men to dig for dozens of feet to find their goods. Many men agreed the crossing was the hardest undertaking of their life.

Boundary disputes had festered between the United States and Canada for years but the gold rush brought the issue to a head as both sides claimed the area. Finally, in February 1898, the NWMP established the border at the summit. Setting up their Maxim machine gun, they began collecting customs duties and ensuring the prospectors met the "one ton rule" to prevent starvation.

THREE STOREYS IN THREE DAYS

Located at the mouth of the Taiya River, the little settlement of Dyea took the full brunt of the stampeder wave as 30,000 to 40,000 people passed through during the winter of 1897 to 1898. From fewer than 1,000 inhabitants in the summer, it grew to an estimated 8,000 by May 1898, full of hotels, restaurants and bars plus a wide array of other thriving businesses. One builder from Vancouver describes one of his jobs as follows: "One day I got an order for the building of a three-storey hotel of about forty rooms, with dining room and barroom, all furnished and the building heated throughout, the keys to be turned over to the owner in three days. I did it!" It's probably safe to say there wasn't much in the way of building inspection going on!

A long line of stampeders snakes up the pass from the Scales to the summit. Note the men sliding back down on the right to take another load up.

THE CHILKOOT LOCKSTEP

The line of stampeders crept up the pass in a constant, unbroken motion that came to be called the Chilkoot lockstep, as men were bent double under the weight of their loads. Step out of line for a moment's rest and it could take hours to get back in. Jack London, who made the crossing in August 1897, later wrote about the ordeal in *A Daughter of the Snows*:

> *Men who had never carried more than parcels in all their lives had now become bearers of burdens. They no longer walked upright under the sun, but stooped the body forward and bowed the head to the earth ... They staggered beneath the unwonted effort, and legs became drunken with weariness ...*

Once over the pass, stampeders still faced the trek to Bennett Lake but it was downhill all the way from here. Locked in by winter's icy grip, the "greatest tent city in the world" sprouted on the lakeshore. There were close to 30,000 people camped

*Bennett Lake, with a motley assortment of boats, scows,
barges. The tent city is in the background.*

here, but they weren't just sitting around. They were stripping the land bare of every tree in sight and feverishly cobbling together what Berton describes as "history's strangest armada – 7,000 homemade boats, fashioned from green lumber," designed to take them to the Promised Land. Once the ice melted, they faced 805 km (500 mi.) of rivers and lakes before they finally arrived at Dawson City, the gateway to the gold fields.

Some had no idea how to build or sail a boat. In May 1898, Harley Tuck recalled, "Our neighbor who is going alone had built a boat that was more like a floating coffin ... [He] loaded his stuff in and pushed out to see how it would float. It turned bottom up and spilled his goods into about four feet of water." Some weren't this lucky. Despite the efforts of superintendent Sam Steele and his NWMP to save lives with checkpoints and boat registrations, many were lost. On May 29, 1898, the ice finally broke and the strange flotilla set sail. Ahead lay the treacherous rapids at Whitehorse and Five Fingers, but at least they were going downriver!

Within a year, the frenetic race over the pass had come to an end. The completion of the White Pass & Yukon Route Railroad from Skagway to Bennett Lake in the

GLENBOW ARCHIVES NA-2615-11

The Canadian customs house manned by the NWMP at the summit of Chilkoot Pass.

THE "LION OF THE NORTH"

He was NWMP superintendent Samuel Benfield Steele, and his life reads like something out of a pulp western. Not only did he help negotiate with Sitting Bull after the battle of the Little Bighorn in 1877, but he played a pivotal role in keeping the peace across the West. Charlotte Gray in her book *Gold Diggers: Striking It Rich in the Klondike* notes he was described as "gruff and bluff, and absolutely fearless of everybody." He and his small contingent maintained law and order at the summits of both White Pass and Chilkoot Pass. Even though he didn't have official authority to do so, he hauled in a Maxim machine gun to each pass to establish Canadian sovereignty. In fact, with no one to overrule him, he really ran the whole show, making up rules on the fly. There is little doubt he saved many lives by requiring every person entering the country at the passes to have a year's supply of provisions and to register their craft. This allowed the Mounties (here they actually used dogsleds and canoes, not horses) to track missing boats. Once the madness of the winter of 1897 to 1898 subsided, Steele moved on to impose "a general cleanup," bringing law and order to the unruly streets of Dawson City. Thanks to Sam Steele, Dawson never experienced the lawlessness that was typical of Skagway.

summer of 1899 and to Whitehorse by the next year spelled the death knell of the Chilkoot Trail as an important transportation route into the Yukon.

THE HIKE

Most outfitters take six or seven days for the entire trip, including up to five days of hiking. Each provides a different variation on travel arrangements to and from the trailhead at Dyea, Alaska, and the end of the trail at Bennett Lake, BC. Whether you are using an outfitter or organizing your own group, be sure to allow yourself enough time to enjoy the stunning beauty of the Coast Mountains and to investigate some of the historical artifacts you will see during the journey. Unless you are one of those suicidal runners with something to prove, remember that exhaustion tends to

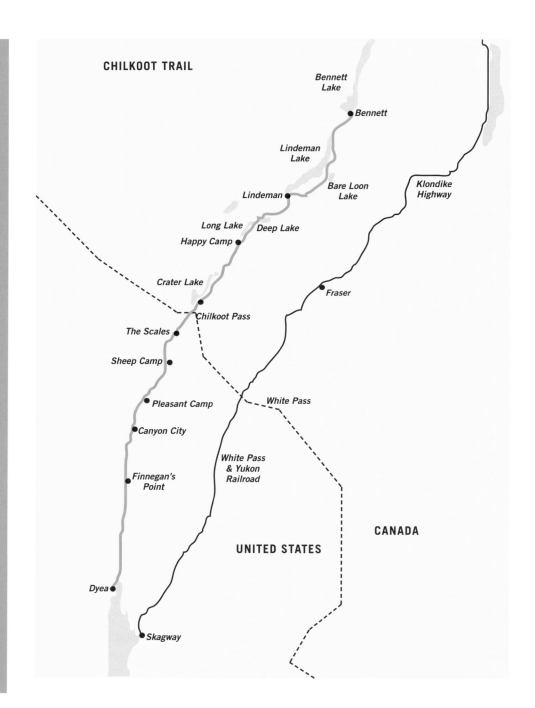

CHILKOOT TRAIL

Bennett
Lake

● Bennett

Lindeman
Lake

Bare Loon
Lake

Klondike
Highway

Lindeman ●

Long Lake   Deep Lake

Happy Camp ●

Crater Lake

● Fraser

Chilkoot Pass
●

The Scales ●

Sheep Camp ●

● Pleasant Camp

● Canyon City

● Finnegan's
Point

White Pass

White Pass
& Yukon
Railroad

CANADA

UNITED STATES

Dyea ●

● Skagway

foster accidents and unnecessary injury, which can be catastrophic in this isolated wilderness.

Please note: Day to day descriptions are based on the itinerary I followed with Sea to Sky Expeditions. See other options in the "How to do the hike" section.

Just as a planning note, our group remained on Yukon time throughout the trip, or one hour ahead of Alaska time. This effectively gave us the jump on hitting the trail ahead of the majority of the hikers and on getting good tent sites at each campground. The long summer daylight hours make this strategy work well.

Day 1 – Whitehorse to Dyea – no walking

The route follows the Klondike Highway from Whitehorse, Yukon, to Fraser, BC. Here the group joins the White Pass & Yukon Route Railroad for the scenic descent into Skagway.

Passport checks are done by US officers on the train trip to Skagway, and by Canadian ones on the return trip to Fraser. Hikers must register at the Trail Center in Skagway, but this is done on your behalf by the outfitter if you are travelling with an organized group.

There is time to have a good look around the historic town of Skagway prior to transferring

A RAILROAD TO HELL!

"Give me enough dynamite and snoose and I'll build a railroad to hell." So boasted railway contractor Michael J. Heney to the skeptics. No doubt many of the 35,000 people who eventually worked on the project believed they had seen the icy equivalent of hell. But Heney made good on his promise to push the railway through the Coast Mountains, following the White Pass route to Bennett Lake and eventually Whitehorse. Starting in May 1898 and finishing just 26 months later, workers battled brutal cold and fierce winter storms. At times they were reduced to just shovelling snow. Once the railway reached Bennett in 1899 and Whitehorse a year later, it effectively ended the need to make the difficult climb over the Chilkoot. Today visitors can still see portions of the White Pass Trail as the railway winds through a stunning landscape of mountains, glaciers and precipitous cliffs. The railway is designated an International Historic Civil Engineering Landmark, in a league with the Panama Canal and the Eiffel Tower.

BOBBIE-LYNNE BROCK

The modern-day tourist train winds through the spectacular White Pass to Skagway.

GLENBOW ARCHIVES PA-3886-9-7

A large group of men assemble in front of City Hall in Skagway to round up Soapy's gang.

ON THE REBOUND

As you make the drive into Dyea, it may seem to be quite a distance from the ocean. The land is actually 1.3 m (4.3 ft.) higher than it was in 1897 when the stampeders arrived. The reason is a phenomenon called "glacial rebound," where the land rises, or rebounds, as the weight of the melting continental ice sheets decrease. The land continues to rise at an annual rate of about 13 mm (0.5 in.).

to the trailhead at Dyea. Skagway is one of the only gold rush towns not destroyed by fire at some time in its history, so many of its buildings have survived for over 100 years. The town has done an excellent job of preserving them. Don't miss the outstanding museum displays at the Visitor Information Center. They also offer free, and highly entertaining, guided walking tours through the historical district.

Skagway was well known for its lawlessness compared to its Canadian counterpart of Dawson City, where the NWMP took law and order seriously. For a time Skagway was controlled by thieves and con men such as the infamous "Soapy" Smith, whose gang of thugs bilked many stampeders with bogus business schemes. "Soapy's" reign eventually ended when he met his demise in a gunfight.

Unlike Dyea, which dwindled to a ghost town after the arrival of the railway, Skagway continues to thrive as a railway, ferry and cruise terminus.

Day 2 – Dyea to Canyon City – 12.5 km (7.8 mi.)

The hike begins with an abrupt introduction to rocks and elevation gain as you begin the climb up Saintly Hill. Not too long after, it descends into the valley, where it follows an old logging road and remains relatively flat to Finnegan's Point. On a clear day you can catch magnificent views of Irene Glacier. Finnegan's Point marks the spot where Pat Finnegan and his sons built a corduroy bridge and road with plans to charge a toll. But they were soon simply overwhelmed by the sheer number of Klondikers passing through. With a shelter and outhouses, it is a good spot for lunch

The abandoned boiler at the site of Canyon City.

CITY OF ELECTRIC LIGHTS!

There is a reason why it is called Canyon City. By May 1898 it had become a busy freight transfer station, with over 1,500 people and 24 businesses. It could even boast electric lights. The settlement sprouted after two freight companies began building tramway houses here to move goods over the canyon and up the pass. Follow the track upstream a short distance to the suspension bridge and then another ten minutes upstream to view some of the artifacts, including a boiler that powered the tramway and the lights. By 1899 it was deserted as freight began moving by rail over the White Pass.

before continuing on the fairly easy trail to the Canyon City campground, where the log cabin shelter is a welcome sight.

Today, until you reach Sheep Camp on Day 3, you are travelling through coastal rainforest, where western hemlock, Sitka spruce and Douglas fir predominate. Plentiful rainfall means the forest is lush with moss, ferns and lichens, making for delightful hiking.

Day 3 – Canyon City to Sheep Camp – 7.8 km (4.8 mi.)

About 15 minutes into the hike, the trail begins climbing up the side of the valley and away from the Taiya River. The trail is almost entirely through forest, with some breakout views along the way. Pleasant Camp, so called because it offered the first place with level ground for camping after Canyon City, is a good rest stop. Expect some excellent ridge views as the hike continues along the forest trail to Sheep Camp.

The camp is large, with outhouses and two group shelters. Almost all hikers will stop here before they tackle the long trek up the pass the next day and on to Happy Camp. National Park rangers offer a regular interpretive program that is well worth catching. Early shut-eye is advised tonight for a very early start in the morning.

Day 4 – Sheep Camp to Happy Camp – 12.7 km (7.9 mi.)

No matter how experienced you are, this will be a hard day with an early start. Parks

D. LARRAINE ANDREWS

Lush forest undergrowth near Pleasant Camp.

GLENBOW ARCHIVES S-227-37

Sheep Camp about 1898.

THE CITY OF TENTS

Sheep Camp was actually a bivouac for sheep hunters long before the stampeders arrived. During the winter of 1897 to 1898, as storms slowed or halted traffic over the summit, Sheep Camp grew into a tent city with more than 60 businesses. Tents and freight lined the lower part of the trail as groups hauled their goods in stages from Dyea to Sheep Camp for the final push up the pass. Pierre Berton describes it as "a bedlam of sweating men, howling dogs and abandoned horses … where an exhausted man could pay two days' wages for a single meal or a small fortune for the privilege of sleeping on the floor, jammed so tightly against his fellows that by nightfall no one could stand up, enter or leave."

BOBBIE-LYNNE BROCK

A section of boulders on the Long Hill.

BOBBIE-LYNNE BROCK

More boulders and unexpected greenery along the Long Hill climb.

Canada recommends you allow at least 12 hours to complete this hike. We were decamped, fed and on the trail by 6 a.m. and took a little over 12 hours to reach Happy Camp.

Once you leave Sheep Camp, the trail begins to rise more steeply and the vegetation makes the transition to high alpine tundra. Here the weather is extremely unpredictable, with harsh extremes almost the norm. Trees become short and stunted, then disappear as you make the long steady climb up the infamous Long Hill. Many stampeders regarded this section as the worst part of the ascent.

Soon the terrain begins to resemble a desolate moonscape of rocks. In 1897 journalist Tappan Adney described them as "great water-and-ice-worn bowlders." Despite the harshness of the climate, an amazing variety of specialized plant life, including dwarf shrubs and lichens, clings to the rocks. You will even see algae growing in the snowfields as evidenced by the watermelon-coloured streaks.

At the top of the Long Hill, you can pause at the Scales for a snack and a short break before the final slog up to the summit.

Approaching the Scales section. Note the artifacts along the trail.

From the Scales the pitch remains relatively moderate until the trail turns left to reveal the last 45 degree ascent up the Golden Stairs. This is not a trail but a route (although the National Park rangers/wardens place orange poles to help guide you up). You will need to find your own way amongst the boulders and take your time doing it.

The good news is that the distance is short (about 0.9 km, or 0.5 mi.). The bad news is that there are two false summits. Just take your time. You will almost certainly encounter snow patches close to the top, which can be very slippery. If it doesn't bother you to look back, and the

A MOST WRETCHED SPOT!

There were plenty of places along the way that qualified as wretched, but Adney called the Scales "one of the most wretched spots on the trail." Here the packers reweighed their loads in order to charge higher rates for the final steep ascent. Many stampeders just gave up here, abandoning their goods, so that many artifacts are still visible all along this part of the trail. Aerial tramways were operating over the pass by March 1898, but most stampeders could not afford the exorbitant rates to have their supplies hauled up to the top.

Climbing the boulders of the Golden Stairs.

weather cooperates, the views down the valley can be magnificent – or so I'm told!

The summit is almost always encased in cloud or fog and the winds are cold and unrelenting. In August 1898 William Zimmer a US customs agent posted at the top of the pass wrote of weather so foul "that a person could not be seen twenty feet away on account of the rain and the fog which has prevailed for nineteen days without exception ..."

Soon you will see the Canadian flag snapping on top of the warming hut and the lonely outhouse overlooking Crater Lake to the north. We arrived to find Thermoses of hot water waiting on the table – courtesy of the Canadian warden! Be sure to rest and eat here and do a little artifact exploring if time and weather permit.

You have completed the toughest part of the day, but ahead lies a difficult 6.4 km (4 mi.) to Happy Camp. The trail descends off the summit but undulates over rough rocky ridges and glacial moraines. Depending on the weather, this section can be hard going, since it is very exposed to the elements. It won't be a minute too soon when you finally see Happy Camp – the name explains itself.

GOLDEN ICON

The Golden Stairs have become the photographic icon of the Klondike Gold Rush as men, bent forward under the weight of their loads, toiled up the 45 degree incline. Tappan Adney called it "a continuous moving train, ... perceptible only by their movement, just as ants are ... zigzagging across the towering face of the precipice, up, up into the sky, even at the very top." Men faced the climb up to 40 times as they ferried their ton of goods up to the summit. Once they reached the top, they hopped on a shovel for a quick slide down to do it all again!

The Canadian flag snaps in the wind at the summit warming hut.

BOBBIE-LYNNE BROCK

Even after the summit, there is still plenty of hard going before you reach Happy Camp.

Day 5 – Happy Camp to Lindeman Lake – 8.8 km (5.5 mi.)

A welcome, shorter day today, but expect plenty of ups and downs over rough, rocky terrain. As you near Deep Lake, you begin to enter the boreal forest zone. Since it is in the rain shadow of the Coast Mountains, it tends to enjoy a drier, sunnier and milder climate, where lodgepole pine, alpine fir and white and black spruce thrive. Adney called it "a new and smiling country," and it is a welcome change from the wind and cold of the pass. As you near Lindeman Lake, the path becomes well worn with easy going through a stand of lodgepole pine.

The hiking trail described above does not follow the one used by the stampeders, who used horses and wagons in the summer and sleds in the winter to haul their supplies to Long Lake. From here they were ferried by boats to Deep Lake, then transferred once again to wagons or sleds for the trip to Lindeman Lake. In the winter it could be used as a "frozen highway" to Bennett Lake.

There are actually two campgrounds at Lindeman. We camped at the lower one with a cozy log shelter by the lake. Don't miss a visit to the excellent interpretive centre and a chance to pick up a certificate showing you have hiked the Chilkoot Trail.

D. LARRAINE ANDREWS

Wildflowers and plenty of firewood at the cozy log shelter by Lindeman Lake.

Day 6 – Lindeman Lake to Bennett Lake – 11.3 km (7.0 mi.)

The trail rises to the top of the ridge between Lindeman and Bare Loon Lakes, travelling through sparse pine forest and frequent bedrock outcroppings. Your efforts are rewarded by a spectacular view over the north end of Lindeman Lake towards Bennett Lake. In 1897 journalist Tappan Adney recalled that Bennett Lake "lies like a trench between towering, rugged mountains of great grandeur." On a clear day there is no disputing his description.

Bare Loon Lake campground (yes, there are loons here) is a wonderful spot for lunch or a rest break in a picnic shelter perched on a rocky outcropping overlooking the lake. From here the trail begins its descent to Bennett Lake. But don't be deceived. There is still another surprise in store as the trail heads through deep sand, making its final elevation gain to a spectacular viewpoint overlooking the lake. The sand, which can be a difficult slog, is the result of erosion from the strong winds that whistle down Lindeman Lake.

The trail passes St. Andrew's Presbyterian Church on its final descent to the campground. The church is the only building still standing from the gold rush days when the town of Bennett was a bustling freight terminus for stampeders and boomed once again with the arrival of the White Pass & Yukon Route Railroad in 1899. By 1900 the railroad had reached Whitehorse and the town rapidly declined to ghost status.

WHERE TO STOP?

Lindeman Lake, named after a German botanist, marked another decision point for stampeders: whether to stop here to construct their boats for the trip to Dawson City or continue on to Bennett Lake. Most opted for Bennett Lake, to avoid the treacherous rapids of One Mile River between the two lakes. Despite this, the place grew to a population of 4,000. They stripped the landscape of trees for boats, fires and shelter. Mosquitoes now figure in diary accounts. Wrote US cavalry lieutenant Frederick Schwatka, "I have never seen their equal for steady and constant irritation in any part of the United States."

At the campground, where Parks Canada has just completed an impressive new log shelter, you will see plenty of visible artifacts scattered amongst the tent sites. Be sure not to disturb them, for they represent an important part of Yukon history. To the east of the town, the WP & YR train station has been beautifully restored and is worth a close look.

Day 7 – Bennett Lake to Whitehorse – no walking!

The afternoon departure of the train for Fraser allows the luxury of a leisurely morning to explore the area, combined with a fabulous breakfast and lunch. The fresh ingredients are a welcome treat delivered the evening before by our own personal "food courier." It is a bit of good planning that has reduced our shared pack weight along the trail – and that is definitely a good thing. From Bennett Lake it is a short train ride back to the van at Fraser and the final return trip to Whitehorse.

Artifacts in the grass on the banks of Bennett Lake.

TRUMP THAT!

It seems "The Donald" (Trump, that is), comes by his realtor instincts honestly. His grandfather, Fred Trump, arrived in Bennett in 1899. Recognizing the opportunities, he and his partner opened a tent restaurant which was soon replaced by a two-storey wooden building. The Arctic Hotel didn't meet the standards of a local journalist, however, who noted in a review: "For single men the Arctic has excellent accommodation as well as the best restaurant in Bennett, but I would not advise respectable women to go there to sleep as they are liable to hear that which would be repugnant to their feelings and uttered, too, by the depraved of their own sex."

BOBBIE-LYNNE BROCK

HOW TO DO THE HIKE

Option 1, guided hike: Can be booked through several different outfitters who offer guided hikes complete with all permits, most camping gear and food supplies. The following are reputable Canadian outfitters:

• Sea to Sky Expeditions **www.seatoskyexpeditions.com.** In 2009 this company was named to *National Geographic* magazine's list of Best Adventure Travel Companies (on Earth) and it is easy to see why. Owner Mark Waldbillig and his crew run a first-rate outfit and are veterans of the trail. When I travelled with Sea to Sky, one of our guides had done the hike 11 times. The food was amazing for the entire trip and our two guides were absolutely top-notch.
• Cabin Fever Adventures **www.cabinfeveradventures.com.**
• Ruby Range Adventure **www.rubyrange.com.**

All these trips leave from and return to Whitehorse. To find other Canadian and Alaskan outfitters, check out **www.skagway.com** and **www.pc.gc.ca**.

Option 2, self-guided independent group: In addition to organizing all your own food and gear, you will need to book the necessary permits and organize transportation to the trailhead at Dyea, Alaska, and at the end of the trail from Bennett Lake, BC. Check the following websites for more detailed booking information:

Parks Canada: Chilkoot Trail National Historic Site of Canada, **www.pc.gc.ca.**

United States National Park Service: Klondike Gold Rush National Historical Park – **www.nps.gov/klgo.**

See additional information in the "Internet resources" section below.

HOW DO YOU SAY THAT?

The Klondike Gold Rush spawned its own peculiar vernacular, including twisted versions of various First Nations words that became part of the language. Here are a few examples:

• cheechako – a greenhorn, someone new to the north
• Chilkoot Pass – called "Kwatese" by the Tagish, meaning "over the mountain"
• Klondike – the native word was "Thron Diuck," meaning "hammer water." Settlers changed it to Klondike, which was easier for them to pronounce.
• Skagway – based on the Tlingit word "Skagua," meaning "place where the north wind blows"
• sourdough – a person who had made it through a Yukon winter
• the three Bs – beans, bacon and bread, the mainstay of a miner's diet and one of the reasons many of them got scurvy

CONSIDER THIS: BEFORE OR AFTER THE HIKE

Even if you just have a few days, don't miss the chance to visit Dawson City. It was, after all, the final destination for the 30,000 Klondikers who endured inhuman conditions and appalling hardships trudging over the Chilkoot Pass in their headlong rush to reach the fabled gold fields on Bonanza and Eldorado Creeks.

Dawson is serviced daily from Whitehorse by Air North or can be reached by road from Whitehorse via the Klondike Highway, a distance of 535 km (332 mi.). If you have the energy and the time, it is also possible to take the water route down the Yukon River, following the path of the original stampeders as they made the final leg of the journey to Dawson City and the jumping-off point for the gold fields. Several outfitters offer the river option; the one guided by Sea to Sky Expeditions is timed to coincide with the conclusion of the Chilkoot Trail hike.

It may seem like a sleepy little town now, but as the stampeders began reaching Dawson from Bennett Lake in June 1898, the scene was chaos. Boats stretched six deep along the river for two miles. Soon the tiny settlement grew to be the biggest Canadian city west of Winnipeg, peaking at 40,000.

THE PARIS OF THE NORTH

As stampeders poured into Dawson, buildings and tents sprouted from the muddy bog almost overnight. Miners lined up to spend their hard-earned gold dust (the accepted currency) at the saloons, dance halls and gaming houses lining Front Street. Prices zoomed to the highest on the continent as men who had existed on the infamous three B's of bacon, beans and bread lined up for delicacies like bananas at $1 each, cucumbers at $5 apiece or tomatoes at $5 a pound. Anyone with the bucks could dine on champagne, oysters on the half shell and lobster Newberg. For a brief time of mad excess, the town became known as "The Paris of the North."

In the process, the native Tron'dek Hwech'en, who had fished for salmon on the Klondike and Yukon rivers for many years, were forced two miles downriver to Moosehide Village. Chief Isaac, recognizing the need to preserve his people's traditions, sent the tribe's most sacred possessions for safekeeping with elders in Alaska.

By the time the newcomers arrived in 1898, it had been almost two years since the original gold strike. All the most lucrative claims had been staked long before. While many stampeders stayed on to work claims of their own or to contract their labour to other established miners, most abandoned their quest once they reached Dawson City. Thousands didn't even bother trying to stake a claim or even visit the gold-laden creeks they had toiled so hard to reach.

Those who did stay on faced more privation as they worked their claims. Bill Haskell, who ended up with a purse of about $25,000, or about $1.5-million today, wrote that food replaced sex as his "most lascivious fantasy," as he dreamt of oyster stew, chocolate cake and cutting into a juicy red steak.

Pierre Berton describes an air of "emotional lassitude" as men wandered the streets with nothing to do and no money left. "Gold had been an excuse. For months they had talked of nothing else. But adventure was what they really hungered for, and that they had achieved. Success was not a sackful of nuggets; it was the satisfaction of having made it." The big winners were those with the savvy to realize the real money lay not in mining gold, but in "mining the miners." Many made (and lost) their fortunes doing just that.

By 1899, news of gold strikes in Nome, Alaska, had cleared the streets and Dawson's fleeting moment of fame ended. Charlotte Gray notes that the final tally from the gold fields between 1896 and 1909 was estimated at $120-million, or the equivalent of over $7-billion today.

Don't be deceived by the small size of the town, which is part of the Klondike Gold Rush International Historical Park. You can easily spend three or four days here and not be able to see everything on offer. Parks Canada, which has preserved more than two dozen buildings from the gold rush era, runs an impressive summer program that includes walking tours and costumed interpreters who do a fabulous job recreating the glory days of Dawson. They offer great value in a "pick-a-pack" option where you can select three tours for the price of two. I ended up doing six and still didn't see everything.

THE RICHEST WOMAN IN THE KLONDIKE

To many, as Charlotte Gray recounts in *Gold Diggers*, she was just "Mom" or "the Queen of the Klondike." An Irish immigrant, she clawed her way over the pass and with showy bravado, threw her last quarter into the Yukon River on her arrival at Dawson. Belinda Mulrooney later recalled, "I saw there was nothing in Dawson I could buy for a quarter. So I threw my last coin into the Yukon and said, 'We'll start clean.'" With sheer determination and guts, and a lot of hard work, the 25-year-old single woman managed to defy all the odds. She proved she was a wily businessperson, eventually amassing a fortune to become the richest woman in the Klondike. Not only did she invest in claims and housing for miners, her Fairview Hotel was the grandest on the riverfront. Sadly, Mulrooney lost her fortune to a cunning and fast-talking suitor named "Count" Carbonneau, who managed to fritter away her hard-won gains. She eventually died in a Washington nursing home in 1967 at the age of 95.

D. LARRAINE ANDREWS

The restored Commissioner's Residence in Dawson City.

Programs change each year, but don't miss the chance to see the Palace Grand Theatre, the Danoja Zho Cultural Centre, the Commissioner's Residence, Dredge No. 4 and the Robert Service Cabin, where a talented stand-in for the bard reminds us why Service's poetry remains as popular as ever.

Other outstanding highlights include the Dawson City Museum, the Jack London Museum, the self-guided audio walking tour and the self-guided walking tour of Dawson's historic buildings. There are plenty of hiking trails around the town, and for those worried about bear encounters, you can join the recreation department for one of their free group hikes.

By an odd coincidence of history, the residences of what are arguably the three greatest writers on the Klondike can all be found on Eighth Avenue within a few blocks of each other. Governor-General's-award-winning author Pierre Berton grew up in Dawson City. His family home has been converted into a writer's retreat and remains a private residence. But you can still visit Robert Service's actual cabin and a reconstruction of Jack London's prospector's cabin that incorporates some of the

The original Robert Service cabin in Dawson City, Yukon.

original logs. London crossed the pass in 1897 and although he never found gold in the ground, he certainly found it in the tales of stampede veterans in the bars of Dawson. His stories made him a millionaire. Robert Service, the "Canadian Kipling," became a wealthy man on the strength of his famous Klondike ballads, even though he didn't come to Dawson until 1908, well after the peak of the gold rush.

ARE YOU READY TO EAT?

By far the best meal I had on this trip was the one at the top of the pass. I suppose it wouldn't have mattered too much what it was, but I won't soon forget the welcome combination of whole-grain wraps, crunchy peanut butter, jam and cream cheese with some pepperoni sticks on the side, all washed down with hot tea. Delicious!

For those with a more discriminating palate, don't pass up the opportunity to try some of the north country's wild game and fish specialties. Whitehorse offers several options, but if the lineups are any indication, Klondike Rib & Salmon is probably the most popular (and best) place in town. Located at Second and Steele, in two of the oldest buildings still in use in the city, they offer everything from Alaskan halibut, Arctic char and sockeye salmon to reindeer stew, bison steaks and elk.

Hygiene standards on the trail were good and we had no concerns about food preparation. The same is true when it comes to eating out anywhere in Alaska or the Yukon.

Tipping is expected. Normally at least 15 per cent of the bill would be considered reasonable.

Vegetarians may have trouble getting enough protein on the trail. You might want to forget it's meat you are eating and just make sure your protein levels are high enough to meet the demands of the trek. As far as restaurants, there may not be a large number of strictly vegetarian establishments, but most menus will offer a vegetarian option.

TOUCH THE LIPS BUT SWALLOW AT YOUR PERIL!

For those up for an adventure of the drinking kind, be sure to stop at the Sourdough Saloon in the Downtown Hotel in Dawson City. The saloon is home to the sourtoe cocktail, the drinking of which has become what can only be described as a rather bizarre and grisly Dawson tradition. The story goes that in 1973 a local character named Captain Dick discovered a long-forgotten toe preserved in a jar of alcohol. It had been amputated with a woodcutting axe when its owner, Louie Liken, a local miner had badly frozen it during a rum-running escapade. For some obscure reason, Captain Dick decided it would be a good idea to plop the toe in a glass of champagne, then down the drink but not the toe. The rule was: "Drink it fast or drink it slow, but the lips have gotta touch the toe." Sadly toe #1 was lost when a miner named Garry Younger accidentally swallowed it trying to set a record with his thirteenth cocktail. Over the years, other frostbite amputees – and one who came too close to a lawn mower – have donated their gnarly digits to the cause. Believe it or not, over 60,000 customers have officially joined the SourToe Cocktail Club and forked over their $5 for a membership card.

INTERNET RESOURCES

Here are some reliable websites to get you started with your research:

www.travelyukon.com is the official travel website for the Yukon Territory.
www.visitwhitehorse.com has information for anyone planning a trip to Whitehorse.
www.travelalaska.com is the state's official travel website.
www.skagway.com features information for anyone planning a trip to Skagway.

www.wpyr.com has information on the White Pass & Yukon Route Railroad.
www.pc.gc.ca is the official site for Parks Canada, with extensive information on the Chilkoot Trail National Historic Site.
www.nps.gov/klgo is the official US National Park Service website, with information on the Klondike Gold Rush National Historical Park.
www.dawsoncity.ca contains information for anyone planning a trip to Dawson City.

RECOMMENDED READING

There is a wealth of information on this famous trail. Here are some of my recommendations:

Chilkoot Trail Heritage Route to the Klondike – David Neufeld and Frank Norris – an in-depth look at the trail, the land, the First Nations connection, the boomtowns and the railroad together with excellent maps. Highly recommended.

City of Gold – commentary by Pierre Berton –an excellent 1957 National Film Board production available from the NFB at www.nfb.ca.

Gold Diggers: Striking It Rich in the Klondike – Charlotte Gray – follows the stories of six very different yet remarkable people as they sought fortune and adventure in the Klondike. Highly recommended.

I Married the Klondike – Laura Beatrice Berton – written by Pierre Berton's mother who made Dawson City her home for 25 years. The book is a Canadian classic for good reason. Highly recommended.

Klondike – Pierre Berton – the definitive work on the Klondike Gold Rush. Highly recommended.

Klondike Trail – Jennifer Voss – a comprehensive hiking and paddling guide for anyone wanting to follow the entire route of the stampeders from the Chilkoot Trail down the Yukon River to Dawson City, Yukon. Good maps, plus chapters on the history and the flora and fauna of the area. An excellent if somewhat dated resource.

Klondike Trail North to the Yukon – Nora L. Deans – a booklet published by Alaska Geographic in conjunction with the Klondike Gold Rush National Historic Park. A good overall introduction to the history of the gold rush with an interesting combination of archival and modern photographs.

The Klondike Gold Rush: Photographs from 1896–1899 – Graham Wilson – another outstanding collection of archival photographs and text. Highly recommended.

The Klondike Quest: A Photographic Essay 1897–1899 – Pierre Berton. An outstanding collection of photographs and text setting the historical context. Highly recommended.

Women of the Klondike – Frances Backhouse – a fascinating glimpse into the stories of the women who braved the hardships of the Klondike and left an indelible mark on its history. Highly recommended.

Robert Service and Jack London both wrote extensively about the Yukon. And they both made fortunes as a result – no doubt considerably more than almost all but the luckiest of the stampeders who inspired their stories.

© FOTOSEARCH.COM

Grizzlies display a large shoulder hump.

FAUNA FACTS:
KING OF THE FOOD CHAIN

Grizzlies seem to attract the fascination of humans like few other wild animals do. These solitary giants are actually a subspecies of the brown bear, but their fur can vary from dark brown to cream to almost black. This tendency to colour variation often causes people to mistake them for their more timid cousin, the black bear. Even if it's black, a grizzly is distinguished by a large shoulder hump and a massive head with a dish-shaped, almost pig-like face. A true black bear will typically be much smaller, with a long face and a straight profile. The name grizzly comes from the long hairs found along the shoulders and back that are grayish, or grizzled, at the tips. Their imposing size – some males have weighed close to 800 kg (1,764 lb.) – means grizzlies really have no predators other than man. Incredibly, much of their diet consists of nuts, berries, fruit, leaves and roots, although they will certainly eat other animals, including everything from small rodents to elk, moose and even black bears. Grizzlies are often seen along rivers in Alaska or the Yukon, scooping out salmon during the summer spawning season. We encountered one on the river right at the trailhead. He was busy eating fish and not concerned with us. Still, we waited for him to move on before we set out. Never underestimate these bears' agility – they may look slow and lumbering, but they can move very quickly, as fast as 48 km/h (30 m.p.h.). If you ever meet one on the trail, back away slowly, speaking in a low, non-threatening voice. Never run; that only makes you look like prey. Do not make direct eye contact, as it may be interpreted as an aggressive challenge. Detour around the bear or leave the area as quickly as possible.

CHAPTER 9 – UNITED STATES – BIG BEND NATIONAL PARK – SOUTH RIM LOOP TRAIL

{ Big Bend is the giant turn the Rio Grande River makes from heading southeast to northeast following the boundary of Big Bend National Park. }

It was a vision of such magnitude as to stir the sluggish soul of a Gila monster. It was so awe-inspiring that it did deeply touch the soul of a hardened human bloodhound ... I resolved that upon the arrival of my ship I would buy the whole Chisos Mountains as a ... playground for myself and friends and that when no longer wanted, I would give it to the State ...

—TEXAS RANGER CAPTAIN E.E. TOWNSEND, "father" of Big Bend National Park, describing the view from Burro Mesa

✳ HIKING RULE 9: It may be tempting at the end of a long hike, but experienced hikers never take shortcuts across switchbacks. Switchbacks, or zigzags, help prevent trail erosion and make the grade easier on a steep slope. Cutting across them may be shorter but it will be harder and can cause considerable trail damage as well.

WHERE IN THE WORLD?

CLAIM TO FAME

Designated a UNESCO International Biosphere Reserve in 1976 and an Important Bird Area in 2001, Big Bend National Park is home to an extraordinary diversity of plant and animal life, superbly adapted to living in the three distinct environments in the park: the oasis of the Rio Grande River, the jagged volcanic peaks of the Chisos Mountains and the sprawling expanse of the Chihuahuan Desert.

Contained within the park's boundaries is the northern third of the latter, a huge arid zone that is considered one of the best examples of desert ecosystem in the United States.

It may look like desolate, uninhabitable terrain, but according to the National Park Service, Big Bend boasts over 1,200 species of plants, including more kinds of cacti than any other national park. Incredibly, an estimated 450 bird species either live in or migrate through the park each year, representing almost half the total number of birds that inhabit or visit North America. The park's location on a migration route between South, Central and North America makes it home to a "river of birds" each spring, with more species travelling through Big Bend than any other national park. What's more, or maybe less, the park's remoteness ensures that its skies are truly dark – the darkest in the lower 48 states. Awarded a Gold Tier certification as a Dark Sky Park by the International Dark-Sky Association in 2012, Big Bend is one of the best places in the entire continental US for stargazing.

DID YOU KNOW?

Apollo astronauts participated in four field trips to Big Bend from 1964 to 1971 in preparation for their moon missions. They were studying the region's volcanic geology to help them identify geologic structures and processes they might encounter on the moon.

WHAT WILL I SEE?

RICHARD REYNOLDS/TEXAS DOT

Scarlet blooms of the claret cup cactus perch on the edge of Big Bend's South Rim.

HIKE PROFILE

The South Rim loop hike begins near the Chisos Basin store at an elevation of 1646 m (5,400 ft.) and follows the Pinnacles Trail and the Boot Canyon Trail to 2248 m (7,375 ft.) at the South Rim for an elevation gain of 602 m (1,975 ft.). It then returns via the Laguna Meadow Trail, descending to the Chisos Basin for a total distance of 20 km

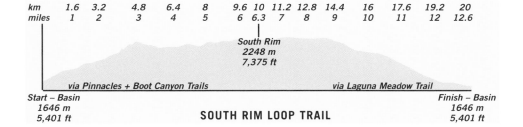

km	1.6	3.2		4.8	6.4		8		9.6	10	11.2	12.8	14.4		16		17.6		19.2	20
miles	1	2		3	4		5		6	6.3	7	8	9		10		11		12	12.6

South Rim
2248 m
7,375 ft

via Pinnacles + Boot Canyon Trails   via Laguna Meadow Trail

Start – Basin
1646 m
5,401 ft

SOUTH RIM LOOP TRAIL

Finish – Basin
1646 m
5,401 ft

(12.4 mi.). The hike can be done in either direction. Although the same elevation gain to the South Rim is required, the trail rises less steeply if done in reverse up the Laguna Meadow Trail and returning via the Pinnacles Trail and the Boot Canyon Trail.

Hazards

As with any hiking on steep or uneven terrain, the normal cautions regarding twisted ankles and injuries from falling apply here. The biggest threats in Big Bend tend to be weather-related. High temperatures and dehydration can cause serious problems with heat exhaustion. Symptoms include dizziness, nausea or an overall feeling of weakness. Cold can also present a problem, especially in the higher elevations where the temperature can quickly plunge as fast-moving storms approach. Hypothermia in such situations is always a danger if you do not have adequate warm clothing and food supplies. Uncontrollable shivering and confusion are sure signs a person is in trouble. They need to stop, eat and warm up.

Flash floods and lightning are always a possibility in mountainous terrain where thunderstorms can develop with frightening speed. Since such storms typically appear later in the afternoon, plan on doing any ridge walking early in the day so you can come back down well ahead of any potential lightning. If you do get caught, go to lower ground and try to find a grove of smaller trees of similar height. Always put your metal poles or packs with metal frames well away from you and wait it out. Such storms generally don't last very long.

Flash floods are always possible in a sudden downpour, so keep an eye on the weather and stay out of narrow box canyons if the weather threatens rain. Flooding can also happen quickly in the desert, with storms rapidly turning desert washes into raging torrents. In his book *Exploring the Big Bend Country*, Peter Koch recalls the days before there were many bridges and a flooded crossing would stop all traffic: "It was the custom for first arrivals to build a fire and have coffee ready for those who followed." Stranded travellers had a good visit while waiting for the water to recede.

The essentials

> **Getting there:** Big Bend is located in the remote southwestern corner of Texas, well away from almost everything, including freeways and shopping malls. There is no public transportation available to, from or in the park, so unless you are on an organized trip with transport provided, you will need to have your own vehicle. The nearest airports are located 523 km (325 mi.) to the northwest at El Paso and 370 km (230 mi.) to the northeast at Midland. Remember, nothing is close in Texas! There are two entrances to Big Bend, on the west side and the north side of the park. The west gate, near Terlingua and Study Butte (pronounced "stew-ty beaut"), is located off Highway 118, 93 km (58 mi.) from Alpine. The other entrance, just north of the Persimmon Gap Visitor Centre, is off Highway 385, 63 km (39 mi.) south of Marathon.

> **Currency:** United States dollar, or USD, or US$. US$1 = 100 cents. For current exchange rates, check out **www.oanda.com**.

> **Special gear:** It is always advisable to have good, sturdy, waterproof boots that are well broken in before you hit the trail. Hiking poles are helpful to maintain balance on uneven or slippery rocks or steps. Of course, you will need a broad-brimmed sun hat, rain gear and adequate supplies of food and water. You might also consider a good pair of gaiters if you are planning to hike in shorts. There are plenty of desert plants with spines and thorns that can cause serious injury to unprotected skin.

HIKE OVERVIEW

The South Rim loop trail is generally rated as a strenuous hike, with an elevation gain of 602 m (1,975 ft.) to the Rim. From the trailhead near the visitor centre, the trail climbs steeply into the Chisos Mountains, with rewarding views of the basin from Pinnacles Pass. It then winds through Boot Canyon past the famous "boot" formation to emerge onto the escarpment of the South Rim. On a clear day, wide, sweeping vistas provide one of the best panoramas in the park over the Rio Grande and far into the Sierra del Carmen in Mexico. From here, it's a steady descent back through the grassy flats of Laguna Meadow and down into Chisos Basin.

Why would I want to?

The South Rim loop hike is often described as the "classic hike of Texas." Tucked away in one of the most remote areas of the continental US, the park has been described as a place of "splendid isolation." Perhaps nowhere else within its boundaries is this isolation more evident than at the edge of the South Rim of the Chisos Mountains, 762 m (2,500 ft.) above the desert floor. On a clear day, a vast, uninhabited stretch of seemingly barren desert and wild, rugged mountains can be seen extending south into Mexico, as far as the Sierra Fronteriza in the Sierra del Carmen, 80 km (50 mi.) away.

The spectacular view from the rim is usually the big drawing card. But the higher elevation and cooler, moister conditions foster an unexpected diversity of plants and animals not found in the low desert lands. Here you will see stands of piñon pine and oak along with relict species of Douglas fir and Arizona cypress left over from a cooler era. In the summer and fall, expect fantastic displays of wildflowers such as scarlet bouvardia and skyrocket gilia. Sparrow-sized grey and yellow colima warblers nest each summer in Boot Canyon, the only place in the US where they are known to stop. In fact, three of the park's birding "hot spots" are included on this trail: the Chisos Basin, Boot Canyon and the South Rim, known for its falcons and swifts.

Lon Garrison, who served as second superintendent of the park in the 1950s, described the beauty of the Big Bend country as "often savage and always imposing. It is magnificent ... The 'Long Look' never fades. The ... view to the horizon ends in a haze of gray or blue or brown as the sky eats up the land. The land disappears but the sky is still there, the forever edge of the world that is always inviting." It's not hard to imagine he had the view from the South Rim in mind when he wrote these words.

The "Long Look" from the South Rim.

When to go

The Park's busy season extends from November to April. Due to its remote location, Big Bend is one of the least visited of all the national parks, but it is often filled to capacity during US Thanksgiving in November, Christmas and college spring break in mid-March. Avoid these prime times and there is a good chance you will have the trails all to yourself. Spring and fall generally bring moderate temperatures, while summer is far too hot for hiking, with temperatures often exceeding 38°C (100°F).

Expect a profusion of wildflowers in the spring. Winters are usually mild and a good time for hiking, although nights can dip below freezing and light snowfall is possible. Of course, these are only guidelines. One day during my February visit, the temperature crept well above 38°C (100°F). But hikers I know who have been to Big Bend in February found the creeks on the South Rim hike frozen all day.

DID YOU KNOW?
Estivation is the converse of hibernation. Summer is when some desert animals sleep during periods of high temperature and aridity.

What's the story?

The country isn't bad. It's just worse. Worse the moment you set foot from the train, and then, after that, just worser and worser.
—Journalist travelling with military expedition led by Major George Langhorne, 1916

It was a sentiment echoed all the way back to the time of the Spaniards. They called the desolate, barren expanse of the Big Bend country El Despoblado, the uninhabited land. American Indians explained the existence of the rugged landscape as a "massive heap of stony rubble" that had been dumped there as leftovers after the Great Creator had finished making the earth. Of course there are less colourful geological explanations for the land we see today, where sedimentary rock, shaped by vast shallow seas, was thrust upward in a process of mountain building over hundreds of millions of years. Combined with the volcanic forces that formed the Chisos and the slow, erosive power of the Rio Grande (sometimes called the Great Excavator), Big Bend is often described as a geologist's paradise.

DID YOU KNOW?
In 1971, fossils of the second-largest flying animal ever documented on earth were found in the park. Sometimes called "the big flap," the pterosaur had a wingspan of 10.7 m (35 ft.).

"Nature armed to the teeth" – prickly pear cactus surrounded by the formidable lechuguilla. Early explorers soon discovered that the sharp leaves of this plant could pierce the legs of horses, while a rider unlucky enough to fall could be impaled.

Early explorers weren't impressed with the weird and beautiful rock formations and sheer walls of the deep, twisting canyons, though. To them they were formidable barriers. In the early 1500s the Spaniards were drawn by the promise of gold. They eventually met resistance by the Chisos Indians and later the fierce Apache and Comanche warriors who had been pushed into the region from their tribal lands to the north. In response the Spaniards established a series of forts, or presidios, along the frontier, but they were no match for the Indians, who knew how to live off the harsh land. After a century of conflict, Spain finally withdrew, relinquishing control in 1821 when Texas became a state of the newly independent Mexico.

No one really wanted much to do with this desolate frontier, where ferocious Indian warriors inhabited the ghostly mountains and the scorching summer heat could kill a man within a day or two. In his book *The Big Bend: A History of the Last Texas Frontier*, Ron Tyler notes that one early traveller to the region called it "... nature armed to the teeth ..." where "each plant ... is a porcupine."

But the strategic location bordering the Rio Grande meant the area could not escape the turmoil and struggle that followed the retreat of the Spaniards. First came hostilities between Mexico and its recalcitrant state, resulting in the creation of the Republic of Texas in 1836. This was followed by conflict between Mexico and the United States, eventually leading to the final cession of the Republic to the United States in 1848. In fact, over the course of its history, six flags have flown over Big Bend.

The Treaty of Guadalupe Hidalgo, signed in 1848 between Mexico and the US, made the Rio Grande the official boundary between the two countries, suddenly bringing the wild, unknown territory to new prominence. Soon military topographical engineers moved in to begin the arduous task of surveying the border and the surrounding country.

Merchants, eager to establish a trade link with Mexico, had opened up the Chihuahua Trail from the Texas Gulf Coast west through Fort Davis and south to

Chihuahua. As travellers headed west in search of gold in California and settlers came in search of land, they realized the Big Bend area was "natural cow country" with its rich grama grasses, shrubs and edible cacti combined with adequate water supplies in the creeks and springs. The Civil War slowed much of this westward movement to a trickle, giving a temporary respite to the Comanches and Apaches still living in the desert grasslands, but by 1881 the last of the Indian tribes in the area had been defeated.

SIX FLAGS OVER BIG BEND

History tended to go on around the Big Bend, long considered an impenetrable and hostile land with no real value. Nevertheless, six flags have flown over the region starting with the Spaniards in 1521. Although Spain's control was punctuated by a brief seven-year interlude that saw the French lay claim to part of the territory from 1682 to 1689, the Spanish flag flew for almost 300 years until Texas became a state in the newly independent country of Mexico in 1821. It didn't take long for Texas settlers to begin clamouring for independence. Although the so-called Texians were defeated in their famous defence of the Alamo, they were ultimately successful in the establishment of the Republic of Texas in 1836, which remained independent until final annexation to the United States in 1848 following the Mexican–American War. Incredibly, they weren't finished yet, seceding from the Union to fight under the Confederate flag from 1861 to 1865, finally rejoining the United States following the end of the Civil War in 1865. The term "Six Flags" has become a popular moniker for shopping malls and theme parks in the state. The six flags even appear on the reverse of the Seal of Texas.

The completion of the railway in 1882 finally connected the Big Bend region to the rest of Texas, opening the way for a steady migration of ranchers who stocked the land with sheep, goat and cattle herds. This led to overgrazing that upset the natural plant population, eventually creating severe erosion. Settlement also brought hunting to eliminate predatory animals like the mountain lion (worth a bounty of $25 per skin in a time when men worked for $1 a day), bears and wolves.

Other settlers came for the curative powers of the dry air for such ailments as asthma and tuberculosis. One of these was J.O. Langford, who suffered from malaria. In 1909 he took up the claim at Hot Springs, sight unseen, with a plan to develop it as a health resort. The development became the first major tourist attraction in the area prior to the establishment of the park.

POCO LOCO AND THE BROKEN BLOSSOM

In 1945, when Peter Koch launched his one-man expedition to photograph the Santa Elena Canyon, he heard murmurs of "poco loco" from the people watching in disbelief from the riverbank. Koch had built a raft from two matched pairs of the dead stalks of an agave plant. (Agave or century plants don't actually live 100 years but often take 30 to 50 years to produce a single large stalk of flowers. The stalk can grow as much as 30 cm (12 in.) a day.)

Koch had wired each pair together, then bound them securely to crossbars with yards of baling wire. Stowed in a five-gallon milk can beneath a waterproof canvas were his cameras and film, while his food and sleeping bag were lashed on in a waterproof bag. Incredibly the contraption, which he christened the Broken Blossom and which had cost a total of 23 cents to build, saw him safely through all the Big Bend canyons as he filmed the first documentary in colour about the park.

Koch knew well the perils he faced, having read accounts of the dangers encountered by the 1852 Mexican–United States Boundary Commission. And he had been warned by Ross Maxwell, the park's first superintendent, about floodwaters from mountain storms that rose dangerously high within minutes. He knew there was no way to leave the canyon once it was entered. Koch recounts his adventures in his book *Exploring the Big Bend Country*, describing his successful navigation of the treacherous rapids of the famous Rock Slide – a "fearsome" pile of house-sized boulders through which the water flows. In 1899, Robert Hill, on a mapping expedition for the United States Geological Survey, had named the spot "Camp Misery," describing the rocks as an almost impassable barrier. He and his men spent "three miserable days" carrying their heavy boats over the rock pile. Koch describes his wild ride "through a narrow opening between two boulders, across a pool, and then down a final steep plunge into the last swirling whirlpool. The "demon of the Rock Slide had been vanquished!" Koch's films and photographs introduced thousands of visitors to the park and are a valuable historical record of its first four decades.

A single large, flowering stalk emerges from a century plant.

COMANCHE MOON TIME

American Indian tribes such as the Chisos, Apaches and Comanches occupied the Big Bend territory almost by default. The harsh and desolate land was considered too inhospitable for anyone but the most hardy, or perhaps the most foolhardy, to tackle. Traditional enemies, the Apaches and Comanches had been forced from their fertile tribal lands farther north, displacing the Chisos, a tribe of hunter–gatherers who were no match for these fierce warriors. The Comanches soon learned that the meagre existence offered by this hard land could be easily supplemented by raiding the vulnerable villages and rancherias across the river in Mexico. Every September, at the time of the Comanche moon, they headed south on the great Comanche War Trail to raid and plunder, driving livestock and other booty back across the river. The Mexicans, like the Spaniards before them, were powerless to defend themselves. The trail split into two forks as it reached the Big Bend area, one near present-day Lajitas and one near Persimmon Gap, on the northeast side of the park. Although it is no longer visible, explorers seldom failed to mention the trail if they saw it. At places it was a mile wide, partly because the Comanches often lit fires behind them to discourage pursuit. According to Ron Tyler in his book on the history of the Big Bend, Colonel Emilio Langberg described the path as "so well beaten that it appears that suitable engineers had constructed it."

21 BATHS IN 21 DAYS

Langford had been duly warned there was nothing at Hot Springs but "rattlesnakes and bandits" and that it was "too far away from anywhere for a sick man to feel like going there to get cured. That damned country promises more and gives less than any place I ever saw." But Langford ignored the dire predictions, drawn by the hope of a cure for his recurring bouts of malaria. After he took the treatment of "21 baths in 21 days" he set about building his resort close to the confluence of Tornillo Creek and the Rio Grande. The site included a two-storey bathhouse over the springs, a post office/store and motor court. A 1933 advertisement claimed, "Sufferers from asthma, kidney diseases, dropsy, jaundice, pellagra, eczema, rheumatism … all kinds of stomach troubles … have left their troubles here and gone home rejoicing. Why not you?" Board and baths were available at $3 per day. Even now, the water maintains a constant temperature of 41°C (105°F). The bathhouse is long gone but visitors can "take the waters" at the foundation remains, while a short walk around the Hot Springs Historic District highlights several of the remaining buildings. Langford later wrote of his life at Hot Springs in his book *Big Bend: A Homesteader's Story*.

Although the Spaniards had never discovered gold here, quicksilver (or cinnabar) ore found at Terlingua and Mariscal led to the establishment of mines. From 1900 to 1930 the Terlingua Mining District, just west of the park boundary, produced about one-third of the country's total output. A listed historic district, the Mariscal Mine (located inside the park) is considered the best preserved mercury mining site in Texas.

Revolution exploded in Mexico in 1910, bringing its share of turmoil and violence to the Big Bend. Bandits and guerilla bands of doubtful allegiance made periodic raids across the border, striking terror into the hearts of residents. The most famous incursions occurred at Glenn Springs and Boquillas, and later at Johnson's Ranch, 26 km (16 mi.) from Castolon. The result was an increased presence of US troops to protect the area, and the establishment of a landing field at the ranch, which operated until 1943.

When peace finally came to the region in the 1920s, talk of establishing a park began to circulate. The seed of the idea had been planted by some of the soldiers. Although they had been fairly bored during their time there, they recognized the unique beauty of the area and suggested it as a site for a national park. Championed by Texas Ranger Everett Townsend, J.O. Langford of Hot Springs and Fort Worth newspaperman Amon Carter, the park finally became a reality in 1933 when it was established as Texas Canyons State Park (the name was changed to Big Bend State Park later that year), and was made a national park on June 12, 1944.

LIQUID GOLD

There may not have been gold in the usual sense, but in the early 1900s C.D. Wood and W.K. Ellis tapped into the "liquid gold" growing at Glenn Springs. There they built a factory to produce wax from the candelilla plant that grew near the springs. The rendering operation employed as many as 60 Mexicans, supporting a thriving village. Wax production, which remains a major industry on both sides of the border, still uses a process that has changed little over the years. The stems of the plants are boiled in large vats of water. When sulfuric acid is added, the wax floats to the surface. It is then skimmed off and allowed to harden. These days the majority of the wax is used in chewing gum.

THE HIKE

Since this is a loop trail, you have a choice of ascending to the South Rim via the Pinnacles Trail and Boot Canyon Trail or the Laguna Meadow Trail for a total distance either way of 20 km (12.4 mi.), not including any side trips. Although the climb up the Laguna Meadow path is less steep, the overall elevation gain is the same. However, if you take this route up, the descent is steeper on the return to the basin and thus

THE LAST INVASION

They were called Roosevelt's Tree Army – the Civilian Conservation Corps, or CCC – established during the depths of the Great Depression in the 1930s to provide work for legions of unemployed men. In 1934 they set up camp in the basin, building

NATIONAL PARK SERVICE

the access road, the Lost Mine Trail and many of the buildings. As recounted in Tyler's book on the Big Bend, approval for the CCC crew hinged on the ability to find water before the application expired. Work began on the well at 9:00 a.m. on April 16, 1934, and by 2:45 p.m. they were successful. Townsend called the well Agua Pronto ("quick water"), referring to the urgency of the task.

The CCC Basin Camp in 1933, framed by the famous "window."

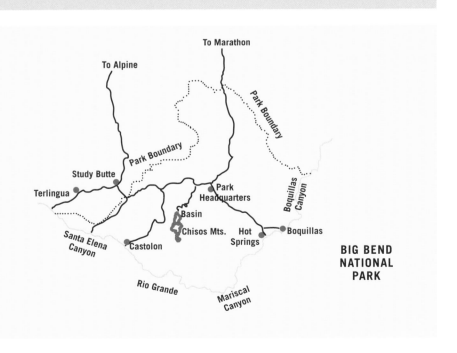

BIG BEND NATIONAL PARK

A view of the basin from the Pinnacles Trail.

The "Boot" resembles an upside-down cowboy boot.

harder on your knees. It is generally agreed that the hike up the Pinnacles route is the prettier of the two and also provides more shade. This is the option described below.

The hike begins at the trailhead near the visitor centre in the Chisos Basin. Within the first 800 m (0.5 mi.) look for a crazy mix of mountain and desert plants growing side by side, such as desert agaves next to an oak tree. Once past Boulder Meadow, the Pinnacles Trail rises steeply over a series of switchbacks through stands of oaks, pines, junipers and madrone trees to Pinnacles Pass. The reward for the climb is a spectacular view of the basin, the Window and the desert to the west. On a clear day you may be able to spot Cathedral Mountain, just south of the town of Alpine. The trail levels out and drops into the north fork of Boot Canyon to follow the Boot Canyon Trail.

Once over the pass you will soon see the junction on your right for the Emory Peak Trail, a 1.6 km (1 mi.) spur that climbs steeply to the summit of Emory Peak, the highest point in the park, at 2387 m (7,831 ft.). Although the views from here cover a full 360 degrees, encompassing almost the entire park, the cliffs at the top are quite sheer and caution is essential, since some rock scrambling is required at the top.

If you climb Emory Peak, return on the same spur to Boot Canyon Trail and continue on through the canyon. It will soon become clear where it got its name. The "Boot" is a volcanic spire that looks like an upside-down cowboy boot, probably named by some imaginative, bored cowboys herding livestock in the area.

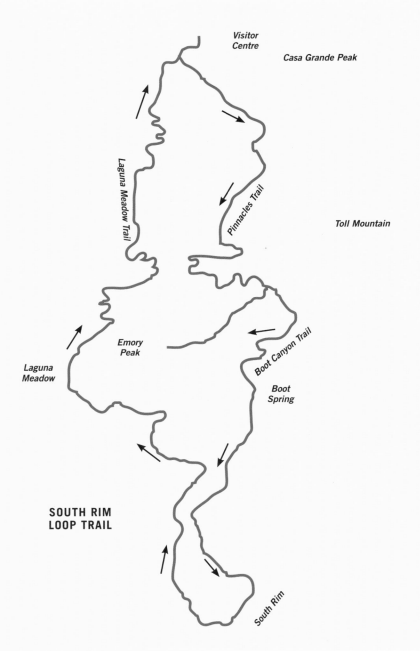

Visitor
Centre

Casa Grande Peak

Laguna Meadow Trail

Pinnacles Trail

Toll Mountain

Emory
Peak

Boot Canyon Trail

Laguna
Meadow

Boot
Spring

**SOUTH RIM
LOOP TRAIL**

South Rim

The view from the South Rim, with the slash of Santa Elena Canyon clearly visible in the distance.

The trail winds past stands of piñon pine, oak and bigtooth maple trees passing Boot Spring and some relict species of Arizona cypress, Douglas fir and Arizona pine that still manage to survive in the cool, moist conditions of the canyon. From April to June, claret-cup cactus and prickly pear bloom along the trails, while summer and fall are the best times to catch the wildflowers. Look for the bright-red flowers of the mountain sage and scarlet bouvardia or for the yellow heliopsis.

Along the way you will see several trail junctions, but ignore these and continue on to the South Rim. It is possible to take the side loop trail from Boot Canyon along the northeast and southeast rim and return to the South Rim. The track provides almost non-stop views as it curves around the rim, including Juniper Canyon,

The panorama from the South Rim: "Look in any direction and see the day after tomorrow."

FINDING A NICHE

From the South Rim it isn't hard to see why the Spanish called the area El Despoblado, the uninhabited land. But look a little closer and it soon becomes clear they had it all wrong. The borderlands of the Big Bend are, as author Fredrick Gelbach put it, "a carpet of interacting plants and animals deftly woven on a geologic loom."

The volcanic peaks of the Chisos Mountains, the "linear oasis" of the Rio Grande and the vast arid expanses of the Chihuahuan Desert have all combined to create a landscape of stunning diversity where plants and animals thrive in ecological niches superbly adapted to the harsh conditions. Well-known writer Edward Abbey called the Chisos Mountains "an island of greenery and life in the midst of the barren, sun-blasted, apparently lifeless, stone-bleak ocean of the Chihuahuan Desert. An emerald isle in a red sea." Here the cooler, moister elevations foster unexpected woodlands with evergreen sumac, mountain mahogany, junipers and small oaks, while mountain lions and black bears still prowl the canyons. Along the thin green ribbon of the river, birds like the summer tanager and vermilion flycatchers are said to be more colourful, while beaver and riverside cottonwood flourish. But it is in the desert, making up 98 per cent of the park, that life depends on the finely tuned cadence of wet and dry for survival. Consider the kangaroo rat, which doesn't drink, but metabolizes water from its food sources. Or cacti, which have spines, not leaves that lose water, and wide, shallow roots to capture rainwater to store in their own reservoirs for the dry season. It may look like a "stone-bleak ocean," but catch it after a spring rain and the carpet of wildflower blooms will forever change your view.

© JOHAN MAERTENS

This bird's nest is a perfect example of how plants and animals interact within the park.

Lost Mine Peak and Toll Mountain. Although the route is rated easy to moderate, it adds another 10.6 km (6.6 mi.), making a very long day hike. This option is probably best tackled as an overnight backpack trip. The southeast rim portion is normally closed to hikers during peregrine falcon breeding season, February 1 to July 15.

Pray that the weather gods are kind on the day you emerge onto the nearly vertical escarpment of the South Rim, 762 m (2,500 ft.) above the desert floor.

In the late 1940s, local rancher Bert Beckett led horseback trips to the South Rim. He would present the vista at the top with the comment, "Folks, you can look in any direction and see the day after tomorrow!" It wasn't an exaggeration. Spread out in a vast panorama is a view that seems almost without limit, capturing the very essence of Big Bend. Below the craggy cliffs of the rim, vast stretches of the wild and rugged Chihuahuan Desert; far to the south, the broad sweep of the Rio Grande; to the west, the slash of Santa Elena Canyon, 32 km (20 mi.) away; to the north, Emory Peak dominates; to the east, Mexico's Sierra del Carmen are visible 48 km (30 mi.) in the distance. On a clear day it is possible to see the Sierra Fronteriza, the most southern group of mountains in the Sierra del Carmen, almost 80 km (50 mi.) away. Here is Garrison's "Long Look" – a perfect place to plan your lunch stop and savour the vista before you begin the trek back to the basin.

From the spectacle of the South Rim, the trail descends below the rocky slopes of Emory Peak, then onto the grassy flats of Laguna Meadow. The meadow is believed to have been used by Indians as a camping spot.

In his book *Exploring the Big Bend Country*, Peter Koch recalls the story of Byron Smith, who at age 14 was hired by local rancher Homer Wilson to trap panthers

THE HEART OF THE MATTER

At the north end of the meadow a sotol pit provides evidence that the spot was used as a camping place. The sotol plant is best described as all-purpose. The evergreen has long, spiny leaves that were used for weaving mats and baskets, while the flower stalk provided a multi-purpose, lightweight wood. Not only are the seeds edible, but the central stem, or "heart," was baked for up to 48 hours in an earthen pit, then pounded into patties and dried in the sun. The chewy snacks are said to taste like nutty molasses syrup. In his memoir *The Life of F.M. Buckelew: The Indian Captive, as Related by Himself*, Buckelew gives a detailed account of sotol bulbs or hearts baked in a rock oven covered with earth, then made into bread. Buckelew was captured by Lipan Apaches in 1866 when he was 14 years old. He lived with them in the Big Bend area until he eventually escaped.

© JOHAN MAERTENS

The spiny leaves of the sotol plant were used for weaving mats and baskets.

(mountain lions) that were preying on Wilson's sheep and goat herds. Smith lived in the Laguna Meadow/Boot Spring area, getting water from the spring and riding down to the ranch every ten days to stock up on "beans, flour, lard, baking powder, salt and pepper and shells to kill deer for meat." He managed to kill six panthers.

From Laguna Meadow the trail descends a series of switchbacks, continuing on to emerge back at the Chisos Basin.

HOW TO DO THE HIKE

Big Bend is very hiker friendly, with over 323 km (201 mi.) of well-marked trails and plenty of front- and backcountry camping options. The best starting place for information is the National Park Service, at **www.nps.gov/bibe**.

If you have at least a week to devote to exploration and want the chance to hike in different parts of the park without the need to camp or organize everything yourself, consider booking with an independent operator who can make all the arrangements so that all you need to do is hike. There are a limited number of operators offering such trips, probably due to the remote location of the park. I hiked with the following operator, a highly reputable company, offering excellent value for money:

• Timberline Adventures **www.timbertours.com**.
I have travelled all over the US with this outfit and have never been disappointed. The company has been in business for over 30 years, which speaks volumes about how they do business. The trips are all-inclusive, with a high standard of accommodation, safety and personal service. All hikes include two knowledgeable guides. I did the six-day Big Bend trip with Timberline, who offer a variety of other hikes in the park as well, including the South Rim loop.

HOW DO YOU SAY THAT?

Naming of places and geographical features in the early days of discovery is often a haphazard affair. And that's what makes the Big Bend story a quirky one to say the least. By the time the topographical engineers began mapping the area in 1902 and 1903 there were only a few names used by Indians or Spaniards that had stuck. For the most part it was a "nameless land."

Arthur Stiles and his helper Stuart Penick, engineers with the US Geological Survey, had set up their three-tent headquarters at Boquillas. M.A. Ernst, the local storekeeper and justice of the peace, decided that the best way to come up with acceptable names to fill in all the blanks on the map was to call a jury. Virginia Madison and Hallie Stillwell tell the story in their book *How Come It's Called That? Place Names in the Big Bend Country*. Stiles recounted that riders were sent out to tell people about the meeting, and on the appointed day, "The jury came on horseback from many distances and directions; and seemed delighted to serve." After a lunch of "roast venison, fried quail, baked sweet potatoes, corn pudding, wild honey, and coffee," the group got down to business. Stiles noted, "Each member of the jury was complimented by having a topographic feature for a namesake. When it came to naming all of the places, it developed that there were barely enough people living in the country to furnish names for all the places." According to Stiles, local names were used if there were any known at the time, with Ernst adding a few of his own inventions as well.

Many geographical features have obvious names, such as the distinctive volcanic spires of Mule Ears Peaks, while others such as Casa Grande, Burro Mesa and Santa Elena clearly show the Spanish–Mexican influence. Here are a few interesting ones:

© JOHAN MAERTENS

Casa Grande towers over the basin.

- Casa Grande – named for its resemblance to a big house or old castle, it dominates the basin.
- Chisos – is the name of the mountains that over-look the park as well as the basin where the Civilian Conservation Corps first set up their camp in 1934 and began building roads and trails for the new park. Chisos is said to mean ghosts or to be based on a Castilian word, *hechizo*, meaning enchantment. The word "basin" is clearly descriptive of the huge depression within the mountains surrounded by some of the tallest peaks of the Chisos. It is now the location of the visitor centre and various tourist services.
- Boquillas – means "little mouths." The name was given to the canyon because of its narrow, high walls.
- Burro Mesa – so named for the wild burros that once roamed there.
- Santa Elena – said to be named after Saint Helena. The famous canyon was origi-nally called Puerto Grande, since it resembled a great door in the face of the cliff.
- Terlingua – said to be a corruption of the words *tres lenguas*, a reference to the three languages of Spanish, English and the various indigenous tongues consid-ered together.
- The Window, or "Pour-off" – is the much-photographed gap between Carter Peak and Vernon Bailey Peak seen from the basin. Bailey was a well-known naturalist

working for the US Bureau of Biological Survey, while Amon Carter, as mentioned earlier, was a newspaper publisher who was instrumental in the formation of the park. The Window drains water from the entire basin into Oak Creek below.

CONSIDER THIS: BEFORE OR AFTER THE HIKE

You've come this far, so don't miss an opportunity to sample everything the park has to offer. There are many choices when it comes to mountain, desert and river hikes. Based on my experience, here are a few alternatives to consider. (Note that all the distances quoted are return.)

The Window: Probably one of the most popular walks in the park, this is a moderate hike of 9.0 km (5.6 mi.) to one of the most iconic spots in Big Bend. The trail begins at the main trailhead near the basin visitor centre and follows a well-maintained path that descends for its entire length, passing through Oak Creek Canyon to the famous Pour-off and a wide vista of the desert beyond. The rocks here can be very slippery, so don't approach the edge, because you won't stop until you hit the bottom, 67 m (220 ft.) below. The Pour-off is the drainage for the entire basin: a thunderstorm can quickly turn the nearly dry creek into a raging torrent. Of course, the elevation drop of 244 m (800 ft.) means you face an uphill climb on the way back, but there are good views of Casa Grande on the way.

The Window is the much-photographed gap between
Carter Peak and Vernon Bailey Peak.

© BETSY DEVLIN

Lost Mine Trail: A not-to-be-missed mountain hike of 7.7 km (4.8 mi.), rated moderate with stunning views. The trail begins just past mile marker 5 on the Basin Road, climbing 381 m (1,250 ft.) to ridgetop views that are some of the best in the park. Be sure to pick up the National Park Service self-guiding brochure available at the trailhead. It is keyed to the 24 markers featured along the trail and offers fascinating details about the flora, geology and history. About 1.6 km (1 mi.) into the hike, the trail reaches Juniper Canyon Overlook, with views of Casa Grande, Toll Mountain and the Northeast Rim of the Chisos. Broad views at the top encompass Pine Canyon, the Sierra del Carmen in Mexico, the East Rim of the Chisos, and Lost Mine Peak. An old legend holds that the Spaniards enslaved local Indians to mine a silver vein found here, but the slaves eventually rebelled and sealed the entry so it couldn't be found. Apparently the rising sun shines on the entrance at certain times of the year, but the mine has never been found.

Santa Elena Canyon: An easy 2.6 km (1.6 mi.) walk into the mouth of one of Big Bend's three major canyons. The trail begins at the end of Ross Maxwell Scenic Drive and is one of the most popular in the park, probably because it is short and easy with much reward for little effort. It can be impassable during the rainy season, though, when it is subject to flooding.

The steep walls of Santa Elena Canyon rise above the Rio Grande.

J. GRIFFIS SMITH/TEXAS DOT

The iconic Mule Ears Peaks rise above the desert.

Mule Ears Peaks: An outstanding moderate desert hike of 11.2 km (7 mi.). With minimal elevation gain and loss of 122 m (400 ft.), it provides an exceptional introduction to the subtle beauty of the Chihuahuan Desert. The well-marked trailhead is located at the Mule Ears Viewpoint parking lot on Ross Maxwell Scenic Drive. Start early because it can get hot by mid-day. Hikers can walk an extra 1.6 km (1 mi.) to Mule Ears Spring for a chance to see leopard frogs and remnants of corrals from the early ranching days. Expect to see a variety of cacti and other desert plants along with ever-changing views of Mule Ears Peaks.

Terlingua: No hiking here, but if you get a chance to stop for a meal at the Starlight Theater, don't miss it. Following a violent

The Starlight Theater is now a popular Terlingua restaurant.

The Terlingua cemetery is one of the stops on the self-guided walking tour.

summer storm, the former movie theatre sat roofless for many years until it was converted into a popular local restaurant with good food and live entertainment.

Located just outside the northwest entrance to the park on Highway 170, the ghost town of Terlingua was once a thriving locale where cinnabar ore was mined to produce quicksilver, or mercury, until the business went bust in the 1940s. Now a designated historic site, and a magnet for artists, musicians and "free thinking individuals," it has put itself on the map as the home of the Terlingua International Chili Championship held every November. The self-guided walking tour of the town's historic structures is worth doing.

ARE YOU READY TO EAT?

Sit-down eating options in the park are limited to the dining room at the Chisos Mountains Lodge, located in Chisos Basin. The restaurant offers spectacular views plus a wide selection of good, reasonably priced food. During my week's stay in the park, we had almost all our meals here with no complaints. The nearest alternatives are about 45 minutes away in Study Butte and Terlingua. There are also four convenience stores in the park, at Rio Grande Village, Castolon Historic Area, Panther Junction and the Lodge, where you can find basic groceries and camping/picnic supplies.

Hygiene standards are high and there should be no concerns about food establishments in the park.

Tipping is expected. Normally at least 15 per cent of the bill would be considered reasonable.

Vegetarians can be easily accommodated at the Lodge dining room. Although this is cattle country, where Texas barbecue reigns supreme, vegetarians can usually eat well in the cities. But it may be more challenging to find meatless alternatives in smaller towns and rural areas, where the concept remains relatively foreign.

INTERNET RESOURCES

Here are a few useful websites to help you plan a trip to the park and surrounding area:

www.nps.gov/bibe, the National Park Service official Big Bend site, provides a wealth of information and good maps.

www.bigbendbookstore.org, compiled by the Big Bend Natural History Association, has an excellent online store plus information on the natural history of the park.

www.traveltex.com is the state's official tourist website.

www.texasmonthly.com "We're the National Magazine of Texas. And the National Home Page of Texas," as their masthead demurely puts it. And a great source of information on food, travel and the arts they are, too.

www.wildtexas.com is a great guide to Texas parks and outdoor recreation, including Big Bend.

www.texasbarbeques.com: you guessed it, everything you ever wanted to know about Texas barbecue.

RECOMMENDED READING

Many of these books can be ordered through the Big Bend Natural History Association at **www.bigbendbookstore.org** or are available at the visitor centre bookstores in the park.

FEEDING THE PASSION

To say Texas barbecue has been elevated to the level of a statewide passion seems to be an understatement. The Texan obsession with slow-smoked barbecue has been likened to a form of "religious devotion," sparking endless debate about the meat. Is beef brisket the best? Should the wood fire be hickory, oak, pecan or mesquite? Should the "rub" be dry or wet? Should the sauce be sweet or spicy, or do you even need sauce? The only way to settle these issues is to try some for yourself. And with barbecue joints promising "real BBQ" on every back road and street corner in Texas, you will have plenty of chances to become an expert.

© BERNIE MCMAHON

Roadrunners often show little fear of humans.

FAUNA FACTS: RUNNING RAMPANT

Many of us first came to know him as the cartoon nemesis of Wile E. Coyote, streaking through the desert with a distinctive and triumphant "beep beep." Real roadrunners may not go as fast as our cartoon friend, but they can reach speeds of 32 km/h (20 m.p.h,) chasing down lizards, snakes and small rodents. They actually peck their prey to death with blows from their beak, getting most of their moisture needs from the body fluids of their meal. Popular tall tales have them deliberately picking fights with rattlesnakes or ensnaring them within fences built of cactus joints. Common myths aside, this member of the cuckoo family can fly but rarely does unless threatened. Although they usually hunt by chasing their prey on the ground, using their long tail as a rudder, they are also capable of jumping straight up in the air to capture small birds or insects. They often display little fear of humans, allowing curious birdwatchers to approach very closely.

Big Bend: A Homesteader's Story – J.O. Langford with Fred Gipson – Langford's story of his life at Hot Springs.

Big Bend: The Story behind the Scenery – Carol E. Sperling – written by a National Park Service Interpretive Ranger, an excellent overview of the Park, including its natural and human history with stunning photographs.

Exploring the Big Bend Country – Peter Koch and June Cooper Price – personal recollections by photographer and film maker, Koch and his daughter June.

Hiking the Big Bend National Park: A Falcon Guide – Laurence Parent – a very comprehensive guide with excellent maps and hike descriptions.

How Come It's Called That? Place Names in the Big Bend Country – Virginia Madison and Hallie Stillwell – great stories on the history behind the names.

Lonely Planet Texas – a comprehensive guide to planning your visit to Texas.

Naturalist's Big Bend: An Introduction to the Trees and Shrubs, Wildflowers, Cacti, Mammals, Birds, Reptiles and Amphibians, Fish and Insects – Roland Wauer and Carl Fleming – obviously a comprehensive guide.

Stray Tales of the Big Bend – Elton Miles – (also by Elton Miles, *Tales of the Big Bend* and *More Tales of the Big Bend*) good collection of stories from the Big Bend region.

The Big Bend: A History of the Last Texas Frontier – Ron Tyler – award winning, highly readable account of the rugged Big Bend country and its history, including an excellent bibliography.

The Republic of Barbecue – Elizabeth Engelhardt – just in case you need to know more about Texas "barbeculture."

CHAPTER 10 – UNITED STATES – YOSEMITE NATIONAL PARK – PANORAMA TRAIL

{ The name Yosemite is a corruption of an indigenous Miwok word for "grizzly bear" or "those who kill," after the fierce Indian tribe inhabiting what came to be known as the Yosemite Valley. It has been spelled variously as "Yo-Hamite," "Yohemity" and "Yo-Semite," and it's pronounced "Yo-*sem*-i-tee," not "*Yose*-might" }

The park is a paradise that makes even the loss of Eden seem insignificant.

—JOHN MUIR

✱ HIKING RULE 10: In his article "A Parable of Sauntering" published in 1911, early Sierra Club member Albert W. Palmer recalled John Muir's advice on hiking (see box below). Muir maintained that "people ought to saunter in the mountains – not hike!" He explained that when people in the Middle Ages made pilgrimages to the "Holy Land," they were going "à la sainte terre," and so became known as "sainte-terre-ers," or "saunterers." Although his folksy approach to the etymology of "saunter" may make experts cringe, he surely got his point across. Muir believed that "... these mountains are our Holy Land, and we ought to saunter through them reverently, not 'hike' through them." Measuring a trail in modern terms of distance covered in the least amount of time were foreign concepts to Muir, who was usually the last person into camp at the end of the day and who often "stopped to get acquainted with individual trees along the way."

WHERE IN THE WORLD?

WHAT WILL I SEE?

D. LARRAINE ANDREWS

A stunning vista greets hikers near the start of the Panorama Trail.

CLAIM TO FAME

Designated a UNESCO World Heritage Site in 1984, Yosemite National Park is described as a place of "exceptional natural and scenic beauty" that "vividly illustrates the effects of glacial erosion of granitic bedrock, creating geologic features that are unique in the world." This glacial action over millions of years has produced a landscape of soaring cliffs, polished domes, hanging valleys, free-leaping waterfalls and sheer granite walls providing a spectacular backdrop for high alpine meadows, giant sequoia groves and over 300 lakes. Within the park's 1,170 square miles (3030 km²), an elevation range of almost 11,000 ft. (3350 m) accounts for a wide diversity of ecological zones that are home to a stunning variety of plants and animals. Although it was not the first national park in the US, its far-sighted protectors developed the basis of the national park concept as it is known today.

HIKE PROFILE

The Panorama Trail begins at Glacier Point at an elevation of 2200 m (7,200 ft.) descending to 1225 m (4,000 ft.) at Happy Isles on the valley floor. Although the trail is mostly down, it involves a climb of approximately 305 m (1,000 ft.) and a descent of 1280 m (4,200 ft.), for a net descent of 975 m (3,200 ft.) over a distance of 13.7 km (8.5 mi.).

Hazards

As with any mountain hiking, the normal cautions regarding twisted ankles and injuries from falling apply here. However, the Panorama Trail does present its own particular hazard if you choose to take Option 1 down the Mist Trail. It is called the Mist Trail for a reason. Since it follows a steep descent over stone steps at the edge of Vernal Fall, the steps can be extremely slippery depending on the time of the year you are there. In the spring, when the fall is at full flow, expect to get drenched from the mist drifting over the stairs. Later in the season, the mist can be relatively non-existent and the steps almost dry. For anyone with vertiginous tendencies, you may consider taking Option 2, avoiding the stairs and the dangerous drop-off that is on your side as you descend. (See the Hike overview section for more details on these options.)

Although it is not normally an issue on the Panorama Trail, altitude sickness can create problems for hikers in other parts of the park, where trails can climb close to 4000 m (13,000 ft.). Classic symptoms include shortness of breath, fatigue, headaches and loss of appetite. If you experience altitude sickness, the only real fix is to descend to a lower elevation.

Visitors often assume bears are a big hazard, but there has never been a bear-related death recorded in the park. Perhaps not surprisingly, car accidents have been the biggest killers, of both bears and humans, followed by drowning, rock climbing, rock falls and suicide.

THE IGNORAMUS WINS!

Right from the beginning, controversy raged on the topic of how Yosemite Valley was actually formed. Because it exhibited sheer cliffs and not the usual U-shape, Josiah Whitney, the head of the California Geological Survey, advanced the "drop down" theory: that the sheerness of the walls was the result of a cataclysmic event that caused the floor of the valley to drop. John Muir disagreed. He wasn't Yale-educated like Whitney and had only briefly studied geology at university. But he had studied the valley on foot from every angle. And he believed that "glaciers have labored, and cut and carved, and elaborated, until they have wrought out this royal road." For his efforts, Whitney branded him an "ignoramus" but his theory, called "Muir's discovery," eventually became the accepted explanation for the stunning landscape we see at Yosemite today.

Although the California grizzly bear still graces the official state flag, the last known grizzly in California was killed in Sequoia National Forest in 1922. The only bears you will find in Yosemite are black bears. Just to confuse the issue, they aren't always black, but often dark brown or cinnamon. Although they are highly intelligent and adaptable to pilfering a free meal if you make it easy for them, they will generally avoid any type of confrontation. That said, all bets are off if you happen to wander between a sow and her cubs, so stay alert.

The essentials

Getting there: Yosemite is located on the western slope of the Sierra Nevada range in northern California. Four entrances provide a number of access alternatives for visitors:

South Entrance off Highway 41 provides access to the closest airport at Fresno and the southern part of the state.

Arch Rock Entrance off Highway 140 provides the most convenient access from northern California through the towns of Merced, Mariposa and Midpines. Merced is serviced by Amtrak (**www.amtrak.com**) as well as Greyhound (**www.greyhound.com**). From there, travellers can opt for a vehicle-free option by purchasing tickets through the YARTS system (Yosemite Area Regional Transportation, **www.yarts.com**), which provides daily bus service to the valley. Once in the park, a free shuttle service is available in the valley and seasonally along parts of Tioga Road. Full details are available in the Yosemite Guide, a free park publication that is widely available in print and online at **www.nps.gov/yose**.

Big Oak Flat Entrance off Highway 120 on the west side of the park, provides the closest access to San Francisco, a four to five hour drive west of the park.

Tioga Pass Entrance off Highway 120 on the east side of the park, provides seasonal access through the town of Lee Vining. The road is subject to heavy snow and is generally open only from late spring to early fall. As it leaves the park at an elevation of 3030 m (9,940 ft.) it follows a short, precipitous and quite spectacular descent of about 915 m (3,000 ft.) to the eastern desert at the base of the mountains.

Currency: United States dollar, or USD, or US$. US$1 = 100 cents. For current exchange rates, check out **www.oanda.com**.

Special gear: It is always advisable to have good, sturdy, waterproof hiking boots that are well broken in before you hit the trail. Hiking poles are helpful to maintain balance on uneven or slippery rocks or steps. Poles are particularly recommended on the Mist Trail, where the descent can be treacherous due to wet conditions. Of course you will also need to carry rain gear and adequate supplies of food and water.

BRUIN REIGNS SUPREME!

John Muir wrote about his first bear encounter in the Sierra in 1869. He had been told they always ran "from his bad brother, man, never showing fight unless wounded or in defense of young." After closely examining a large cinnamon bear in a meadow, he decided to "see his gait in running" so he shouted and waved his hat "expecting to see him make haste to get away. But to my dismay he did not run or show any sign of running.... Then I suddenly began to fear that upon me would fall the work of running; but I was afraid to run, and therefore, like the bear, held my ground." The two eventually called a truce in their stare down when the bear "with magnificent deliberation turned and walked leisurely up the meadow." But Muir had learned his lesson. "In the great cañons Bruin reigns supreme."

HIKE OVERVIEW

The Panorama Trail provides several different options, depending on how ambitious you are. In theory the hike can be done as a loop, but most people hike it one way from Glacier Point, at the end of Glacier Point Road, to the valley, which requires a ride to the trailhead.

WACKO'S THE WORD!

Although it is no longer accessible (I can't imagine why not), Overhanging Rock at Glacier Point attracted its share of wacko daredevils. The granite slab protrudes over the valley – one wrong step and it's free fall all the way to the bottom. Over the years, death-defying stunts were recorded in many famous photos, including acrobatic flips and hanging handless from a pole extended over the drop. This one shows Kitty Tatch and her friend Katherine Hazelston doing high kicks in their long dresses.

Kitty Tatch and Katherine Hazelston dance on Overhanging Rock at Glacier Point.

HANGING OUT WITH THE SIERRA SUPERSTARS

Today the paved road to Glacier Point gives easy access to one of the park's most stunning viewpoints. Spread out at your feet, like a larger than life Technicolor postcard, is the entire eastern Yosemite Valley. Sierra superstars like Half Dome, Yosemite Falls, North Dome, Clouds Rest, Tenaya Canyon and Royal Arches compete for your attention with Nevada Fall, Vernal Fall and Liberty Cap, creating a panorama that seems almost too perfect to be real. Right from the beginning, the spectacular view made this one of the most popular spots in the park, but it wasn't always so easy to get there. As early as 1872, an enterprising James McCauley opened his toll path from the valley up the steep Four Mile Trail to the top, where tourists could stay at his Mountain House Hotel. It was McCauley's idea to push burning embers over the edge to create a spectacular "firefall" that could be viewed from the valley below. The tradition was taken up by David and Jennie Curry, who in 1899 established Camp Curry at the base of the cliff. The nightly display continued each summer with a few brief interruptions until halted by the Park Service in 1968 as being incompatible with the objectives of a national park. (Check **www.yosemitefirefall.com** for more information.)

Just one of the many superb views from Glacier Point.

If you are travelling with an outfitter, the details of getting to Glacier Point will be taken care of for you. If you are on your own, you will need to arrange a car shuttle or make a one-way reservation on the bus that runs mid-June to mid-September, departing several times a day from the valley. The bus is not exclusively for hikers, and since the viewpoint is very popular, you should reserve in advance to assure a place.

The trail is generally considered the most scenic of all the trails in the valley, (and arguably the entire park), with views of some of Yosemite's most iconic images spread out in picture-perfect splendour all the way to the bottom. Hikers have several choices.

Option 1 is shorter and steeper, at 13.7 km (8.5 mi.). The final descent includes the Mist Trail, one of the most popular routes in the park. Although this portion can sometimes resemble "a trip to the mall," it is worth it for the unsurpassed views of Vernal Fall.

Option 2, at 14.9 km (9.3 mi.), is longer but less steep, making it easier on the knees and avoiding the crowds often encountered on the Mist Trail.

Option 3 is the full loop, starting from the valley floor and climbing to Glacier Point on the steep Four Mile Trail, then descending the Panorama Trail to the bottom. Unfortunately, despite its name, the Four Mile Trail is actually 4.6 mi. (7.4 km) long! (All of these options are described in more detail under The Hike section below.)

PAUL LYCETT

IS IT "FALL" OR "FALLS"?

Why is it Yosemite Falls but Nevada Fall and Vernal Fall? Both Nevada and Vernal are free-leaping – they fall without being broken on ledges or outcroppings. The plural version, as in Yosemite Falls, means the water meets one or more obstacles as it descends. Vernal and Nevada form the "Giant Staircase" as they plunge in two major steps from Little Yosemite Valley. On a clear day the phenomenon is clearly visible from Glacier Point and the Panorama Trail.

Vernal Fall is an example of a free-leaping cataract.

LIFELONG STUDENT OF THE WILDERNESS

No other single individual's name is more closely associated with Yosemite National Park than that of John Muir. A tireless advocate for the park and the preservation of nature in general, he was a self-described "poetico-trampo-geologist-botanist and ornithologist-naturalist etc. etc.!!!!" Muir didn't consider himself a "natural writer." In fact, he expressed surprise "that I could earn money simply with written words …" Many of his books and articles are considered classics that remain widely available and widely read today.

Muir's mountaineering exploits began when he was a boy in Scotland, where he and his mates "tried to see who could climb highest on the crumbling peaks and crags" of nearby Dunbar Castle. When the family moved to a farm in Wisconsin he escaped a life of toil and brutal beatings to attend university, studying botany and geology. It was an experience that sent him "flying to the woods and meadows in wild enthusiasm," to enter "the University of the Wilderness."

The wilderness was to be his teacher for the rest of his life. Following a 1600 km (1,000 mi.) trek to Florida in 1867 and a six-week walk from San Francisco to Yosemite the following year, he signed on as a summer sheepherder in 1869 to follow a flock of close to 2,500 animals into the high Sierra at Tuolumne (pronounced "To-*all*-uh-me") Meadows. (His account of that summer was eventually published as *My First Summer in the Sierra* in 1911.) It may seem slightly incongruous that someone who regarded these "wool bundles" as "hoofed locusts" would sign up for such a job. But his boss told him his main task was to keep an eye on Billy the shepherd, assuring Muir "that I could study plants and rocks and scenery as much as I liked." And he did just that. The sheer joy and passion of his writing still captures the reader over 100 years later.

John Muir co-founded the Sierra Club in 1892 to "make the mountains glad."

Why would I want to?

Because John Muir said so! In his book *The Yosemite* (1912), Muir advises anyone "so time-poor as to have only one day to spend in Yosemite" to start out at three o'clock in the morning (!) "with a pocketful of any sort of dry breakfast stuff, for Glacier Point, Sentinel Dome, the head of Illilouette Fall, Nevada Fall and the top of Liberty Cap..." Muir was famous for wandering the mountains for days with little more than a blanket, his notebook, some tea and a "crust" of bread tied to his belt. (Bread was important to Muir, who was serious when he wrote, "Just bread and water and delightful toil is all I need." He was recounting his first summer in the Sierra, in 1869, when the party had run out of bread before new provisions arrived and had to rely on a diet of mostly meat. Almost a full six pages is given over to a discussion of camp food and the effects of a lack of bread on an unhappy stomach that "begins to assert itself as an independent creature with a will of its own.")

Muir's one-day excursion is basically the Panorama Trail with the Four Mile Trail and a "glad saunter" up Liberty Cap added in for good measure. This is described below, in the section on "The hike," as Option 3 without the climb to the summit of the Cap. In typical Muir style, he advises hikers to linger at Nevada Fall "an hour or two, for not only have you glorious views of the wonderful fall, but of its wild, leaping, exulting rapids and, greater than all, the stupendous scenery into the heart of which the white passionate river goes wildly thundering, surpassing everything of its kind in the world." Convinced yet?

When to go

The valley remains open all year, but the high elevation in the northern part of the park along Tioga Road means heavy winter snow generally restricts access from late spring to early fall. The park is famous for its dry, sunny summers, when you can expect huge crowds in the valley (complete with traffic jams) and waterfalls at a trickle or even dry. Springtime, when "the snow is melting into music," with waterfalls running at their peak and meadows full of wildflowers, generally avoids the crowds but lingering snow usually means access to Glacier Point and Tuolumne Meadows remains restricted. Autumn is really the best time to visit. The summer hordes have finally left. The oaks, maples and dogwoods provide brilliant displays of fall foliage and the days are cool and crisp, making for almost ideal hiking conditions.

What's the story?

The most extravagant description I might give of this view to any one who has not seen similar landscapes with his own eyes would not so much as hint its grandeur and the spiritual glow that covered it. I shouted and gesticulated in a wild burst of ecstasy ...

— John Muir, *My First Summer in the Sierra*

When Muir caught his first glimpse of the Yosemite Valley in 1869 it was already part of the Yosemite Grant, signed by President Abraham Lincoln in the midst of the Civil War on June 30, 1864. The grant entrusted the Yosemite Valley and the Mariposa Grove of giant sequoias south of the valley to the State of California to be preserved for public use "for all time."

Muir would eventually become one of the most eloquent advocates for the establishment of the park. But well before his arrival a few extraordinary visionaries, including Frederick Law Olmstead and Israel Raymond, had already begun a strong lobbying campaign that led to the enactment of the land grant. Their remarkable foresight, combined with the tireless efforts of John Muir, eventually resulted in the creation of the incredible wilderness sanctuary we now call Yosemite National Park.

And it all happened within a remarkably short time. As early as 1776, Spaniards colonizing the San Francisco Bay area wrote of a snowy range of mountains they christened the Sierra Nevada – *sierra* because the peaks were jagged and sawtooth, *nevada* because they were snowy.

The Spanish gave the mountains a name, but no white man would actually venture into the spectacular valley we call Yosemite until the arrival of the Mariposa Battalion in March 1851. Almost two decades earlier in 1833, Joseph Walker and his team of trappers met heavy snow as they climbed the east slopes of the Sierra Nevada. Walker later confirmed that he and his men knew of the existence of a great valley close to their route, but lack of food and supplies meant they were not equipped to explore it. Reduced to eating some of their horses, their main concern was survival.

What Walker and his crew didn't know was that the valley was the territory of a Miwok tribe who had seen the white men pass their secret mountain home. They called the valley Ahwahnee, "the place of the big mouth," because of its shape, and they called themselves Ahwahneechee, the people of that place. Walker's failure to

A RANGE BY ANY OTHER NAME?

John Muir's vision of the mountains he came to know so intimately was typically more poetic: " the mighty Sierra, miles in height and so gloriously colored and so radiant, it seemed not clothed with light, but wholly composed of it … Then it seemed to me that the Sierra should be called, not the Nevada or Snowy Range, but the Range of Light."

DID YOU KNOW?

The Sierra Nevada is the longest and highest continuous mountain range in America, stretching over 645 km (400 mi.) and covering close to 17 per cent of the state of California. The Rockies may be longer in total but are actually comprised of a series of smaller ranges.

investigate the valley bought the tribe another 18 years of peace before disaster overtook them with the arrival of James Savage and his soldiers.

It was the beginning of what would be a very quick end to the Ahwahneechee way of life, in an astonishing series of events spanning a mere four years. In 1851 the valley was a secret stronghold known only to the natives. By 1855 they had all been killed or driven onto reservations and the first tourists had arrived.

Savage was commanding officer of the volunteer militia called the Mariposa Battalion, which the governor of California had authorized to deal with now hostile tribes in what became known as the Mariposa Indian War.

The conflict between miners, traders and native tribes had arisen following the discovery of gold in January 1848 at Sutter's Mill on the American River northwest of Yosemite. With white men encroaching on their land and hunting their game without negotiation, the natives could be expected to retaliate. Following raids on two of his trading posts, Savage set out in search of a fierce tribe they mistakenly called the "Yosemetos," an apparent corruption of the Miwok word "uzumati," or grizzly bear. The name recognized their reputation as ferocious fighters.

Fortunately for us, a young recruit named Lafayette Bunnell, who accompanied the battalion, recorded his eyewitness account of the group's discovery and subsequent naming of the valley in his book called *Discovery of the Yosemite and the Indian War of 1851 Which Led to That Event*. The first view came at a place he called Mount Beatitude, later named Inspiration Point. Bunnell describes his awe at the sight, admitting that "a peculiar exalted sensation seemed to fill my whole being, and I found my eyes in tears with emotion." Bunnell seems to have been one of the only soldiers moved by what he saw. He wrote later in the book that "very few of the volunteers seemed to have any appreciation of the wonderful proportions of the enclosing granite rocks…" One member recalled, "If I'd known that the valley was going to be so famous, I'd have looked at it."

The group descended to camp near Bridalveil Fall. That night Bunnell suggested the valley be called "Yo-sem-i-ty" in recognition of the tribe they were effectively forcing out of this magical place. He felt the name was "suggestive, euphonious, and certainly American."

By 1855 the first tourists were arriving to see the wonders of the valley for themselves. They were led by James Hutchings. A miner turned journalist with an entrepreneurial

DID YOU KNOW?

Bridalveil Fall gets its name from the white, lacy, veil-like appearance it displays because of frequent wind gusts that cause the lower portion of the fall to fan out. The Ahwahneechee name was Pohono, for "Spirit of the Puffing Wind."

bent, he recognized the potential for promoting the grandeur of the valley in his new, illustrated *California Magazine*.

Hutchings was accompanied by artist Thomas Ayres, whose drawings were later used in books and articles published by Hutchings to promote the valley. Ayers was the first of many artists and photographers whose images would capture the imagination of the world.

Hutchings spoke of the "luxurious scenic banqueting" the valley offered and soon became the owner of Hutchings House, a hotel accommodating visitors willing to undertake the arduous journey to see these wonders. He actually employed John Muir for a season to build a sawmill. Hutchings, who was associated with Yosemite for close to 48 years, eventually grew to bitterly resent the growing popularity of his former employee, to the point where he refused to acknowledge Muir and his accomplishments in any of his writings.

To the south of the valley, Galen Clark had arrived that same year with the second tourist party. Clark returned in 1857, claiming land near the giant sequoia trees in Mariposa Grove. He had been diagnosed with a lung disease that he was told would shortly end his life. Clark decided to go to the mountains "to take my chances on dying or growing better, which I thought were about even." His chances turned out better than even, as he spent most of the next 53 years in Yosemite, eventually dying there at the age of 96.

As travellers began arriving to see the "Big Trees" and to venture farther north into the valley, Clark became a reluctant innkeeper, guiding visitors through the marvellous wonders of the Mariposa Grove and stressing the need for protection of these centuries old giants. When the Yosemite Grant was made in 1864, Clark was appointed the first "Guardian of Yosemite." He later became a friend of John Muir and a charter member of the Sierra Club. Muir described him as "the best mountaineer I ever met, and one of the kindest and most amiable of all my mountain friends." It was high praise from a man who was certainly no slouch himself when it came to climbing mountains.

The arrival of tourists was soon followed by indiscriminate development – trails were built, forests logged, orchards and gardens planted. Sheep were moved to high alpine meadows where their sharp hooves destroyed the delicate wildflowers and fragile grasses.

In an unbelievably fortunate series of events, a few of the right people were in the right place at the right time with a shared vision that was unusual for the times. They saw the impending destruction of one of the world's wonders and sounded the alarm to protect it.

Although John Muir's name is forever linked with the formation of Yosemite National Park, his formidable legacy has overshadowed the contribution of several

EXPRESSING THE SOUL

Of all the artists and photographers associated with Yosemite over the years, perhaps none have captured the essence of the park more than the black and white images produced by Ansel Adams. Adams was a talented concert pianist, but he was considering abandoning a promising music career in favour of photography. Adams later recalled that friends and family warned him, "Do not give up your music; the camera cannot express the human soul." But eventually the camera won. He commented, "I found that while the camera does not express the soul, perhaps a photograph can!" One of his signature photographs, "Monolith, The Face of Half Dome," was shot one afternoon on his last glass plate for the day. He knew he wanted "a brooding form, with deep shadows." Adams recounted, "I felt I had accomplished something, but did not realize its significance until I developed the plate that evening. I had achieved my first true visualization! I had been able to realize a desired image: not the way the subject appeared in reality but how it *felt* to me ..."

D. LARRAINE ANDREWS

The brooding form of Half Dome with Clouds Rest just behind it.

THEY'RE BIG!

Giant sequoias aren't the oldest trees in the world, nor are they the tallest. At 4,600 years old, the bristlecone pine exceeds them by at least 1,500 years. And while the coastal redwoods grow up to 115 m (378 ft.) tall, the tallest of the giant sequoias is only around 94 m (310 ft.). But in total volume, they are the biggest living organism in the world.

It wasn't until the 1960s that scientists realized a policy of fire suppression was putting sequoias at extreme risk by allowing smaller conifers to compete for space, sunlight and moisture and to blanket the forest floor with needle debris. Sequoia seedlings need direct sunlight, good moisture and bare mineral soil to germinate. Finally a series of controlled burns was started to help reduce the dangerous forest litter and foster new sequoia growth.

John Muir understood so well these complex interactions in nature, as evidenced in his book *The Yosemite*, where he turns another common belief on its head: that sequoias are only found in well-watered places. Explained Muir, "… it is a mistake to suppose that the water is the cause of the grove being there; on the contrary, the grove is the cause of the water being there." The immense root system forms a thick sponge "that absorbs and holds back the rain and melting snow, only allowing it to ooze and flow gently … dispensing it as blessings all through the summer, instead of allowing it to go headlong in short-lived floods." Even a century ago Muir understood what today is called complexity theory. As he says in *My First Summer in the Sierra*, "When we try to pick out anything by itself, we find it hitched to everything else in the universe." It is a fitting mantra for the twenty-first century.

YOSEMITE NATIONAL PARK SERVICE LIBRARY

Galen Clark at the base of the Grizzly Giant in the Mariposa Grove.

men who came before him. Without their initial foresight, who knows what would have happened to the precious treasure we know today as Yosemite.

Thomas Starr King was a Unitarian minister well known for his nature book *The White Hills: Their Legends, Landscapes and Poetry*, about the mountains in New Hampshire. In 1861 he set out to see if all the hype about Yosemite was warranted. He was quickly convinced. King chronicled his journey in a series of long letters that appeared in the *Boston Evening Transcript*, and trumpeted its wonders when he returned to his church in San Francisco. His letters created great interest back in New England, but his plans to create a companion book to *The White Hills* and use his influence to promote preservation of the valley were cut short by his untimely death just months before the Yosemite Grant.

King was followed in 1864 by Frederick Law Olmsted, the landscape architect who designed Central Park in New York City. He was overwhelmed with his first view of the valley, writing, "The union of the deepest sublimity with the deepest beauty of nature, not in one feature or another, not in one part or one scene or another, not any landscape that can be framed by itself, but all around and wherever the visitor goes, constitutes the Yo-Semite the greatest glory of nature."

Olmsted teamed up with Israel Raymond, an influential San Francisco business-man who was concerned about the fate of the giant sequoias in Mariposa Grove. Raymond enlisted the help of US Senator John Conness (California), convincing him to introduce a bill in Congress to transfer Yosemite Valley and the Mariposa Grove to the State of California "for public use, resort and recreation ... for all time." The bill passed in 1864, unchallenged by a government totally preoccupied with the bitter Civil War being waged in the east.

The creation of the Yosemite Grant was an improbable and unprecedented victory in a time when the concept of conservation and the preservation of wilderness based solely on its natural and inherent beauty was totally foreign to most people.

It may have represented an historic milestone, but it soon became obvious that protection was in name only. Government appropriations for improvements were almost non-existent, while the administration of the grant lands degenerated into a quagmire of mismanagement and "fat cat" appointments to the governing board. Uncontrolled development resulted in a hodgepodge of roads and hotels, and pastures full of cattle and sheep.

Muir had once written that he wanted "to entice people to look at Nature's loveliness." But he admitted it was not an easy task, noting in 1890 that "... the love of Nature among Californians is desperately moderate." It seemed Californians' love of profit was putting any love of nature at serious risk. Muir had left Yosemite in 1874 to explore the Sierra Nevada, marry, and raise a family on a fruit farm acquired from his father-in-law, with only occasional visits to his beloved Yosemite. His wife eventually sold some of their lands to allow him to return to his first loves of exploration and the study of nature.

A sightseeing trip in 1889 with his friend Robert Underwood Johnson was a catalyst for action. Muir had not seen the valley since 1884. He was dismayed and sick at heart to see thousands of "meadow mowers" destroying the pristine grasslands of Tuolumne Meadows. "To let sheep trample so divinely fine a place seems barbarous," he wrote.

Johnson, the influential editor of *Century Magazine*, convinced Muir to take on the challenge of promoting the formation of a national park to protect the wilderness areas surrounding the land grant. His magazine provided Muir with a national platform to conduct a campaign in which he wrote some of his most enduring and evocative prose in support of the new park. The power and passion of his writing were clearly evident when he wrote: "But no temple made with hands can compare with Yosemite. Every rock in its walls seems to glow with life ... as if into this one mountain mansion Nature had gathered her choicest treasures..." Muir's and Johnson's efforts were instrumental in the designation of Yosemite as a national park on October 1, 1890.

Thanks to the efforts of John Muir and Robert Johnson, the pristine grasslands of Tuolumne Meadows are forever protected from the destructive forces of thousands of "meadow mowers."

LISA P. FREEMAN

But another challenge loomed. The valley and the Mariposa Grove remained under state control and they were in bad shape. By 1895 Muir was in despair, noting, "It looks ten times worse now than ... seven years ago. ... As long as the management is in the hands of eight politicians appointed by the ever-changing Governor of California, there is but little hope."

Hope did come, however, in the person of President Teddy Roosevelt, who visited Yosemite in 1903. Incredible as it may seem now, Muir and Roosevelt camped out together in the *real* Yosemite for several nights. Under Muir's persuasive guidance, Roosevelt was convinced of the need to protect this special place and on June 11, 1906, following bitter resistance by Yosemite businessmen, a bill was finally passed to transfer the Yosemite Grant lands to the national park.

Muir wrote in triumph to his old friend Robert Johnson: "Sound the loud trimble and let every Yosemite tree and stream rejoice... " In the years to come, the park would face, and continues to face, many challenges, not the least of which is its incredible popularity. It regularly attracts close to four million visitors every year. But thanks largely to the incredible persistence and dedication of John Muir, the marvels of this "mountain mansion" are protected forever.

THE HIKE

The Panorama Trail is normally done as a one-way hike beginning at Glacier Point and descending to Happy Isles in the valley. As described in the "Hike overview" section, if you are travelling on your own, you will need to arrange a car shuttle to Glacier Point or take the bus that runs from mid-June to mid-September. It runs several times a day from the valley, but seats should be reserved in advance. It is not exclusively a hikers' bus and is very popular with tourists who take the round trip tour. Check the free park publication called the *Yosemite Guide* for information on the shuttles and practically everything else you need on park essentials.

If you are travelling in your own vehicle, Glacier Point is reached by taking the signed junction along the Wawona Road and driving 25 km (15.5 mi.) to the end of Glacier Point Road. The "Hike overview" section describes three hiking options. Options 1 and 2 follow the same path until you reach the turnoff for the Mist Trail. Option 2 provides a longer but gentler descent, but you can decide when you get there how your knees are doing. Option 3 is basically the loop described by John Muir for hikers with one day to spend in the valley. (See the "Why would I want to?" section above.) This route makes for a long hiking day, adding another 7.4 km (4.6 mi.) to the total and requiring a strenuous climb of 975 m (3,200 ft.) up to Glacier Point, with the views at your back. The good news is it is mostly downhill after that as you follow the Panorama Trail to the valley floor. If you choose Option 3, the trailhead is below Sentinel Rock on Southside Drive at road marker v18. All three options end

YOSEMITE NATIONAL PARK

Tioga Pass

Tuolumne
Meadows

Tioga Road

Hw 120

Hw 120

Yosemite
Falls
El Capitan

Clouds Rest
Half Dome
Glacier Point

Yosemite
Valley

Hw 140

Mariposa
Grove

at Happy Isles in the valley, where you can take the free shuttle back to Yosemite village.

Once you have reached Glacier Point and taken some time to absorb the spectacular view in front of you, head to the Panorama Trail sign-post near the snack bar. The route follows a fire-scarred hillside that is regenerating from a 1987 natural fire. Head left at the fork.

As you descend, magnificent views of Half Dome open up on your left. This Yosemite icon will be visible in all its glory from many places along the trail, clearly revealing the fact that it is not actually a dome, but a ridge.

Magnificent views of Half Dome are revealed along the fire-scarred hillside.

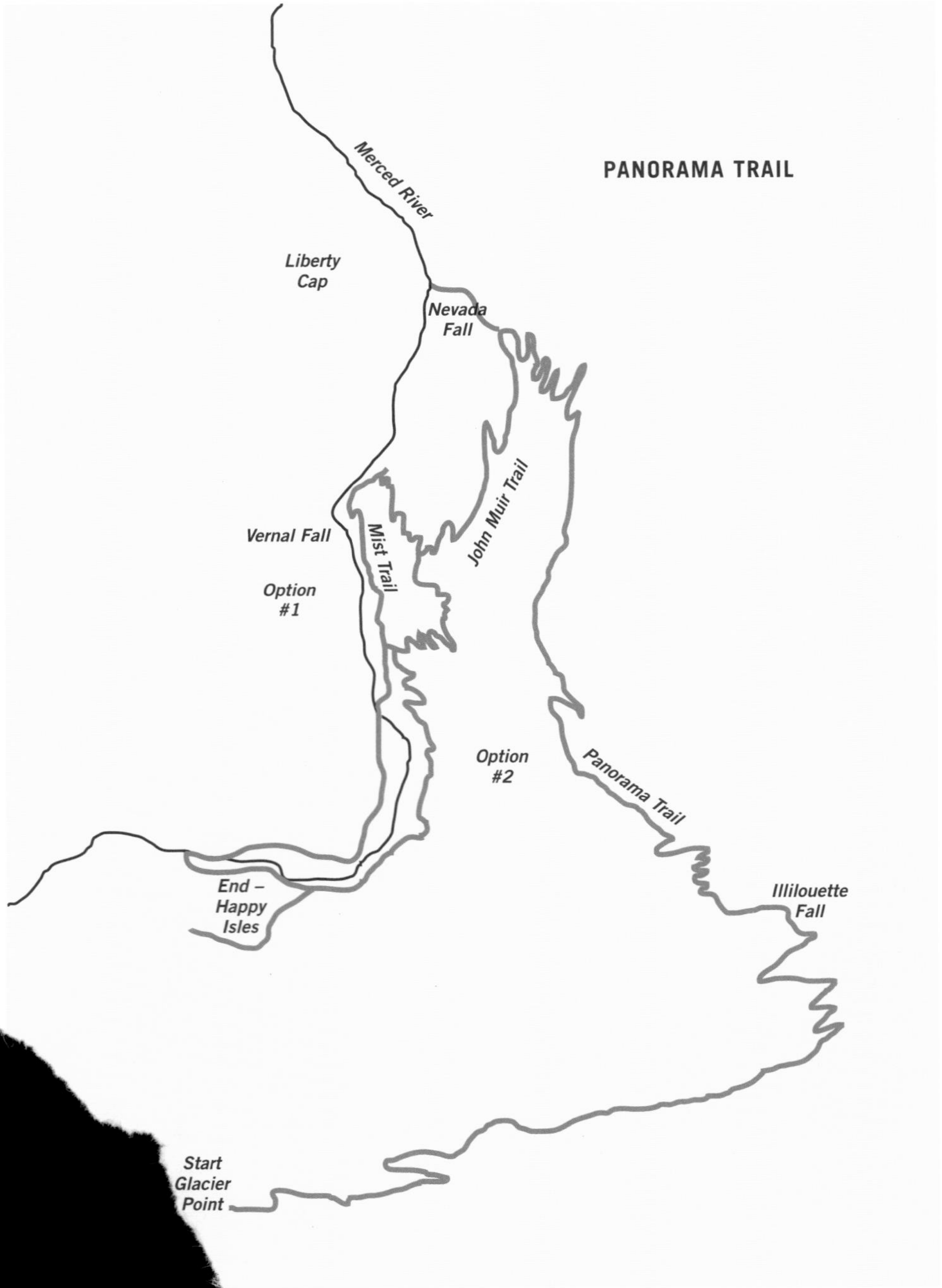

PANORAMA TRAIL

Merced River

Liberty
Cap

Nevada
Fall

Vernal Fall

Mist Trail

John Muir Trail

Option
#1

Option
#2

Panorama Trail

End –
Happy
Isles

Illilouette
Fall

Start
Glacier
Point

SHATTERING THE ILLUSION

Half Dome is probably the most recognizable icon in the park. But it's not really a dome at all. From the valley it appears to have been sliced in half like a loaf of bread, but from Glacier Point and the Panorama Trail it becomes obvious that it is actually a thin ridge with a rounded backside that is almost as sheer as the famous face. Josiah Whitney, the state geologist for California back in John Muir's day, called it "a new revelation in mountain forms; its existence would be considered an impossibility if it were not there before us in all its reality." Whitney judged Half Dome "probably the only one of all the prominent points about the Yosemite which never has been, and never will be, trodden by human foot." Over the years, thousands of hikers have proven him wrong. But the final 45-degree slog to the top would not have been accessible without the ingenuity of a local blacksmith named George Anderson. In 1875 he installed a rope system anchored to bolts he had drilled into the granite. The ropes have since been replaced with steel cables. The hike is so popular that it is now necessary to obtain a permit to climb the cable portion, where overcrowding was creating lineups and dangerous conditions.

D. LARRAINE ANDREWS

This view of Half Dome seen from the Panorama Trail clearly shows it is not really a dome but a thin ridge with a rounded backside almost as sheer as the famous face.

Mules are still a common sight on the trail at the top of Nevada Fall.

D. LARRAINE ANDREWS

LISA P. FREEMAN

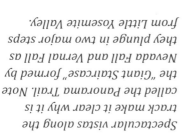

Spectacular vistas along the track make it clear why it is called the Panorama Trail. Note the "Giant Staircase" formed by Nevada Fall and Vernal Fall as they plunge in two major steps from Little Yosemite Valley.

The trail is clearly marked and easy to follow as you descend a series of switch-backs to Illilouette Fall with more views of Half Dome and Mount Starr King. You will descend to a wide bridge and then begin the only major climb on the trail, following the slopes above Panorama Cliff. It soon becomes clear why it is called the Panorama Trail as vantage points along the track provide stunning vistas from Upper Yosemite Falls east past Royal Arches, Washington Column and North and Half Dome. Just when you think it can't get any better, more views of Half Dome, Mount Broderick, Liberty Cap, Clouds Rest and Nevada Fall come into view.

The trail eventually switchbacks down about 1.6 km (1 mi.), intersecting with the John Muir Trail. Make sure to take the short spur to your right and the Nevada Fall viewpoint, a perfect lunch stop.

ELEVEN FEET OF SNOW ALL SUMMER

It was called La Casa Nevada – the Snow House. And for close to 20 years in the 1870s and '80s Emily and Albert Snow welcomed visitors to their hotel near the base of Nevada Fall. Emily often told guests they could expect 11 feet of snow there all summer – a fact they couldn't dispute when she informed them Albert was six feet tall and she was five feet. Emily was famous for her baked beans, one visitor lamenting in the guest book, "Where shall I see their like again?" She also served up copious amounts of doughnuts, chops, pies and bread. James Hutchings noted in his book *In The Heart of the Sierras* that "although they do not know whether the number to lunch will be five or fifty-five, they almost always seem to have an abundance of everything relishable." Emily was well known for her quick rejoinders to odd questions. When one guest asked how they raised foods like tomatoes, she replied, "Oh! Madam, we *raise them* – on the backs of mules!"

Liberty Cap towers next to the free-leaping Nevada Fall. Muir suggested hikers consider a "glad saunter" to the top of the Cap as part of their one day excursion on the trail.

Once you have enjoyed the spectacular views from the top, head back to the John Muir Trail. On your right, Nevada Fall thunders into the valley. The trail can be slippery (I speak from experience here), so take your time on the descent. Soon you will reach Clark Point and decision time. From here you can head right along a connector trail to descend to the Mist Trail (Option 1) or stay on the slightly longer but gentler John Muir Trail (Option 2), which is largely viewless from this point but less steep and much easier on the knees. (It can be quite dusty, though, since it is also a horse trail.) Both trails end at the Happy Isles bus stop, where you can catch a free shuttle back to Yosemite Village.

Assuming you turn right at Clark Point, you will soon pass a sign for the Upper Mist Trail. Ignore this and descend to a viewpoint at the top of Vernal Fall. Then veer south and walk up along the fence to a gate-like opening where you turn right to enter the lower half of the Mist Trail. The trail is one of the most popular in the park, so expect crowds. In the spring it can be quite treacherous, as mist from Vernal Fall saturates the steep steps and you as well. In the autumn the steps can be relatively dry. Portions of this trail are among the steepest in the park, so just take your time on the descent and stop to enjoy the view along the way. There is a steep drop off on your side of the steps by the fall, so if that could be a problem for you, consider taking the safer John Muir Trail.

Muir described Vernal Fall as "a staid, orderly, graceful, easygoing fall, proper and exact in every movement and gesture, with scarce a hint of the passionate enthusiasm of ... the impetuous Nevada, whose chafed and twisted waters hurrying over the cliff seem glad to escape into the open air..." As usual, he seems to have nailed it.

His description of tourists could have been written for the Mist Trail too: "Up the

The stairs next to Vernal Fall are often dry in autumn.

LISA P. FREEMAN

mountains they go, high heeled and high hatted, laden … with mortifications and mortgages … , some suffering from the sting of bad bargains, others exulting in good ones …" Expect to see everything from people in dress shoes to flip-flops, with tiny babies strapped to their backs or three-year-old children running amok on the steps. Just take your time and try not to knock anyone over the edge! The trail eventually descends to cross the Vernal Fall bridge and continues on down to the shuttle-bus stop at Happy Isles and free transportation back to Yosemite village.

HOW TO DO THE HIKE

Yosemite is extremely hiker friendly, with an abundance of information available for anyone who wants to plan their own adventure. Guided day hikes and overnight backpacking are also available through organizations closely associated with the park, including the Yosemite Conservancy, the Sierra Club and Delaware North, the park's concessionaire. (See the "Internet resources" section below for more details.)

If you have at least a week to devote to exploration and want the chance to hike in different parts of the park without the need to camp or organize everything yourself, consider booking with an independent operator who can make all the arrangements so all you need to do is hike. Here are a couple of ideas to consider. I have hiked with both these operators. They are highly reputable and offer excellent value for money. I did the six-day Yosemite trip with Timberline, which covers a variety of hikes around the park, from easy to strenuous, including the Panorama Trail.

- Timberline Adventures **www.timbertours.com**
  I have travelled all over the United States with this company and have never been disappointed. The outfit has been in business for over 30 years, which speaks volumes about how they do business. The trips are all-inclusive, with a high standard of accommodation, safety and personal service. All hikes include two knowledgeable guides, who always seem to find a variety of the absolute best places to eat on every trip.
- New England Hiking Holidays **www.nehikingholidays.com**
  Despite the name, they do hikes all over the United States and parts of Europe.

HOW DO YOU SAY THAT?

The park is full of place names attributed by various explorers and early settlers, often reflecting the Spanish and American Indian influence on the language. Here are a few interesting ones:

- **El Capitan** – the name given to the famous granite monolith by the Mariposa Battalion. Each year, it draws hundreds of death-defying climbers to its vertical cliffs. The name is supposed to be a Spanish translation of the Indian word "To-to-kon-oo-lah," for rock chief.

- Glen Aulin – now the site of a High Sierra camp, is a Gaelic phrase for beautiful valley, or glen.
- Half Dome – has actually had many names over the years, including Rock of Ages, Cleft Rock, Goddess of Liberty and Spirit of the Valley.
- Happy Isles – named for the three nearby islands in the Merced River. It was the site of a massive rock fall in 1996 that knocked over 700 trees and killed one hiker.
- Illilouette – may sound French but is thought to be an English translation for the Indian word "Too-lool-a-we-ack." James Hutchings said it meant "the place beyond which was the great rendezvous of the Yosemite Indians for hunting deer."
- Mono – said to derive from a Yokuts Indian word for "flies." American Indians at Mono Lake harvested the pupae of a fly found there for use as a favourite food.
- Tenaya – the chief of the Indian tribe who lived in the valley when the Mariposa Battalion arrived in 1851. The battalion named Tenaya Lake after the chief, replacing the Native name of "Py-we-ack," or Lake of Shining Rocks.
- Wawona – represents the American Indian name of "Who-who'-nah" for the big trees. The word sounds similar to the hoot of an owl, which they regarded as the guardian spirit of the sequoias.

CONSIDER THIS: BEFORE OR AFTER THE HIKE

Yosemite, it seems, can only be described in superlatives and none of them seem to be entirely adequate. But while much of the focus tends to be on its crown jewel of the valley, there is plenty more to explore outside this narrow and spectacular sliver. The park is the size of Rhode Island, with 95 per cent of it designated wilderness and not accessible to cars. With over 1300 km (800 mi.) of trails, you could literally spend years exploring. Fortunately, even in the valley, the number of people on the trails tends to decrease quickly once you get past the one or two kilometre mark. Ask five Yosemite veterans about their favourite hike and you will get five different answers. It is impossible to say. Here are a few alternatives to consider.

Clouds Rest: A strenuous hike of 23.3 km (14.5 mi.) return, climbing to a 360-degree panorama of the park, with awesome views of Half Dome and the valley. The trail begins at the Sunrise Lakes trailhead off Tioga Road at the west end of Tenaya Lake and is well marked. It involves an elevation gain of 541 m (1,775 ft.), 305 m (1,000 ft.) of which occurs over the course of about 1.6 km (1 mi.) up a series of rocky, ankle-busting switchbacks. Although the hike only tops out at 3025 m (9,925 ft.), I experienced altitude problems on this hike, probably because it climbs so quickly. Acrophobics and klutzes beware. Anyone who can't handle heights, narrow ledges and sheer drop-offs should not plan on completing the final short bit of this hike to the very top, but you will still be rewarded with good views on the ridge. Muir writes of running up to Clouds Rest to get some primulas for a botanist friend, then running home in the moonlight with the sack of roses on his shoulder!

The vista from Clouds Rest provides outstanding views of Half Dome, El Capitan and the Yosemite Valley.

Mono Lake as seen from Mono Pass.

Mono Pass: A moderate high-altitude hike of 12 km (7.5 mi.) return that climbs past streams and meadows to the historic Mono Pass. Be sure to continue a further 500 m (0.3 mi.) into the Ansel Adams Wilderness for fantastic views of Mono Lake and the desert to the east. I would vote this my favourite High Sierra hike but there are many more that I haven't done, of course. The trailhead is located off Tioga Road, just 1.6 km (1 mi.) west of the Tioga Pass entrance and is well marked. The hike is one of the highest-elevation day hikes in the park, topping out at 3230 m (10,600 ft.) with an elevation gain of 275 m (900 ft.). Although it is higher than Clouds Rest, the climb up is gradual and I had no altitude problems. You will pass two forks along this hike. Keep to the left at both. Muir's description of his climb over Mono Pass to the shores of the Lake in *My First Summer in the Sierra* is worth a read, as he describes in great detail the trees and the wildflowers "in lavish abundance."

Glen Aulin: A moderate hike of 21 km (13 mi.) return. Parking is available at the trailhead near the stables close to Tuolumne Meadows off the Tioga Road. This is a very pretty hike as you head past Soda Springs and Parsons Lodge, following the river and the meadows, meandering through lodgepole pine forests and over white burnished granite worn smooth by glaciers. The trail eventually descends steeply to a

Glacier-sculpted rocks are clearly visible along Glen Aulin Trail.

D. LARRAINE ANDREWS

wonderful lunch spot by the White Cascade. The Glen Aulin High Sierra Camp is just over the bridge if you want to partake of the toilets. From here, it's uphill most of the way back, with an elevation gain of 180 m (600 ft.).

Mariposa Grove: Located at the south end of the park, this may be out of your way, but try not to miss the chance to wander amongst the giant sequoias. It's not hard to understand how Ellsworth Huntington came to think of them as old friends.

The giant sequoias in Mariposa Grove seemed like old friends to Ellsworth Huntington during the two summers he spent studying them.

PAUL LYCETT

THIS GUY GOT IT RIGHT!

Washington Lewis, Yosemite's first superintendent, had a brilliant idea. Why not let hikers see the high country without the need to carry a heavy pack? Starting in 1924, a series of High Sierra camps were established to provide beds and meals for hikers, eliminating the need to carry an "irksome" load of equipment. The camps have evolved into hike-in hotels with tent cabins, showers and hearty meals. All you need to bring is a sheet and a towel, plus your clothes. The camps are extremely popular and are booked far in advance by lottery at **www.yosemitepark.com**.

OLD FRIENDS

We may think it is a new concept, but in 1912 Ellsworth Huntington of Yale University published the results of his research into climate change obtained over two summers spent studying some of the giants in Mariposa Grove. After many weeks spent living by the trees, Huntington came to regard them as "friends in a sense more intimate than is the case with most trees. They seem to have the mellow, kindly quality of old age, and its rich knowledge of the past stored carefully away for any who know how to use it."

Troop F on the Fallen Monarch. Visitors to the grove are no longer allowed to climb on the tree.

ARE YOU READY TO EAT?

Food outlets in the park tend to offer standard American fare that is often overpriced but usually provides good fuel before or after a hike. In the valley, the Mountain Room Restaurant at Yosemite Lodge at the falls and the pricey dining room at the Ahwahnee Hotel both offer stunning views along with excellent food. The historic Wawona Hotel, close to the Mariposa Grove in the south of the park, is also a good bet for an upscale meal.

Hygiene standards are high and there should be no concerns about food establishments within the park.

Tipping is expected. Normally at least 15 per cent of the bill would be considered reasonable.

Vegetarians will find no strictly meatless establishments, but most places will offer a vegetarian option.

HORSE SOLDIERS TO THE RESCUE

When the federal government established Yosemite National Park in 1890 it did not appropriate any funds to administer it. The following year, US cavalry troops were assigned the task of patrolling the new reserve, largely because the use of soldiers didn't involve any extra money. They had to be paid anyway, so they were paid to protect the park. The troops were originally stationed just north of the site of the Wawona Hotel but were moved to Camp Yosemite when the valley and the grove became part of the national park in 1906. Once administration was turned over to the new National Park Service in 1916 the camp became the site of Yosemite Lodge and many of the buildings were used for guest accommodations. If you decide to enjoy a meal at the lodge's Mountain Room Restaurant, have a thought for the soldiers camped here so many years ago. Not only did they manage to drive out the illegal miners, hunters, ranchers and sheepherders whose flocks were destroying the high alpine meadows, they built most of the backcountry trails, mapping the vast wilderness as they went. John Muir praised them, saying, "Blessings on Uncle Sam's soldiers ... They have done their job well, and every pine tree is waving its arms for joy."

INTERNET RESOURCES

There is a vast amount of information related to Yosemite available on the Internet. Here are some reliable sources to get you started:

www.nps.gov/yose is the official park website maintained by the National Park Service.

www.yosemite.ca.us/library includes thousands of pages of digital books and articles.

www.sierraclub.org includes a feast of everything related to John Muir, including his complete books and many essays and articles. The Sierra Club also offers guided day hikes and backpacking trips.

www.yosemiteconservancy.org, dedicated to park preservation, offers guided hikes and backpacking trips.

www.yosemitepark.com is the official website of the DNC Parks & Resorts at Yosemite, the park's concessionaire. Reservations for camping and lodging can be made here. They also offer guided hikes and backpacking trips.

www.yosemitehikes.com is an excellent source for trip notes and maps.

RECOMMENDED READING

There have been hundreds of books written about Yosemite and the Sierra Nevada. A good place to look is the website for the Yosemite Online Library as well as the

SANDY BRENNAN

FAUNA FACTS: NO FEAR

Marmots like this guy often show little fear when you pass them on the trail sunning and grooming themselves. The yellow-bellied species frequent the park, where they live in colonies, burrowing in rocky terrain where outcrops provide spots to sunbathe and watch for predators. Marmots respond to danger with a distinctive whistle or an undulating scream to warn the colony of potential threats such as badgers, bears and hikers. The cheeky rodents can spend up to 80 per cent of their lives in burrows, 60 per cent of it hibernating. Because they are estimated to lose up to 50 per cent of their body weight during this time, survival depends on sufficient weight gain by the fall to carry them through their winter sleep. So if they look a bit chubby by the end of the season, there's a good reason!

Sierra Club noted above. Following is a list of books with which I am familiar from my research:

Complete Guidebook to Yosemite National Park – Steven P. Medley – award winning, if a little dated now; gives a concise overview on the basics of the park.

Lonely Planet: Yosemite, Sequoia and Kings Canyon – full of practical information on everything you need to know about the park, plus good maps and hike descriptions.

My First Summer in the Sierra – John Muir – the classic tale of Muir's 1869 trip herding sheep in the high Sierra.

The Secret of the Big Trees: Yosemite, Sequoia, and General Grant National Parks – Ellsworth Huntington – a fascinating piece on climate change research done in the early 1900s. A free copy can be accessed at www.archive.org.

The Yosemite – John Muir – another classic about the park.

Yosemite, a National Treasure – Kenneth Brower – a lavish *National Geographic* park profile with the text and photographs we expect from *National Geographic*.

Yosemite and the Range of Light – Ansel Adams – Adams at his best.

Yosemite and the Wild Sierra – Galen Rowell – a collection of some of Rowell's best images.

Yosemite National Park: A Complete Guide – Jeffrey P. Schaffer – a very comprehensive guide on hiking in the park, including over 80 detailed hike descriptions, chapters on history, flora and fauna, geology and a great bibliography.

Yosemite: The Complete Guide – James Kaiser – an excellent guide to the park, its history and its hikes, with great maps and outstanding photographs by the author.

Yosemite: The First 100 Years 1890–1990 – Shirley Sargent – just what it says: a good history of the park, with lots of archival photos.

Yosemite Trivia – Michael Ross – the answers to all your questions about Yosemite.

Yosemite's Yesterdays, Volumes I and II – Hank Johnston – a fascinating collection of stories about the park that weren't necessarily the biggest newsmakers but certainly merit a read. Includes many wonderful archival photos.

CHAPTER 11 – PATAGONIA – PARQUE NACIONAL LOS GLACIARES – LAGUNA TORRE AND CAMPAMENTO DE AGOSTINI; PARQUE NACIONAL TORRES DEL PAINE – W CIRCUIT

> The name Patagonia, or "Land of the Bigfeet," comes from the word "patagoni," for the big feet of the native Tehuelche people. Tribe members were described as "giants" by Antonio Pigafetta, the chronicler of Ferdinand Magellan's voyage of discovery, 1519–1522.

Justino awoke me this morning by shouting that the wind was blowing, which is like telling a sailor that the sea happens to be salty this morning ... the fact that the air is in rapid motion becomes almost as elemental as the fact that there is air. It is a condition of life here ...

—GEORGE GAYLORD SIMPSON, naturalist, 1932

✳ HIKING RULE 11: In Patagonia, don't bother bringing a hat unless you can attach it securely to your head. Even then, bring an extra one to replace the one that blew away.

WHERE IN THE WORLD?

HOW TO CHOOSE?

Even a cursory browse of information about hiking in Patagonia will present you with the need to make a choice between two spectacular destinations: Parque Nacional Los Glaciares (referred to here as Fitz Roy), and Parque Nacional Torres del Paine (referred to as Paine). It isn't an easy decision.

Paine, located in Chile, seems to get most of

the attention, probably because serious hikers have more choices for routes of different lengths and degree of difficulty. These routes can be done completely backpacking or as a combination of camping and comfortable, serviced huts called refugios or completely refugios. Fitz Roy, located in Argentina, is often overlooked by serious hikers who are not hell-bent on scaling some of the most serious climbing rock in the world. But this park affords access to stunning viewpoints in easy day hikes with no need to camp, although a three- to four-day backpacking alternative allows views of the Fitz Roy Range from many angles.

To my way of thinking, unless you absolutely cannot make the logistics work, you should do them both. Fortunately, in South American terms, the two parks are not far apart, and connections between them are usually not difficult to arrange. You have come all the way to the end of the earth, so don't miss two of the prime hiking locations in all of Patagonia. Obviously, I didn't make a choice. In a departure from all the other chapters in this book, I am including both options. The choice is yours.

WHAT WILL I SEE?

© DEBRA GARSIDE PHOTOGRAPHY

The iconic Cuernos del Paine (Horns of Paine) in Parque Nacional Torres del Paine.

CLAIM TO FAME

Parque Nacional Los Glaciares, or Fitz Roy, is one of the largest national parks on the continent. A UNESCO World Heritage Site, it contains the largest ice mantle outside Antarctica, with a total of 47 glaciers and an additional 200 smaller glaciers separate from the main icefield. Most sedentary tourists flock here to see the spectacular Perito Moreno glacier west of El Calafate in the southern portion of the park. Climbers from all over the world are willing to sit for months playing cards in a base camp waiting for a weather window to challenge the sheer rock spires of Cerro Fitz Roy and Cerro Torre tucked in the northern end of the park. Hikers, however, will find this magical spot a much kinder place, where easy day hikes offer spectacular rewards of scenery for relatively little effort.

Parque Nacional Torres del Paine, or Paine, was recognized as a UNESCO World Biosphere Reserve in 1978. Tourists are drawn by the ability to see the park's most iconic peaks and glacial lakes from the comfort of a bus. Hikers can easily spend a week or more exploring the "wow power" of its massive stone towers, ancient beech forests, massive glaciers and impossibly blue lakes.

HIKE PROFILES

Fitz Roy

Altitude is not a factor in this park. Cerro Fitz Roy, for example, rises to about 3350 m (11,000 feet), but because it is surrounded by rolling plains, it displays more relief than most peaks of that height, accentuating the sheer drama of its glacially carved spire. There is no significant elevation gain on the highlighted walk for this park to Laguna Torre.

WHERE IS PATAGONIA?

Neither a province nor a country, Patagonia is almost a state of mind. Some guidebooks would have you believe it is a clearly defined geographical region covering a vast portion of southern South America. Precise delineations of latitude and longitude will be used to identify the boundaries, devoting a good deal of discussion to how much, if any, of southern Chile should be included. Many Argentines consider Patagonia to include everything south of the Río Colorado all the way to Tierra del Fuego. Many Chileans would describe the "true" Patagonia as the extensive southern steppes of Argentina called *la pampa*. Chile wouldn't even figure on their map of Patagonia. In the end, it seems there is no precise definition. The region encompasses enormous swaths of both countries – from barren tablelands to lush rainforest, from pristine lakes and fertile farmland to glaciers, fjords and jagged peaks. They are all part of this elusive place called Patagonia.

© DEBRA GARSIDE PHOTOGRAPHY

Mount Fitz Roy and its cohorts.

MOUNT TERROR?

Mount Fitz Roy was named after Robert FitzRoy by Argentine explorer and naturalist Francisco Moreno in 1877. FitzRoy was the captain of HMS *Beagle* during two voyages of discovery to the southernmost reaches of the continent. The peak is the tallest in the range that bears the same name. The native Tehuelche name, Chaltén, means "smoking mountain" because of the wind-whipped wisps of cloud that make it resemble a volcano. Some authors have suggested Chaltén signifies "terror," which would seem entirely appropriate for anyone seriously considering the climb up its massive spire. Several attempts to reach the summit were aborted, until members of a French team led by Lionel Terray and Guido Magnone were finally successful in the summer of 1952.

Paine

Altitude is not a factor in this park either. Hikers have the option of doing the full circuit hike, which can take from eight to ten days, or the shorter W trek, so-called

Los Cuernos, or the Horns of Paine, rise above Lago Pehoe.

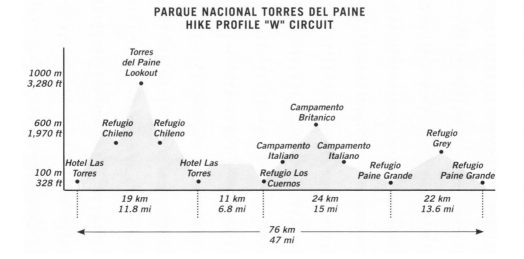

PARQUE NACIONAL TORRES DEL PAINE
HIKE PROFILE "W" CIRCUIT

because the route resembles a W when drawn on a map. This chapter describes the W version. There are several options for doing the W which affect the distances covered and the number of days you'll need for completing it. The route illustrated here begins on the east side of the park heading west, providing the best views of the famous Cuernos del Paine, or Horns of Paine. Hikers usually take about four days to cover about 76 km (47 mi.), with the greatest elevation gain of close to 800 m (2,625 ft.) experienced on the ascent to the Torres del Paine lookout.

Hazards

There are no poisonous or predatory animals (other than the elusive puma), and besides the usual chance you could turn an ankle or take a fall, there are few other hazards. Except, of course, the challenges presented by the wind and the fickle weather. The mental and physical effects of the constant, unrelenting wind combined with the possibility of experiencing all four seasons in one day should not be underestimated. Every travel narrative from Magellan's onward makes some reference to the wind. It blows its fiercest from October to March, during prime hiking time, "stripping men to the raw," according to writer Bruce Chatwin, who did a fair amount of walking for his book *In Patagonia*. Patagonia is the only place in the world where I have hiked all day wearing a Gore-Tex jacket over several layers, and the only place other than Iceland where I have literally been blown off my feet.

WIND TALES

The wind is legendary in Patagonia. George Simpson, on an expedition with the American Museum of Natural History in 1932, commented, "Going into the wind down a slope that was too steep to stand on at all ordinarily, we could walk leaning forward at an apparently fatal angle, supported by the constant gale in our faces ... just there the wind was blowing such large pebbles that we had to remove our goggles for fear of their being hit and broken." Chatwin recalls the "relentless" wind he encountered during a long two-day walk. "Sometimes you heard a truck, you knew for certain it was a truck, but it was the wind. ... Sometimes the wind sounded like an unloaded truck banging over a bridge. Even if a truck had come up behind you wouldn't have heard it." Sometimes the wind actually stops, creating an eerie effect after you have become accustomed to the unremitting pounding. Explorer Eric Shipton described it as "the sudden cessation of an artillery barrage, the silence was uncanny, almost oppressive." A similar experience occurred during almost two days I spent in Ushuaia, located further south in Tierra del Fuego, where the unnatural calm became an almost constant source of comment.

The essentials

Travelling in Patagonia requires compliance with requirements for both Argentina and Chile. Border crossings are frequent and can be slow. They need to be factored into your travel time.

Getting there: Both Argentina and Chile are regularly serviced by a number of major airlines or their partners including, among others, Air Canada, American Airlines, British Airways, Delta, LAN, Qantas and United Airlines. There are a number of options to access southern destinations in Patagonia, depending on whether you are arriving in South America through Santiago de Chile or Buenos Aires.

By air: Aerolíneas Argentinas (**www.aerolineas.com.ar**) provides regular service through the domestic airport Jorge Newbery near downtown Buenos Aires, to El Calafate and Ushuaia. If you are connecting through an international flight, be aware that flights arrive at the international airport Ezeiza, requiring a transfer that must be factored into your travel plans.

LAN (**www.lan.com**) provides service to Punta Arenas from Santiago (through Puerto Montt) and Ushuaia (through the domestic airport in Buenos Aires).

By bus: Bus services connecting the main cities in Patagonia are generally frequent and quite good. Check the "Internet resources" section for websites with links to information on travelling by bus. Of course, if you are using the services of a tour operator/outfitter, you can avoid the hassle of arranging your own connections.

Currency: Both Argentina and Chile use a unit of currency called the peso – referred to as ARS, or AR$, and CLP, or CH$, respectively. AR$1 and CH$1 = 100 centavos, although centavos are no longer circulated in Chile. For current exchange rates, check out **www.oanda.com.**

Special gear: Make sure you have good, sturdy, waterproof walking boots. Hiking poles are highly recommended to maintain balance in the strong winds. A hat you can tie on, sunscreen and water bottles are essential, as are layers of warm clothing and good rain gear. No special gear other than a good day pack are required for hiking in Fitz Roy, since many of the viewpoints are easily accessible in day hikes using the town of El Chaltén as your base. Several options are available in Paine, including full backpacking and camping or a combination of camping and staying at comfortable serviced huts called refugios. Camping equipment is generally available for rent at many campsites, and meals can be purchased at the refugios, which offer beds (you will need a sleeping bag), hot showers and full or partial board. Your choice of route and mode of travel will determine the amount of gear and the size of your backpack.

THE HIKES – AN OVERVIEW

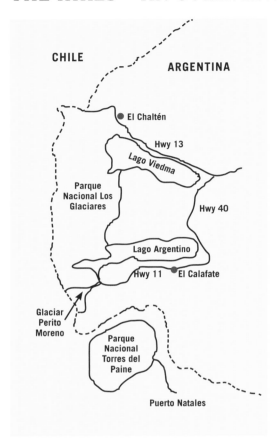

Fitz Roy

Hikes in the park begin and end in the small town of El Chaltén. The trailhead for the walk to Laguna Torre and Campamento de Agostini is easily accessed at the northwestern edge of town. This is a relatively easy, well-marked track involving minimal elevation gain or loss and with stunning views of Cerro Torre.

Paine

The W circuit described in this chapter travels from east to west, capturing the best views of the famous Horns of Paine. The park is accessed via road from Puerto Natales, 112 km (70 mi.) to the south. The first leg of the W begins near the Hostería Las Torres and follows the Río Ascencio to the base of the Torres del Paine. Retracing your steps to Hostería Las Torres, the hike skirts Lago Nordenskjold to Refugio Los Cuernos. The next leg of the W heads into the Valle de Frances, then on to the Mountain Lodge Paine Grande. The final portion of the W follows Lago Grey north to its terminus at Glaciar Grey for a return boat trip to the southern tip of the lake. There are various options available to hikers along the circuit, but this is a basic description of the route I followed. The trails are well marked, and other than a challenging climb over boulders to the Torres del Paine lookout on the first day, the trek does not involve a significant amount of elevation gain or loss. The biggest challenges are the wind and the weather. Since this is a multi-day hike, you must be prepared with sufficient gear as well as both mentally and physically to deal with the wild wind and the possibility of cold, wet conditions even in the middle of summer.

Why would I want to?

Fitz Roy

The northern sector of the park is serviced by the small town of El Chaltén, which is accessed by road from El Calafate. Crossing the barren Patagonian steppes and skirting the shores of Lago Argentino and Lago Viedma, the drive is one of the highlights of the entire trip. Long before you reach El Chaltén, the ramparts of Cerro Fitz Roy rise above the plains, dominating the horizon with their singular beauty.

Veteran Patagonian climber Gregory Crouch sums it up superbly in his book *Enduring Patagonia*. He makes his case (and mine) rather well:

> An otherworldly range of mountains exists in Patagonia ... It is a sublime range, where ice and granite soar with a dancer's grace. Cerro Fitz Roy and Cerro Torre are the two crown jewels of the range. ... Fitz Roy's stone bulk towers ... over the arid plains and dominates the landscape like a barbarian king. Beside and a bit behind the king rises Cerro Torre, his royal consort, a graceful obelisk: tall, slender, vertiginous, elusive ... Cerro Torre stands at the left end of a line of towers, all divided from Fitz Roy and his satellites by a deep valley and a flowing glacier. Anywhere else, the peaks that flank Fitz Roy and Cerro Torre would be centerpiece summits; here in Patagonia they are the palace guard.

Crouch sees these towers with the eyes of a climber. Fortunately a hiker can see the "barbarian king" and his "palace guard" with a pair of sturdy boots planted firmly on the ground and a good day pack.

Paine

Many regard this park as South America's finest. Dominated on the northeast side by its monolithic Torres del Paine and the distinctive Cuernos del Paine to the south, the jagged peaks of the Paine Massif lie at its core. But it's not just about mountains. Open steppes and ancient beech forests compete for your attention with the tongues of immense glaciers jutting into electric blue lakes fringed by shockingly pink flamingos. Somehow it hardly seems surprising to see Andean condors soaring above herds of graceful guanacos and flocks of large, flightless birds the size of small horses (called rheas) darting madly about this magical place. Best of all, it's easily accessible in a moderate four-day hike to anyone of reasonable fitness.

When to go

Seasons are reversed in this part of the world, with January and February the height of the summer. Since these months are also summer holidays for South American school children, trails can get crowded at this time of the year. Fitz Roy receives heavy snowfall during the winter, so hiking is confined to November to April, subject of course to the vagaries of the weather. Although Paine is open all year, the peak hiking period is considered to be December to late March. Hiking in the shoulder seasons of November and April can be less crowded, with the added benefit of reduced wind later in the season.

What's the story?

Patagonia. The very name evokes a place of myth and mystery at the end of the earth.

Renowned travel writer Bruce Chatwin calls Patagonia "a metaphor for The Ultimate, the point beyond which one could not go." He explains, " ... in the opening chapter of *Moby Dick*, Melville uses 'Patagonian' as an adjective for the outlandish, the monstrous and fatally attractive" when he refers to "all the attending marvels of a thousand Patagonian sights and sounds ... "

W.H. Hudson grew up in Argentina and became a well-known author and ornithologist. He helped perpetuate the myth in his book *Idle Days in Patagonia*, first

An impressive panorama of peaks in Parque Nacional Torres del Paine.

© DEBRA GARSIDE PHOTOGRAPHY

published in 1893. Hudson vividly recalls his arrival following a near disastrous shipwreck. "At last, Patagonia! How often I had pictured in imagination, wishing with an intense longing to visit this solitary wilderness, resting far off in its primitive and desolate peace, untouched by man, remote from civilization! ... the ancient habitation of giants ... "

Even as late as the 1970s a famous outdoor equipment firm decided to capitalize on the allure of the name when it switched from the solid but rather dull Chouinard Equipment to "Patagonia." They explained, "To most people ... Patagonia was a name like Timbuktu or Shangri-La: far-off, interesting, not quite on the map. [It] brings to mind romantic visions of glaciers tumbling into fjords, jagged, wind-swept peaks, gauchos and condors."

Chris Moss, in his book *Patagonia: A Cultural History*, maintains, "Patagonia was mysterious even before it came into being."

Well before Ferdinand Magellan rounded the Cape of 11,000 Virgins on October 21, 1520, and stumbled into the strait that would eventually carry his flotilla to the Pacific, Europeans believed in the existence of a *terra australis incognita*, an "unknown land of the south" on the basis that the lands of the Northern Hemisphere must be balanced by land in the south.

DAD SITS IT OUT

Rheas, or nandu, are ostrich-like, flightless birds that once populated the vast Patagonian plains before settlers established huge estancias (ranches) and filled them with sheep and cattle. The birds can still be seen but in much reduced numbers. In an unusual reversal of roles, the male rhea incubates the eggs and cares for the chicks once they hatch. They were hunted by natives and settlers alike for their tasty meat. Aboriginals and after them the gauchos used boleadoras comprised of three medium-sized stones covered with rawhide, attached to three long strips of hide. The contraption was spun around the head and then thrown like a lasso to wind around the bird's legs, stopping it instantly in its tracks.

Antonio Pigafetta, Magellan's Italian diarist, claimed they already knew of "a very mysterious strait by which one could sail" through a southern passage leading to the Southern Sea. He maintained the map had been made by an "excellent man called Martin de Boemia," a well-known German cartographer. It seemed logical there would be a water channel between the two worlds of north and south.

Hell was thought to exist somewhere in the far south, so it wasn't much of a leap to believe the Land of Fire – Tierra del Fuego – reported by Pigafetta, was the land of Satan. Maps showed Fire Land at the edge of some great contrarian Antarctic continent, the antipodean reverse of the north, where trees grew down and snow fell up.

WHY SO MUCH WIND?

You will not escape it. Wild and unrelenting, the "terrible wind" blows from the west with the force of a locomotive, in gusts that will knock you off your feet. Why is it so fierce? Crouch explains in *Enduring Patagonia*: "[The great peaks of Patagonia] stand squarely athwart what sailors refer to as the 'roaring forties' and 'furious fifties' – that region of the Southern Hemisphere between 40° and 60° south latitude known for ferocious wind and storm. The violent weather spawned over the great south sea charges through the Patagonian Andes with gale-force wind, roaring cloud, and stinging snow … Patagonia is a land trapped between angry torrents of sea and sky." As a relatively small land mass in the huge expanse of the southern ocean, it bears the full, brute force of the raging storms. The wind is forced up over the mountains, dumping the snow and precipitation that has gradually formed the great glaciers and ice caps. As it plunges down the other side, it accelerates, not unlike the famous chinook of the Canadian Rockies. Be prepared if you are standing in the way!

© DEBRA GARSIDE PHOTOGRAPHY

A weathered tree shows the effects of constant wind.

The fires they reported were actually those of the Fuegian Indians, but until the region was properly mapped, fantastical images of monsters, mermaids and condors big enough to carry off elephants persisted. How could reality possibly compete with that?

Myths continued to abound. Pigafetta documented a land of "giants," which he christened "patagoni," for their big feet, hence the name Patagonia. But as Bruce Chatwin points out, "Patagonia cannot, and never could have, meant Big-Foot. 'Pata' is indeed a 'foot' ... in Spanish but the suffix '-gon' is meaningless." And they didn't even actually have big feet in the first place. Apparently the large footprints Pigafetta had seen were the result of the furs the natives wrapped around their feet to protect them from the cold.

A more fanciful explanation for the origin of the name Patagonia comes from the romantic tale of the great "Patagon." As Chris Moss recounts in his book *Patagonia: A Cultural History*, Patagon was said to be "born of an animal ... and the most monstrous being on earth; ... He looks like a dog, with big ears that reach down to his shoulders ..." It finally took the reasoned logic of Charles Darwin to put an end to the hyperbole, but by then, of course, the name and the myths were firmly entrenched. Darwin recalled an interview "with the famous so-called gigantic Patagonians ... Their height appears greater than it really is, from their large guanaco mantles, their long, flowing hair, and general figure; on an average their height is about six feet ..."

11,000 VIRGINS?

When Magellan finally rounded the cape and entered the strait that would eventually bear his name, it was the Catholic feast day of St. Ursula and the 11,000 Virgins. The legend of St. Ursula has countless variations. One claims that an entourage of 11,000 virgins accompanied her on a pan-European pilgrimage. They were all beheaded in a massacre by the Huns, while St. Ursula herself was shot dead. (The number 11,000 seems improbable, to say the least – it has been suggested "some blundering monk" wrote it down wrong.) Magellan apparently named the cape in honour of the feast day, although there could have been more subtle influences at play in his choice of names, considering he and his crew had already been at sea for a long time. Ahead of them lay 38 days of tortuous navigation through a 538 km (334 mi.) maze of islands and dead ends before they would finally emerge successfully into the Pacific Ocean.

But that wasn't the end of the fantastical stories. By the early 1600s, rumours were circulating about the existence of a magical City of the Caesars, variously called the Wandering City or Trapalanda, a prosperous city rich with gold, silver and diamonds located somewhere in a valley of the Andes. Many versions concerning

© DEBRA GARSIDE PHOTOGRAPHY

Andean condors are big but not big enough to carry off elephants.

its location and its founders persisted well into the late 1700s. A history of very real discoveries of untold wealth in the Aztec and Inca cities to the north sparked a renewed effort to find this elusive place where Spaniards were claimed to be immortal. Historian Enrique de Gandía sums up the magical notion of the place: "This city of illusions was finally lost in the unknowable immensity of silent, tragic Patagonia, where there are still dreamers who, without admitting, search for it and dream of it."

The real tragedy of Patagonia was postponed until the last quarter of the nineteenth century when the rising strategic importance of the region to both Chile and Argentina inevitably drove the push for colonization. It would ultimately mean obliteration of the native tribes who had occupied these harsh lands for thousands of years. But in the meantime the extreme climate, to which they were superbly adapted, bought them some time.

In response to perceived threats from British pirates like Sir Francis Drake, the Spanish had attempted to establish colonies along the Magellan Strait in the late 1500s, but with disastrous results. With names like Cape Famine, it isn't hard to conclude they were a dismal failure.

It wasn't until 1848 that the first Chilean settlement was successfully established at Punta Arenas. Known to English sailors as Sandy Point, it became an important stopping point for ships rounding the Horn on their way to the California Gold Rush, but declined in importance after the completion of the Panama Canal.

In 1831 British naturalist Charles Darwin accompanied the second voyage of the

Beagle. Even today the account of his travels remains readily available and widely read. Although Darwin wrote with the keen eye of a scientist, he was deeply affected by his journey, later recalling, "No one can stand unmoved in these solitudes, without feeling that there is more in man than the mere breath of his body. In calling up images of the past, I find the plains of Patagonia most frequently cross before my eyes."

Darwin managed to capture that sense of the empty unknown that continues to pull travellers to this place almost two centuries later. But his writings also had a profound influence on the fate of the natives. Darwin called them "ape people," stating, "One can hardly make oneself believe they are fellow-creatures, and inhabitants of the same world." His comments helped fuel a campaign that would eventually mean genocide for the indigenous peoples.

In his book *In Patagonia* Chatwin describes it this way: "In the 1890s a crude version of Darwin's theory, which had once germinated in Patagonia, returned to Patagonia and appeared to encourage the hunting of Indians. A slogan: 'The Survival of the Fittest,' a Winchester and a cartridge belt, gave some European bodies the illusion of superiority over the far fitter bodies of the natives."

Ironically, Darwin later forecast the demise of the native population, following a

THE KING OF PATAGONIA – BELIEVE IT OR NOT, THIS ONE IS ACTUALLY TRUE

To call it an unlikely alliance is a bit of an understatement. In the early 1550s, the Spanish began a period of conquest in what would eventually become part of Chile. They were met with ferocious and unexpected resistance by the native Mapuche people. This fiercely independent tribe had managed to successfully consolidate their power over a number of scattered groups in a process called Araucanization. By 1777 the Spanish grudgingly admitted they could not control these militants and officially recognized a separate kingdom called Araucanía, outside the rule of the Spanish authorities. When Orllie-Antoine de Tounens arrived from France to establish what he called his "single constitutionally monarchic federation," he found the Spanish patently uninterested. But it seemed a match made in heaven when he began to find support amongst the Mapuche. They probably believed their case might be better served by a European speaking on their behalf. By November 1860, de Tounens declared himself king of a constitutional hereditary monarchy called Araucanía, a territory embracing all the lands of Patagonia as far south as the Strait of Magellan. In 1862 the Chilean authorities arrested him for fomenting revolution amongst the indigenous peoples. Although he insisted his intentions were purely philanthropic, he was tried and declared "loco." De Tounens eventually died in France in 1878, while the Mapuche fell victim to so-called "pacification." They called it "the Last Massacre" as their traditional lands were overrun with thousands of foreign settlers.

meeting with Argentine dictator Juan Manuel de Rosas. "Every one here is fully convinced that this is the justest war, because it is against barbarians. Who would believe in this age in a Christian civilised country that such atrocities were committed?"

Native tribes did put up a fight, but in the end they were ruthlessly hunted for a bounty or fell victim to diseases of the white man from which they had no protection. Even an alliance with the King of Patagonia could not avoid the inevitable "pacification."

A flood of immigrants from around the world began settling wide swaths of Patagonia, encouraged by the governments of Chile and Argentina. Both countries were determined to grab as much of the territory as possible. Boundary disputes and threats of war continued well into the twentieth century. Welsh, German, English, Scots, South Africans, Yugoslavs filled the empty lands. Soon the guanaco herds were replaced by huge estancias filled with sheep and cattle, while farther north, in the Chilean Lake District, farmers settled the rich agricultural lands.

Both Argentines and Chileans would eventually come to know the terror of brutal totalitarian regimes where opposition often courted torture and death. Fortunately both countries have emerged from those dark times to enjoy new democratic freedom and economic prosperity, fed in no small part by the continued growth of tourism. But even as Patagonia continues to become more and more accessible to the average traveller, it still retains that mythical sense of the "back of beyond," a place of ethereal beauty at the end of the world.

THE HIKES

Fitz Roy – Laguna Torre and Campamento de Agostini – 19 km (11.8 mi.)

This hike is often referred to as one of the most classic in the park. Elevation gain or loss is minimal.

The walk begins at the northwestern end of the small town of El Chaltén, the self-proclaimed trekking capital of Argentina. From a signpost on Av San Martin, head west on Eduardo Brenner, and then right where a post indicates the beginning of the trail. (An alternative start can be found behind the Hotel Los Cerros located in town.)

Whether you take the main trail or the alternative, the two meet at a junction. The track then heads west to a mirador, or lookout, with extraordinary views of Cerro Torre and the Río de las Vueltas valley.

Follow the trail through stands of lenga (a species of beech tree) and across glacial moraines, eventually passing a junction on the right that is a short cut route to Campamento Poincenot. Ignore this path and continue on up the valley, eventually bearing left to cross an alluvial plain and follow the waters of Río Fitz Roy to arrive at Campamento de Agostini. A further 15-minute walk from the camp brings you to the shores of Laguna Torre where it is common to see icebergs that have calved off the face of the glacier below Cerro Torre. Once you have taken in the remarkable panorama of granite spires and massive glaciers laid out before you, return via the same route to El Chaltén.

If you have time to fit in another day hike, consider the walk to Laguna de Los Tres. Beginning at the north end of El Chaltén, the trail climbs onto open slopes of salt bush and tussock grasses, passing through patches of beech forest before eventually arriving at Campamento Poincenot. Good views of Mount Fitz Roy are the reward on this trek, with even more spectacular vistas if you make the final ascent from the camp up to Laguna de Los Tres.

© DEBRA GARSIDE PHOTOGRAPHY

For many years, Cerro Torre was considered impossible to climb.

IMPOSSIBLE TO CLIMB

One look at the sheer granite spires of Cerro Torre and it isn't hard to see why it was declared impossible to climb by some of the world's best mountaineers. But that only spurred on members of the climbing community to take up the challenge. Controversy dogged several attempts to reach the summit, beginning with the assault by Cesare Maestri and Toni Egger in January 1959. Egger was lost in an avalanche on the descent, along with the evidence captured on his camera. Maestri claimed they had reached the top, but he had no proof. He returned in 1970 to make his claim official, sparking even more debate when he used a compressor and two high-powered drills to install safety spikes along the route. Even then he failed to climb the final "ice mushroom" at the summit, claiming it was nothing more than a piece of snow and not part of the mountain. The dispute was finally settled once and for all when an Italian team led by Casimiro Ferrari finally made it to the "real" top in January 1975.

The view down the Río de las Vueltas valley.

HIKE 1 – LAGUNA TORRE
HIKE 2 – LAGUNA DE LOS TRES

Paine – the W Circuit – 76 km (47 mi.)

This hike can be done from either direction, although the description is from east to west over four days. This provides the best views of the Horns of Paine as you walk west. Logistics and distances may vary depending on whether you go with an outfitter or independently. (See the "How to do the hike" section below.)

Day 1 – Hotel Las Torres to Torres del Paine Lookout – 19 km (11.8 mi.) return

This is the only day with significant elevation gain/loss of about 800 m (2,625 ft.). The trail begins just past the hotel, where it crosses a bridge and heads steeply uphill (but not for long). It follows the Río Ascencio, with fine views back over the valley if you need an excuse to stop and catch your breath. The route passes the Refugio Chileno, a good place to stop for a warm drink on a cold day, and then continues past Campamento Torres. (A refugio supplies meals and sleeping accommodations, while a campamento is a campground.) For the next hour the trail climbs steeply (about 400 m or 1,312 ft.) over a large, "knee-popping" boulder field to the treeless tarn at the base of the towers. Once you have rested and enjoyed the view, return by the same route.

There are no guarantees you will see anything for your efforts. This goes for anywhere in Patagonia, of course, but I speak from personal experience here. I have done this hike twice – the first time in miserable cold, rain and wind, with only cloud shrouded Torres to greet us at the top. The second time was luckier – we actually

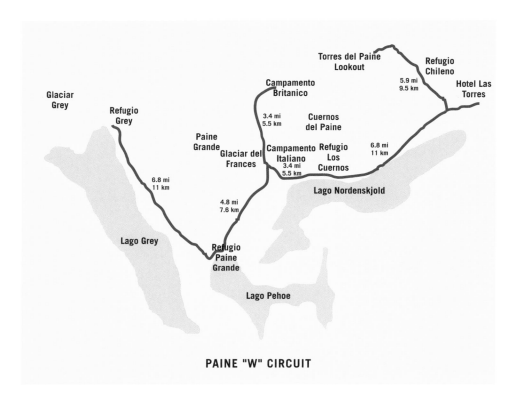

PAINE "W" CIRCUIT

WHAT A PAINE!

Chileans claim their park is "one of the most beautiful and unique places on the planet." The name "Paine" is from a native Tehuelche word meaning "blue," for the electric-blue glacial lakes, while "Torres" refers to the Torres del Paine. These are the three granite towers – Torre Sur, Torre Central and Torre Norte – that form the centerpiece of the park. Torre Norte was conquered in 1958 by an Italian expedition, but it wasn't until 1963 that a British team scaled Torre Central and Italians made the first climb of Torre Sur. It is hard to believe that prior to its creation in 1959, the park was actually part of a large sheep estancia.

saw the Torres, although I must admit the view from the Hotel Las Torres was pretty good without any effort at all! There are several options for accommodations here ranging from the luxurious hotel to camping. We stayed at a private camp with meals provided by the outfitter.

Day 2 – Camping Las Torres to Refugio Los Cuernos – 11 km (6.8 mi.)

The trail is moderate, with a number of uphill and downhill

The spires of the Torres del Paine.

CLEOPATRA'S NEEDLES

"[W]e still directed our march along the grassy plain which led direct towards the three huge Cleopatra peaks rising from out of the snow glaciers far ahead of us." The summits were the Torres del Paine – "three tall peaks of a reddish hue, and in shape exact facsimiles of Cleopatra's Needle …" (This was the popular name for three ancient Egyptian obelisks relocated to London, Paris and New York City in the nineteenth century.) The year was 1879. Lady Florence Dixie, the daughter of the eighth Marquess of Queensberry, had set out the year before on a journey of discovery with her husband, two brothers and a family friend.

Lady Dixie was weary of "the shallow artificiality of modern existence" and was looking for an adventure. She certainly found it here, as she describes in her account of the voyage, *Riding Across Patagonia: A Victorian Equestrian Adventure*. The woman was clearly no slouch when it came to facing the challenges of hunting wild rheas, outrunning prairie fires and surviving a horse fall which she describes as follows: "Unconscious of anything but the exciting chase … I am suddenly disagreeably reminded that there *is* such a thing as caution …" When her horse steps in a hole and crashes on his head, "he turns completely over on his back, burying me beneath him in a hopeless muddle." But Florence is up in no time, rejoining "the now somewhat distant chase."

ROBERT A. MITCHELL JR.

Before she left on her adventure, incredulous friends had wondered why on earth she would choose "such an outlandish part of the world to go to." Florence replied simply, "Precisely because it was an outlandish place and so far away …" And she did it all in skirts and riding sidesaddle!

Cleopatra's Needles as Lady Florence Dixie would have seen them from the plains below.

sections. It follows the shore of Lago Nordenskjold to the refugio. On a clear day, the lake seems impossibly blue. Winds can be fierce along this section. The refugio provides bunks, hot showers and full or partial board. Camping is also available. We stayed at the refugio. It was warm and very comfortable, with good food, a welcome respite from the cold wind. Vertigo alert: the bunks are stacked three high and it's a long way to the top one!

Day 3 – Refugio Los Cuernos to Refugio Paine Grande via Valle des Frances - 24.1 km (15 mi.)

This can be a long day if you do the whole hike, which involves backtracking along part of the middle leg of the W. I must confess I have tried this hike twice and never made it past Campamento Italiano, because of pouring rain and cold wind. On a good day (or so I'm told), the views of Paine Grande to the west and the Torres and Los Cuernos to the east are quite spectacular. You will need to assess whether you think it is worth the effort to hike all the way to Campamento Britanico if you aren't going to be able to see anything. Conditions on this part of the trail can be slippery, but it can be easily bypassed during inclement weather.

The trail to Campamento Italiano follows the shore of the lake, then climbs up to the camp. With any luck you will catch some good views of the Glaciar del Frances and Cerro Paine Grande to the west. From Campamento Italiano to Campamento Britanico it is a full 11 km (6.8 mi.) return before heading off to Refugio Paine Grande. You can decide how far you want to go. From Campamento Italiano it is another windy 7.6 km (4.7 mi.) over rolling, open terrain along the shores of Lago Skottsberg and Lago Pehoe. The views of the Cuernos and Cerro Paine Grande along this stretch can be outstanding.

Refugio Paine Grande is a huge complex offering several accommodation options and full or partial board. We stayed at the campground with wonderful hot showers and outstanding views of the Cuernos. We took our meals at the refugio, which offered good, substantial hiking fare.

ROBERT A. MITCHELL JR.

Cerro Paine Grande rises from the mist.

Day 4 – Refugio Paine Grande to Glaciar Grey and Refugio Grey – 11 km (6.8 mi.) one way

There are a number of options for finishing up this leg of the W and the last day of the hike. The walk from Refugio Paine Grande to the glacier follows a relatively easy trail along Lago Grey to the lookout just past the refugio. (The refugio is a good place to stop for a

© DEBRA GARSIDE PHOTOGRAPHY

The Cuernos del Paine exhibit distinctive dark caps.

cup of tea on a cold day.) You can head back the way you came or take the passenger boat to the southern end of the lake, with fantastic up-close views of the glacier and the Cuernos. (The boat launch is located near the refugio.) Again, don't underestimate the force of the wind. It certainly made for an interesting boat trip at the end of the hike. From here you can choose whether to overnight in the park or head back to Puerto Natales.

HOW TO DO THE HIKES

Fitz Roy

As noted in "The hikes" section, the logistics of hiking in this park are quite easy. Some of the most spectacular viewpoints can be reached via day hikes that begin and end in El Chaltén. You will only require a good day

ON THE HORNS OF A DILEMMA

It can be hard to keep your Torres straight! In Fitz Roy, the peaks are often referred to interchangeably as Cerro, Monte or Macizo (massif). Along with Cerro Fitz Roy, Cerro Torre dominates the Fitz Roy range, but it should not be confused with the Torres del Paine, which are the three distinctive, iconic towers in the northeast section of Paine. The Cuernos, or "Horns," are also located in Paine, south of the Torres. The Cuernos are easily recognizable due to their distinctive dark caps, remnants of a heavily eroded, softer sedimentary layer sitting atop a band of exposed granite.

Glaciar Grey as seen from Lago Grey.

SLIP SLIDING AWAY

Patagonia's colossal glaciers are really nothing more complicated than huge masses of surplus snow that did not manage to melt from season to season, but accumulated over hundreds of years. All it took was enough cold winters followed by some not very warm summers to eventually give rise to these vast icy formations. Old unmelted snow becomes compacted into ice as new deposits accumulate over successive millennia. Once the glacier reaches a critical mass, it will begin to overflow the accumulation zone and move under the force of its own weight. These rivers of ice exert tremendous pressure on anything standing in the way, ripping up and dragging enormous quantities of rock and debris. In the process they literally shape the landscape, chiselling mountains, valleys and lakes as they finally grind to a halt on flat ground. It is hard to believe it all started with something as simple as a snowflake.

pack, some food and your rain gear. Variations on the described hike allow for two- or three-day extensions that provide more spectacular views of the Fitz Roy Range. Permits are not required but you will need to carry your food and camping gear with you. See the "Internet resources" section for links to information on the park as well as El Calafate and El Chaltén.

Paine

As noted in "The hikes" section, there are several alternatives when it comes to hiking in the park that can require everything from full backpacking and camping to just carrying sufficient clothing and personal gear for the duration of the trip while using the services of the refugios for board and lodging. In theory, camping equipment can be rented at the refugios, but it may not be available in the high season. Trekkers must register and pay an entry fee. See the "Internet resources" section for links to information on the park and the refugios. Bookings must be made far in advance of arrival.

For those who prefer to leave all the planning and logistics to the experts, here are some recommended outfitters who offer hiking trips in both parks. I have travelled with all of these operators in various parts of the world and have found them to be reputable and reliable. I travelled twice with G Adventures (formerly GAP Adventures) to Patagonia. They specialize in South America and offer excellent value for money.

- G Adventures (formerly GAP Adventures) **www.gadventures.com**
- World Expeditions **www.worldexpeditions.com**
- Exodus **www.exodus.co.uk**
- Explore! **www.explore.co.uk**

HOW DO YOU SAY THAT?

Spanish is the official language of both Chile and Argentina. Although locals may not be fluent in English, it is usually not difficult to find someone who understands at least some, especially in the areas most commonly frequented by tourists. Here are a few useful phrases to help you along the way:

- hello – hola
- goodbye – adios
- thank you – gracias
- Do you understand English? – Entiende el ingles?
- Where is … ? – Donde esta … ?
- How much does it cost? – Cuanto cuesta?
- I don't understand – No entiendo

CONSIDER THIS: BEFORE OR AFTER THE HIKE

Even if you don't make the trek to El Chaltén and Fitz Roy, you should seriously consider including a trip to El Calafate, the jumping-off point for the spectacular Glaciar Perito Moreno. The town has boomed in recent years as tourist travel to view the glacier has been facilitated by the new international airport. The glacier is located about 80 km (50 mi.) southwest of town and is well serviced by a number of operators.

Other attractions close to town include the Reserva Municipal Laguna Nimez, a former sewage pond that now boasts more than 100 bird species. Guided walks are available or you can wander on your own. A new Glaciarium, located on the road to the famous glacier, tells the story of Patagonia's icefields, tracing the history and work of Glaciar Perito Moreno's namesake, explorer and conservationist Francisco Moreno (1852–1919). The term "perito," which means "expert," commemorates Moreno's extensive knowledge of geology, archaeology and anthropology and his crucial involvement in gathering information to settle the boundary disputes between Chile and Argentina. But for many Argentines, the nickname El Perito Moreno is used as an endearing term. Don't get confused by the little-known national park that also bears his name. I remember a young traveller relating the tale of having taken a long bus ride to the park, only to discover she had missed the glacier by several hundred miles.

Ease of access has made this glacier one of the biggest tourist draws in Patagonia, but don't let that put you off. It is well worth battling the crowds to see and hear this enormous natural wonder as it grinds and rasps its way down the valley. Size estimates vary, but the more or less 30 km (18.6 mi.) long river of ice is about 5 km wide (3 mi.) wide at its terminus. With an average height of 74 m (243 ft.) above the water, the blue monster calves off massive icebergs almost daily in a stunning display of the sheer, raw power of ice in perpetual motion.

Strategically placed catwalks make it possible for visitors to safely view this gigantic river of ice as it butts into the Iceberg Channel separating the two arms of Lago Argentino. It is also possible to view the glacier by boat, an excursion that is highly recommended. Occasionally the moving ice forms a natural dam which eventually gives way under the immense pressure in an astonishing eruption. Glaciologists debate whether the glacier is actually advancing or it is only the peculiar shape of the valley that keeps it flowing in its original direction.

Glaciar Perito Moreno – the blue monster

ARE YOU READY TO EAT?

Meat and mate are two words synonymous with the Argentine focus on food and drink. To be fair, the dining scene in both countries is as cosmopolitan as you would hope to find anywhere in the world. But beef is still king in Argentina, where gigantic steaks are served hanging over the side of the plate and "vegetable" often means your choice of potato cooked one of three or four ways. A staple of the restaurant scene is the parilla, or steakhouse, where meat of every description is grilled in full view of potential customers strolling by. And although salad bars are frequently included on the menu, the meat is definitely the centre of attention. Chile's long coastline and fertile farmland provide an abundance of seafood and fresh produce, but beef remains the entrée of choice there as well.

North Americans frequently have a hard time adapting to the late evening dining habits in both countries, where eating at 9 p.m. is considered early. Fortunately, many tourist areas cater to the odd habits of North Americans and Europeans who can't wait that long for their evening meal. (Both Argentines and Chileans cheat by snacking on a fairly substantial late afternoon tea, called *te* in Argentina and *onces* in Chile, including a sandwich and dessert.)

Hygiene standards are generally fairly high and tap water is potable almost everywhere.

Tipping is not expected in family-run eateries, but a gratuity is commonly added to the bill in formal restaurants.

Vegetarians: At first glance it doesn't sound like good news for vegetarians, but although meat usually dominates the menu, fresh ingredients are relatively easy to find and salads are usually large and quite safe in either country.

MATE MUSINGS

The sipping of yerba mate tea is a Patagonian ritual. Although it is more common in Argentina, the ubiquitous mate gourd and bombilla, or straw, is everywhere. Boiling water is poured over the tea leaves and sucked through the straw – natives will often nurse the brew all day, carrying the gourd with them and adding hot water as needed. Lady Florence Dixie, in her travelogue *Riding Across Patagonia*, notes her party brought a sack of it along with them: "[W]e all grew so fond [of it] that we ultimately used it to the complete exclusion of tea and coffee …" Bruce Chatwin, in his book *In Patagonia*, describes gauchos reclining with their mate after a big feed of lamb roasted on a spit. "One man presided over the ritual. He filled the hot brown gourds and the green liquid frothed to the neck. The men fondled the gourds and sucked at the bitter drink, talking about mate the way other men talked about women."

INTERNET RESOURCES

Curated from the wealth of Patagonia information available on the Internet, here are some useful English-language sites to get you started. Additional sites are listed in the "The essentials" and "How to do the hikes" sections.

www.argentinaturistica.com is a good source of general information on Argentina.

www.gochile.cl provides general tourist information on Chile.

www.interpatagonia.com presents tourist information on the region of Patagonia.

www.losglaciares.com has good information on Parque Nacional Los Glaciares, with links to El Calafate and El Chaltén, among others.

www.verticepatagonia.com contains information on accommodations at various camps and refugios in Paine.

www.torresdelpaine.com features information on accommodations at various camps and refugios in Paine.

RECOMMENDED READING

Travelogues and books about Patagonia abound. This is a selection of some I recommend.

A Book-Lover's Holidays in the Open (1916) – Theodore Roosevelt – chronicles the former United States president's Patagonian travels.

Enduring Patagonia – Gregory Crouch – written by a climber, provides a hair-raising perspective of the peaks of Patagonia, particularly in Fitz Roy. Highly recommended.

Idle Days in Patagonia – W.H. Hudson – follows Hudson's travels during a year-long trip to Patagonia in the late 1800s; Far Away and Long Ago, also by Hudson, is his childhood memoir of growing up on the isolated Argentine pampas in the 1840s.

In Patagonia – Bruce Chatwin – the book put Chatwin on the map as far as travel writing is concerned. It remains the one source consistently cited as a must read on Patagonia. Although he has been criticized for adapting the facts to make a good story, it is still a good starting point. Highly recommended.

"FAT-BEHIND-THE-EYE" REIGNS SUPREME

In Riding Across Patagonia, Lady Florence Dixie waxed positively poetic about some of their meals cooked over a fire at the end of a long day of riding and hunting. One meal, which she described in great detail, included roast ribs and head of guanaco, fried ostrich (rhea), roast goose and duck, ostrich wings and liver, blood pudding, mate and biscuits. Another meal included roast "chorlitos," a native bird which she described as "so seductively succulent, so exquisitely flavoured, so far beyond anything the gourmet might dream of in the sublimest flight of his imagination …" But even the legendary chorlitos didn't match a delicate morsel found in the head of the guanaco – "whatever other culinary novelties we discussed, and they were as numerous as strange, 'Fat-behind-the-eye' always retained its supremacy in our affections as the ne plus ultra of pampa delicacies."

ROBERT A. MITCHELL JR.

FAUNA FACTS: GENTLE GRACE

Although the huge guanaco herds reported by Francisco Moreno during his explorations no longer exist, these graceful relatives of the camel family continue to thrive in Patagonia. They are a common sight in Paine, where they tend to roam in small herds of females with their young, defended by a protective dominant male. Bachelor males form separate herds and fight violently during mating season to establish breeding rights.

Small herds of graceful guanacos are a common sight in Parque Nacional Torres del Paine.

They are superbly adapted to the steppe, with highly prized thick, soft wool that protects them from the cold wind. Unlike the sheep that replaced them, guanaco have hooves that do not damage the grasses on which the species feeds. In *Riding Across Patagonia*, Lady Florence Dixie mentions the tame guanacos kept at Sandy Point (Punta Arenas), noting, "… their gentle ways and amiable dispositions make them charming pets."

Lonely Planet: Trekking in the Patagonian Andes – Carolyn McCarthy – somewhat dated but still an excellent guide to the entire region.

Moon Handbooks: Patagonia, Including the Falkland Islands (2011 edition) – Wayne Bernhardson – a comprehensive guide to the entire region, with good maps.

Nowhere Is a Place: Travels in Patagonia – Bruce Chatwin and Paul Theroux – a collection of impressions and accounts by two well-known travel writers, together with a stunning array of photographs by Jeff Gnass.

Patagonia: A Cultural History – Chris Moss – written by a former journalist at the Buenos Aires *Herald*, this book provides a fascinating glimpse into the history and myth that is Patagonia. Highly recommended.

Patagonia Glaciers and the Southern Andes – Alejandro Winograd and Daniel Rivademar – stunning photos and text on Parque Nacional Los Glaciares.

Riding Across Patagonia: A Victorian Equestrian Adventure – Lady Florence Dixie – a classic tale of adventure during a trip in 1879. Highly recommended.

Rounding the Horn, Being the Story of Williwaws and Windjammers, Drake, Darwin, Murdered

Missionaries and Naked Natives – Dallas Murphy – a fascinating history of the end of the earth.

Voyage of the Beagle – Charles Darwin – still in print after almost 200 years, the classic account of his five-year voyage, including his time in Patagonia.

Wind, Sand and Stars – Antoine de Saint-Exupéry – an autobiographical account of life in Patagonia from the perspective of a famous author and aviator.

INDEX